4

1/9

Policy Studies Institute

GOVERNMENTS AND TRADE UNIONS

Policy Studies Institute

GOVERNMENTS AND TRADE UNIONS

The British Experience, 1964–79

DENIS BARNES and
EILEEN REID

 Heinemann Educational Books · London

Heinemann Educational Books Ltd
22 Bedford Square, London WC1B 3HH
LONDON EDINBURGH MELBOURNE AUCKLAND
HONG KONG SINGAPORE KUALA LUMPUR NEW DELHI
IBADAN NAIROBI JOHANNESBURG
EXETER(NH) KINGSTON PORT OF SPAIN

© Policy Studies Institute 1980
First published 1980

ISBN 0 435 83045 7

Filmset by Northumberland Press Ltd,
Gateshead, Tyne and Wear
Printed by Richard Clay (The Chaucer Press) Ltd,
Bungay, Suffolk

Contents

PART III EDWARD HEATH, 1970–74 – 'A NEW STYLE OF GOVERNMENT'

PART IV JACK JONES, 1972–79 – 'A NEW SOCIAL
CONTRACT'

Acknowledgements

We would like to thank all who have contributed to the writing of this book: the Wolfson Foundation for making it possible to undertake the work, the secretarial staff at Political and Economic Planning and the Policy Studies Institute who dealt patiently with the various drafts, the staff of the Department of Employment Library who coped expertly with our many demands and those who assisted by reading the manuscript and discussing it with us. We are especially grateful to Rose Parton, who deciphered and typed a great deal of our work, and to Elspeth Robinson, who prepared the bulk of the final draft. The responsibility for the facts, figures, judgements and conclusions of the book is that of the authors.

Denis Barnes
Eileen Reid
Policy Studies Institute
October 1979

Introduction

Since 1945 all governments have been concerned about the consequences of trade union power. They have regarded the wage increases produced by collective bargaining as impeding their attempts to maintain full employment, stable prices and a satisfactory balance of payments and to increase the rate of economic growth and generally 'manage the economy'. They have been concerned also about industrial relations – the effect on the economy of strikes, restrictive practices, demarcation and overmanning. It was not until the mid-1960s, however, that concern over these different, though related, issues fused and 'trade union power' became a major political issue.

This study is mainly concerned with the period 1964–74, when events surprising to me took place: the extent of the breakdown in relations between the Wilson Government and the unions which led in 1969 to *In Place of Strife* and the accompanying excitement within the labour movement; Edward Heath's belief in 1972 that a Conservative government could reach an agreement on incomes policy with the General Council and his decision in 1974 to have an election on the issue of trade union power. I decided, however, that the book should include some background to show how and why the events of 1964–74 took place and should try to assess their effects in the years which followed. The study thus refers to some relevant features of government–union relations during the years following the trade union legislation of the 1870s and includes some discussion of events between 1974 and 1979 – the wages explosion and inflation of 1974 and 1975, the legislation which increased union power and the 'confrontations' under the Callaghan Government which, in the light of what happened between 1964 and 1974, seem even more surprising than those of 1969 and 1970–74.

After the war governments responded to the problems of trade union power in two ways. First, there were attempts to recreate the partnership with the unions brought about in 1940 by the war and continued under the Attlee Government until 1950. These attempts included Harold Macmillan's abortive efforts to reach an agreement on wage restraint in 1956 and the establishment of the National

Economic Development Council in 1961, the partnership of the Wilson Government with the unions from 1964 to 1966, the protracted bargaining by Edward Heath in search of an agreement in 1972 and 1973 and Jack Jones's 'social contract' of 1974 to 1978. Partnership with shared responsibility in managing the economy was, it appeared, a possibility open only to Labour governments – and the partnership did not necessarily produce the results hoped for by government. The first partnership, with the Wilson Government in 1964, did not restrain wage increases effectively and was abandoned after eighteen months. The period of the social contract between 1974 and 1978 saw a higher rate of wage increase than at any time since the war, a spectacular gap between the rate of wage increase and the rate of increase in productivity and the highest rate of inflation for centuries.

Secondly, there were attempts to assert government authority and to restrain the bargaining power of the unions – Macmillan's incomes policy of 1961–62, Wilson's statutory incomes policy of 1966–69, Heath's 'confrontations' in 1970–72 and his statutory incomes policy 1973–74. Failure to impose restraint led governments to attempt to reduce the power of the unions: to Wilson's *In Place of Strife* in 1969 and Heath's Industrial Relations Act, 1971.

The result of the policies of governments, whether seeking partnership or attempting to exercise authority, has not been what was intended. Governments have failed to maintain full employment, inflation has continued for longer, has accelerated and reached higher levels than ever before and the rate of economic growth has not increased. Trade union membership has grown and, so far from being reduced or contained, union power has increased. Unions now exert power in areas in which, twenty years ago, they were not effectively organised. They have become more militant. Governments have made changes in the law so that unions can use their power more effectively.

In the last ten years three successive Prime Ministers have been prevented by the industrial and political power of the unions from pursuing policies they declared essential in the national interest. All lost the elections which followed the defeats of their policies. The conflict has been about money and power – depressingly, not about real money but the money of inflation and not about constructive power but the power to interfere with each other's activities.

Lady Avon is said to have commented that in 1956 she felt as though the Suez Canal was flowing through her drawing room. Some of the issues to which we refer in this book – industrial relations, wage claims, negotiations, strikes, confrontations and settlements, differentials, low pay, free collective bargaining, wages policies, norms, productivity – have dripped into our homes for years. I hope we are not simply adding to this persistent drip, for the book is not about these issues in themselves. It is an account of some of the political problems they caused and the reactions of governments and unions to these problems.

Eileen Reid has worked with me on the study from its inception, first at Political and Economic Planning and latterly at the Policy Studies Institute.

D. C. B.

This coal strike is the beginning of a revolution.... Power has passed from the King to the nobles, from the nobles to the middle classes and through them to the House of Commons and now it is passing from the House of Commons to the trade unions.

Sir Edward Grey, 1912.

This is an attempt to take over the functions of government by a body that has not been elected. If they succeed it will be the end of parliamentary democracy which we have taken centuries to build. There can be no negotiations. It can only end in a complete surrender.

Stanley Baldwin, on the General Council of the TUC calling a General Strike in support of the miners, 1926.

If we yield now to the TUC we shall never be able to call our bodies or souls or intelligences our own.

Ramsay MacDonald, 1931.

It has always been my aim ... to seek to avoid, as far as that is possible, revealing the impotence of authority in these matters.

Sir F. Leggett, Chief Industrial Commissioner, on industrial relations, 1942.

The eyes of the world are turning to Great Britain. We now have the moral leadership of the world and before many years we shall have people coming here as to a modern Mecca learning from us in the twentieth century as they learned from us in the seventeenth century.

Aneurin Bevan, 1948.

I sometimes wonder, Mr. Deakin, who governs this country – the government or the Transport and General Workers Union.

That is a question I would prefer to leave you to answer, Home Secretary.

> Chuter Ede, Home Secretary and Chairman of the Emergencies Committee and Arthur Deakin, General Secretary of the Transport and General Workers Union, during a dock strike, 1948.

The power which challenges the rule of law most is the power of the great British unions at present.... One of the biggest problems of the law today is how to restrain the misuse or abuse of power.

> Lord Denning, Master of the Rolls, April 1979.

PART I

1870–1964

Chapter 1 looks briefly at the period 1870–1945 before going on to examine in more detail the events of the years 1945–51. Its aim is to pick out the legislation and events which are relevant to the main subject of the study, the years from 1964 to 1974. For example, Harold Wilson's proposals to 'reform' industrial relations threatened to change (if marginally), and Edward Heath's Industrial Relations Act did change, legislation passed between the 1870s and 1906 which was crucial to the central activities of the trade unions and the exercise of their industrial power. In pressing on with *In Place of Strife* Wilson temporarily disregarded the realities of trade union political power within the labour movement and called up the spectres of Ramsay MacDonald and the disagreeable political consequences of 1931; the Heath Government's 'confrontations' recalled the early 1920s, the disputes with the miners, the General Strike and the Baldwin Government.

Until the years immediately before the First World War, when some politicians became seriously concerned about trade union power,[1] the trade union 'problem' was not a major political issue. There were periods when governments were concerned about industrial unrest. The legislation of the 1870s was prompted by this and there was similar concern in the 1880s and 1890s. There were times when ministers – even prime ministers – became involved in industrial troubles and acted, not always successfully, as mediators or conciliators. For the most part, however, it was accepted that such affairs should be left to employers and unions, with assistance from government – or other sources – available on request. Except for occasional excitements, industrial relations and the trade unions were, in these years, issues of low political priority compared with imperial and foreign affairs, Ireland, free trade or protection, taxation and national insurance, education, the vote and the reform of the House of Lords. Despite

[1] Sir Edward Grey, *see* page xii.

this low priority, however, the legislation which still in 1969 formed the basis for the exercise of the industrial power of the trade unions, together with the legislation which formed the basis of their political power within the labour movement, was passed between 1870 and 1913.

The years between 1870 and 1950 can be divided into four periods:
1. the years from 1870 to the First World War, during which the foundations of the industrial and political power of the unions were laid;
2. the period 1920–40, which saw the first general 'confrontation' between government and the trade union movement and a decline of union power;
3. the Second World War, when the unions firmly established their position and power;
4. the years of the Attlee Governments 1945–51, with policies to give effect to trade union objectives and during which the causes of the continuing disputes between post-war governments and the trade union movement emerged.

Chapter 2 reviews the period of Conservative governments which began with the election in 1951 and continued under Churchill (1951–54), Eden (1954–57), Macmillan (1957–63) and Home (1963–1964). There were general elections in 1955 and 1959, in both of which the Conservatives increased their majority.

The most consistent feature of the policy of successive Conservative governments towards the trade unions was the desire to avoid serious conflict. Ministers became, however, increasingly concerned about the country's relatively poor economic performance, inflation, the balance of payments and the pound, with the result that there were moves to secure wage restraint which threatened to jeopardise the policy of 'conciliation'. There was concern also about industrial relations – unofficial strikes, restrictive practices, low productivity – the poor state of which was thought to contribute to the country's comparative economic failure. As the period progressed it became increasingly difficult to reconcile the policy of full employment with the outcome of free collective bargaining.

1   Background, 1870–1951

The Growth of Trade Union Power, 1870–1920

Following the report of the Royal Commission set up in 1867 to inquire into the organisation and rules of trade unions and employers' associations and their effects on industrial relations and trade and industry, the legal position of trade unions and their activities (until then for the most part criminal conspiracy) was revolutionised by the Trade Union Act, 1871 and the Criminal Law Amendment Act, 1871. The intention of these Acts was temporarily thwarted by a legal judgement that it was still a criminal offence to interfere with an employer's right to conduct his business and further legislation was enacted to reverse the effect of this judgement – the Conspiracy and Protection of Property Act, 1875, accompanied by the repeal of the 1867 Master and Servant Act. The effect of this legislation was to abolish criminal liability for combination in restraint of trade and hence to protect unions as corporate bodies from action under the criminal law when they called their members out on strike or took certain other measures in pursuit of their objectives.

Protection from liability under the criminal law still left trade unions in a position where the exercise of their industrial power could have serious consequences. Following the Taff Vale judgement in 1901 that a union could be sued for damages caused by a strike, the government appointed a Royal Commission to inquire into the subject of trade disputes and combinations and the law affecting them. The majority recommendations of the Royal Commission were unacceptable to the trade unions but a political understanding between the Liberal government and the Parliamentary Labour Party resulted in the amendment of the original legislation based on the Commission report and the enactment of the Trade Disputes Act, 1906, which exempted trade unions from liability to be sued for tort and gave protection from civil suits for certain acts in furtherance of trade disputes. The legislation between 1871 and 1906 provided the legal framework for the use of industrial power by the unions.

During this period the unions sought also to increase their political power. Organisation at the centre for political purposes became a feature of the trade union movement and the first Trades Union Congress was held in 1868, followed in 1871 by the establishment of a Parliamentary Committee to influence the legislation then under consideration. The unions secured direct representation through elected Members of Parliament in the House of Commons, at first within the Liberal Party but towards the end of the century through an independent Labour Party. The development of this political activity was strengthened and formalised by the establishment in 1900 of the Parliamentary Representation Committee and by the decision that the trade unions should give first priority to support of a Parliamentary Labour Party.

Again there was a challenge from the courts. In the Osborne case in 1910 it was ruled *ultra vires* for a trade union to make a levy on its members for political purposes. This was reversed by the Trade Union Act, 1913, which provided that unions could raise such a levy so long as members had the right to contract out of paying it.

Three features of the legislation are worth comment. First, much of it was passed to reverse legal decisions inimical to an increase in trade union power. These decisions generated a distrust and suspicion of the law and hostility to the courts within the trade union movement which continued until 1974. Secondly, the majority recommendations of the Royal Commissions of 1867 and 1903 which preceded the legislation were not accepted by the politicians and the legislation which followed did not conform to them. These features were repeated in the period 1964–70. The Wilson Government's appointment of the Donovan Commission was provoked by the legal judgement in the case of *Rookes* v. *Barnard*. The government did not consider the recommendations of the Commission adequate and their proposals for legislation did not conform to them. The Heath Government's Industrial Relations Act, 1971 rejected the basic assumptions and major recommendations of the Donovan Commission. Thirdly, although the early legislation was politically controversial and opposed in Parliament, no alterations were made with any change of government until 1927. Concern about the trade union vote and respect for trade union power meant that the key principles of protection from criminal and civil liabilities were not questioned by governments until the late 1960s.

Confrontation and Failure, 1920–40

This period divides very roughly into two – the years up to the General

Strike in 1926, followed by a period in the late 1920s and the 1930s when trade union influence was at its lowest ebb since the early 1900s.

The increased membership, industrial power and political influence of unions during the 1914–18 war (there were trade union members in the Lloyd George Coalition Government) inspired changes in the political activities of the trade union movement after the war. The Trades Union Congress was re-organised, with a General Council which had a wider purpose, and apparently more authority, replacing the old Parliamentary Representation Committee. It was authorised to help co-ordinate industrial action, to help settle inter-union disputes, to speak for the industrial side of the labour movement and to be responsible for the relations with international trade unionism. A National Joint Council was set up in 1922 on which the General Council of the TUC and the Labour Party Executive each held half the seats. The TUC and Labour Party agreed to co-operate in establishing departments for research, public relations and international affairs. The trade unions, which had continued to be represented in the House of Commons in the Liberal Party, though on a diminishing basis, now committed themselves wholly to representation through the Parliamentary Labour Party. The Labour Party was to be the political spokesman and the promoter of trade union interests.

The industrial and political power which the unions had gained during the war was, however, reduced with the collapse of the post-war boom in 1921 (unemployment rose from around 170,000 in 1918 to 2½ million in 1921) and the end of the government's concern with the maintenance of war production. Government policies now gave priority to checking inflation, re-establishing the position of sterling and increasing the competitiveness of industry. These policies involved wage restraint, which in many sectors took the form of a reduction in real wages, and from 1921 to 1926 unions were engaged in a series of strikes or lock-outs in defence of wage levels. Membership dropped from nearly 8½ million in 1920 (more than double the 1914 total) to 5½ million in 1925 and it continued to decline until late in the 1930s.

The new arrangements with the Labour Party did not provide an effective substitute for the direct political influence which the trade unions had exercised during the war period. The first Labour government of 1924 was a minority government, unable to take action to further trade union interests or to pursue economic policies more favourable to those interests. It resigned in November 1924 and was succeeded by a second Conservative government under Stanley Baldwin.

The industrial troubles in which governments had been involved since 1921 developed into direct and general confrontation between the unions and the Baldwin Government. In its final stages the conflict centred on the coal industry, culminating in the General Strike of 1926. Although the dispute was primarily about wages and costs and between the Miners' Federation of Great Britain and the Mining Association, other factors complicated the issue, including relics of government involvement in the industry during the war, such as subsidies the government now wished to remove, and arguments about royalties and nationalisation. The Baldwin Government made attempts to settle the dispute, including the appointment of a Royal Commission, conciliation between the miners and their employers and discussions with the General Council. After a lock-out of miners, the General Council called a 'general' strike in their support, which was called off after nine days.

This was the first general confrontation between government and the trade union movement. Baldwin viewed it as raising the most serious constitutional issues.[1] It was denounced as an attempt by the unions to coerce the government by use of industrial power – a view apparently shared by the majority of the public, by important members of the Parliamentary Labour Party (PLP) and some members of the General Council of the TUC.

Given the enormity of the challenge to parliamentary democracy which Baldwin and other politicians regarded the General Strike as presenting, the Trade Disputes and Trade Union Act passed in 1927 might be thought surprisingly moderate. (It was, however, the first anti-trade union Act since the 1870s.) Even more surprising, given the nature of Baldwin's concern, it penalised the Labour Party, the instrument for the pursuit of trade union objectives by constitutional means. The Act made general and sympathetic strikes illegal and changed the provisions of the Trade Union Act, 1913 by providing that members must 'contract in' to pay the political levy instead of being required to 'contract out'. It also prohibited civil servants from belonging to unions in membership with the TUC.

There were two important longer-run consequences of the General Strike and its failure. First, the use of industrial power against government policies had failed, and the direct use of industrial power for political purposes was discredited until the 1970s. Secondly, the

[1] *See* p. xii.

possibility of the TUC's exercising authority or even effective influence over individual unions, except on limited domestic issues and in very special circumstances, was destroyed. Individual unions had surrendered their powers to the General Council in 1926 with disastrous results – for them – and they would not repeat the operation.

The election of a second Labour government in 1929 might have been expected to provide relief and encouragement for the unions in their period of decline. The MacDonald Government of 1929 was, however, again dependent on Liberal support, which limited its powers to carry measures desired by the trade unions and to which it had declared its commitment in the election. It was not able to repeal even the hated Trade Disputes and Trade Union Act, 1927. For this and other reasons, relations between Ramsay MacDonald and trade union leaders, including Ernest Bevin, General Secretary of the Transport and General Workers Union (TGWU) and by now the most effective member of the General Council, were not good and the situation was not helped by the fact that Arthur Henderson, the leading spokesman for trade union interests in the government, was also MacDonald's most serious rival in the Cabinet and Party.

What limited power the unions could exert through the government was swept away in the political consequences of the sterling crisis of August and September 1931. MacDonald gave priority to saving the pound. The implications of his decision have become depressingly familiar. The conditions for the necessary overseas loans included cuts in public expenditure and the government's proposed cuts included reductions in unemployment benefit. The reaction of the General Council of the TUC was predictable. Walter Citrine, General Secretary of the TUC, backed strongly by Bevin, declared that the government's proposals meant a continuation of the deflationary policy and that the General Council was opposed. MacDonald described the attitude of the trade union representatives as 'practically a declaration of war', reflecting, 'If we yield now to the TUC we shall never be able to call our bodies or souls or intelligences our own'. The opposition of the TUC to the proposed measures was backed up by a group in the Cabinet led by Henderson. This group withdrew support from MacDonald, who resigned and, supported by a few of his colleagues, formed a national government in August 1931.

In the 1931 election, the representation of the Parliamentary Labour Party was reduced from 288 to 52. Many of its important figures were defeated. It spent the thirties recovering from 1931 with a new generation of leaders.

Trade union leaders could be forgiven if by 1931 they had the same suspicious view of politicians and the political system as they had of judges and the courts. After the political debacle Bevin and others, including Citrine, made moves to re-establish more effective relations between the General Council and the Labour Party. They hoped to ensure, by increasing the influence of the unions, that a future Labour government would not repeat MacDonald's mistake and would keep to commitments agreed with the unions. The TUC prepared a detailed programme which the Labour Party could include in an election manifesto and implement in government. This programme, set out in *Trade Unionism and the Control of Industry*, published in 1932, contained proposals for greater government intervention in industry and for a national industrial council on which employers and unions would be represented. Complete socialisation of the economy and the elimination of private enterprise was ruled out, but industries to be 'nationalised' would, the report stated, be identified in later reports. In an effort to ensure that union influence prevailed, the joint council representing trade unions and the Labour Party, which had been set up in 1922 following the TUC re-organisation and birth of the General Council, was replaced in 1934 by a National Council of Labour. The unions made efforts to ensure that it functioned on the lines they wished.

This was for the future. Immediately after 1931 relations between trade unions and government were probably as distant as at any time since the early 1900s and the influence of the trade unions on government less than at any time since then. Union suspicion of, and hostility to, government economic and industrial policies was as great as in the twenties and, after 1935, extended to government foreign policy. In a period when unemployment did not drop below $1\frac{1}{2}$ million, was regularly above 2 million and sometimes stood at nearly 3 million, the industrial power of the unions was in decline. Nevertheless, the years up to the war showed the relative strength and stability of the trade union movement, as opposed to the weakness of the Parliamentary Labour Party.

The Foundations of Post-war Power, 1940–45
It is fair to describe this period as one of government–trade union coalition which revolutionised the position and power of the unions. With the prospect of war, the Conservative Government, under Neville Chamberlain, prepared plans which took full account of the

manpower and related problems experienced between 1914 and 1918. There would be, the government knew, shortages of skilled labour. These manpower shortages would lead to the bidding up of wages and could present a threat of serious inflation. Production might be threatened by strikes. In its plans to meet these problems the government accepted that trade union co-operation was essential. The threat and outbreak of war did not, however, remove trade union hostility to the Conservative government.

The rearmament programme caused shortages of manpower in engineering and ship-building as early as 1939. The government made moves to secure trade union co-operation in dealing with this problem before war was declared on 3 September 1939. Ernest Brown, Minister of Labour, held discussions with the General Council in July, but as the General Council took the view that the problem should be left to the unions and employers, the attempt to secure co-operation did not prosper. Immediately after war was declared the government introduced the Control of Employment Bill, which prohibited employers from advertising for labour and from engaging labour except through employment exchanges. The TUC was not consulted until a few hours before publication. The General Council protested that the government had not given it reasonable notice and attacked the Bill as an infringement on the voluntary character of the labour market. It pressed that the provisions of the Bill should not become effective without an Order and that any Order should be made only after the minister had referred it to an advisory committee consisting of an equal number of trade union and employer representatives. The government accepted the proposals, amended the Bill and changed its approach.

Ernest Brown met representatives of the General Council and employers' organisations and announced that he was setting up a National Joint Advisory Committee with members from each side of industry. The General Council met the Prime Minister. The General Secretary, Citrine, made it clear that collaboration with the government could be given only if the government extended 'the fullest recognition of the trade union function on [the workers] behalf'. The Prime Minister issued instructions, cleared beforehand with Citrine, to all departments to consult with the TUC and individual unions on any matter that might affect them directly or indirectly.

In May 1940 the Labour Party entered the coalition government headed by Winston Churchill. In Parliamentary terms the important Cabinet appointments were those of Clement Attlee and Arthur

Greenwood, but the most significant in terms of the labour movement was the appointment of Ernest Bevin as Minister of Labour. Bevin had been a leading figure on the General Council for twenty years. He was the 'creator' of the Transport and General Workers Union and by now the most influential trade unionist in the country. As Minister of Labour he was, in effect, the representative in the Cabinet of the trade union movement and the key figure from the labour movement in the government. His major responsibilities were to ensure that the manpower was available to achieve the highest level of war production, to contain the inflationary wage pressures which had begun in 1938–39 and which were likely to be intensified, to operate the machinery of conscription to the services and to avoid industrial troubles which would have an adverse effect on the first objective.

In the crisis of May 1940 (after the defeat of France), Parliament passed an Emergency Powers (Defence) Act under which the government could by Order exercise dictatorial powers over property and persons. Orders were made under this Act giving the Minister of Labour power to prevent employers engaging workers except through labour exchanges, to direct people to particular jobs and prevent them leaving essential jobs, to protect them from dismissal and to regulate some working conditions. These Orders provided a legal framework for the mobilisation of labour. All the Orders were agreed with the General Council and, if appropriate, with individual unions.

Bevin insisted that these – and other powers taken to prevent strikes – must be agreed amongst government, trade unions and employers and that they must be reserved for use in the last resort. The civilian manpower operation for which he was responsible would work only if it was generally accepted, and the co-operation and active support of the unions was essential for this purpose. A Joint Consultative Committee of union and employers' representatives met throughout the war and ensured continuing trade union involvement at the top level. This was the focal point of the wartime partnership between the government and the trade union movement.

Bevin's policy on wages and industrial relations was based on the same belief that agreement and consent must be the basis of policy and that legal powers could be used only where these had failed. It was agreed on the Joint Consultative Committee that collective bargaining should continue, but subject to certain restrictions. These restrictions, set out in Order 1305, required that if a dispute could not be settled the parties must give 21 days notice to the Minister of Labour, who could then attempt to settle it by conciliation or other methods or refer it to a new body – the National Arbitration Tribunal. Strikes (or lock-outs) before the 21 days notice or against awards of the National Arbitration Tribunal were illegal.

There were no official strikes in breach of Order 1305 during the whole period of the war, but a number of unofficial strikes took place. Legal action was taken in six cases only. The coal industry was particularly badly affected and in 1941 a thousand strikers at Betteshanger Colliery in Kent were prosecuted. As a result union officials were imprisoned and the rank and file were fined. The outcome was a settlement of the dispute, more or less on the strikers' terms, by a process of negotiation with the jailed union officials, the release of the officials and non-payment of the fines.[2] After this there were no further war-time prosecutions under the Order.

The effectiveness of compulsory arbitration in restraining wage increases and countering inflation was questioned as early as 1941 by Kingsley Wood, Chancellor of the Exchequer, and other ministers, who argued for direct wage controls. Bevin, who on labour affairs had an effective veto on proposals put to the Cabinet, rejected alternative policies and his policy based on collective bargaining within the restrictions of Order 1305 was maintained throughout the war.

From 1940 to 1945 trade union views on mobilisation of labour, wages and industrial relations, as expressed in Bevin's policies, prevailed. Union influence on related issues which could directly affect war production – rationing, prices, the protection of the civilian population – was considerable and at times decisive; their industrial power reached a new peak. Membership increased from 6¼ million in 1939 to over 8 million in 1945. The trade unions' great, and at times overriding, political power was, however, limited to policies directly affecting the prosecution of the war. While they influenced the development of policies for the post-war period, the extent of this influence is less easy to assess. On one issue of major importance to them they were certainly ineffective: Ernest Bevin failed to persuade Winston Churchill and the Cabinet to repeal or to amend the Trade Disputes and Trade Union Act, 1927, or to secure a commitment to repeal it after the war. The Beveridge Report on social insurance,

---

[2] The Betteshanger affair was to be a showpiece in the evidence to the Donovan Commission appointed in 1965.

published in December 1942, which provoked more popular enthusiasm than any other proposal for post-war 'reconstruction', was
supported by the trade unions, but it was not an issue to which
they gave high priority. Other post-war plans, including the reform
of the educational system prepared for by the Education Act, 1944,
proposals for the re-organisation of health services and housing
policies, reflected a consensus within the Coalition Government in
which the trade union influence was only one of many.

For the unions the crucial pronouncement on post-war policy was
the White Paper, *Employment Policy* (Cmnd. 6527), published in May
1944. This accepted the expansionist economic policies designed to
create jobs which the TUC had pressed on governments since 1929,
though it also, of course, represented a general movement in the
views of economists and politicians in all parties. It committed
post-war governments to having 'as one of their primary responsibilities the maintenance of a high and stable level of employment' and to
using government policies, including public expenditure, to influence
demand to achieve this.

The commitment was in general terms and was guarded. The
problems of a policy of 'full' employment were emphasised and the
conditions for the success of the policy, including, in particular, those
for which the trade unions would carry responsibility, were set out.
The White Paper stated that the success of the policy ultimately
depended on the understanding and support of the community as a
whole and especially on the efforts of employers and workers in
industry. The efforts needed included keeping wages and prices stable,
maintaining mobility of workers between occupations and localities
and the requirement that 'trade unions examine their trade practices
to ensure that they do not constitute a serious impediment to an
expansionist economy and so defeat the object of a full employment
programme'. The General Council welcomed the commitment to full
employment, pointing out that it had urged this on governments since
1929, but made it clear that these policies alone did not meet its
view of the economic and industrial requirements of the post-war
period.

The TUC had been preparing for the post-war period since 1943
and shortly after the publication of *Employment Policy 1944* set out its
objectives in its *Interim Report on the Post-War Reconstruction*, published
in July 1944, which stated that the trade union movement was
determined to have a 'decisive share in the actual control of the
economic life of the nation'. The report fully supported a policy of

full employment but insisted that trade unions should function without state interference and represent their members through free collective bargaining. It 'pledged' the unions to act reasonably and responsibly, as they had done during the war, so that full employment would not be prejudiced.

Specific proposals in the *Interim Report* for the most part repeated those in *Trade Unionism and the Control of Industry, 1932* and reports of the later 1930s. They included the establishment of a national industrial council, which would advise the government on all aspects of industrial policy and would have representatives of trade unions and employers and its own administrative staff, state control over banking and the nationalisation of the fuel and power, transport and iron and steel industries. Industries which remained in the private sector would be influenced by government through its control of purchasing and licensing and the continuation of price controls. Some of the proposals were repeated in the Labour Party proposals for 'reconstruction', *Full Employment and Financial Policy*. The Labour Party manifesto for the election in July 1945 included commitments to all the major points in the TUC *Interim Report* and to policies on education, housing, health services and social insurance based on the plans for reconstruction developed within the Coalition Government.

By 1945, after twenty years of unrewarding opposition to governments and government policies, the war had transformed the position of the trade union movement in relation to government and the country at large. The unions could claim to have decided the manpower policies vital to the war – and they had worked in partnership with the government to administer them. As the war had been won, it could be assumed that their policies had been right and their contribution to government indispensable. Bevin had become the most important and powerful national figure so far produced by the labour movement.

The success of the Labour Party in the election of 1945 meant that the decision of the trade unions in 1900 to create the labour movement was at last rewarded. Their industrial and political power was finally established.

The Attlee Governments, 1945–51

The Attlee Government which came into office in 1945 determined the main features of economic and social policy for the next thirty years – full employment, the extension of public ownership and the welfare state. Given the history of the movement and particularly the setbacks of the 1920s and 1930s, the euphoria expressed by Aneurin Bevan[3] over the government's achievements was almost forgivable.

Full employment ensured that the industrial power of the trade unions would not again be destroyed, as had happened in the 1920s. The extension of public ownership and other measures met the trade union objectives of the 1930s and earlier.[4] The government had at the same time, however, to meet the immediate problems arising from the return to a peace-time economy – problems which continued for thirty years or more and which came to form the background to relations between governments and the trade unions – the balance of payments and the level of the pound, inflation, wages and collective bargaining.

On wages the government decided in the autumn of 1945 to continue Bevin's war-time policy of collective bargaining subject to compulsory arbitration. The Trades Union Congress in September passed a resolution pressing for an end to compulsory arbitration, but the General Council and the employers agreed to the continuance of Order 1305, on the understanding that it would be ended whenever either side wished. It was soon clear that the policy would be less effective than it had been during the war as labour shortages caused by pressures to increase production rapidly to meet peacetime needs created pressure on wages and costs. The rate of increase in wages accelerated almost immediately: in the twelve months from October 1945 wage rates rose by about $9\frac{1}{2}$ per cent compared to an annual average of about 7 per cent in the war years. There was a general reduction in normal working hours in 1946 which added to labour costs. The Treasury and some ministers were alarmed and justifiably sceptical of the argument put forward by the Ministry of Labour that the first post-war wage round and the reduction in hours should be regarded as exceptional post-war adjustments. The argument was destroyed by a further wage round in which increases averaged about

[3] *See* page xii.

[4] Legislation deriving directly from these objectives included the repeal of the Trade Disputes and Trade Union Act, 1927 and 'nationalisation' of the Bank of England, electricity, railways and road transport, civil aviation, gas and steel. The decasualisation of dock labour was made permanent by the Dock Labour Act, 1946. Although the government did not establish the national industrial council advocated by the TUC, it set up an Economic Planning Board on which the TUC was represented. Other legislation included that which implemented the Beveridge Plan and established a National Health Service – policies agreed within the Coalition Government and supported by the unions.

9 per cent. The post-war phenomenon of the 'annual wage round' had appeared and the warnings in *Employment Policy 1944* of inflation as a consequence of full employment were confirmed.

As in 1940–42, there was again pressure within the government, this time from Stafford Cripps, Aneurin Bevan, Emmanuel Shinwell and others, supported by the Treasury, for a 'wages policy'. There were discussions in the autumn of 1946 with the representatives of the General Council of the TUC and the employers on the National Joint Advisory Council,[5] followed by the publication at the beginning of 1947 of a White Paper, *Statement on the Economic Conditions Affecting Relations Between Employers and Workers* (Cmd. 7018). The Paper reviewed the economic situation but made no specific recommendations on wages.

In 1947 – the year of a fuel crisis – pressure within the government for more effective wage restraint increased. Ministers were, however, divided over possible alternatives to the 'Bevin' policy, while the Trades Union Congress re-affirmed strongly its commitment to free collective bargaining. Under pressure from Cripps, George Isaacs, Minister of Labour, asked joint bodies negotiating wage claims to take account of the difficult economic situation and referred back Wages Council proposals for increases. The General Council protested to Attlee and this initiative came to an end.

The problem for the government and union leaders was how to reconcile a policy for the restraint of wage increases – even members of the General Council accepted that wages should not continue to rise at the same rates as in 1945 and 1946 – with the freedom of unions to engage in collective bargaining. The problem for union leaders was whether they would be able to persuade their members to accept any form of wage restraint: by 1947 there had already been a considerable number of unofficial strikes in breach of Order 1305.

In late 1947 the TUC published its *Interim Report on the Economic Situation*. The report emphasised the importance of government in maintaining price stability and argued for continuation of subsidies. On wages, it argued in favour of the *status quo* and in defence of collective bargaining. The government issued a White Paper, *Statement on Personal Incomes, Costs and Prices* (Cmd. 7321), in February 1948, which declared that there was no justification for wage increases

---

[5] The National Joint Advisory Council had for the most part been superseded during the war years by Ernest Bevin's Joint Consultative Committee. Sir Stafford Cripps, President of the Board of Trade, also appointed a National Production Advisory Council for Industry.

without increases in productivity. The General Council protested that it had not been consulted about the White Paper, but after a meeting with Attlee, Bevin and other ministers, agreed to recommend its acceptance on the understanding that the government would freeze prices at their levels of 31 January 1948, control profit margins and refuse increases in prices which were in response to increases in wages. The employers would be asked to submit to the Chancellor of the Exchequer a plan for reducing prices and profits. The acceptance of the wage restraint implied in the White Paper would be reviewed every three months. A Special Conference of Trade Union Executives approved the recommendations of the General Council.

The policy of wage restraint thus adopted proved effective. Wages had increased to around $6\frac{1}{2}$ per cent in the 9 months between June 1947 and the adoption of the new policy in March 1948. In the eighteen months from March 1948 to September 1949 they increased by only about 4 per cent. In the same period prices increased overall by about 5 per cent while food prices increased by 7 per cent, reflecting the government's policy of reducing subsidies. The wage restraint assisted the government to overcome its major economic problems, though only temporarily. During the same eighteen months exports increased faster than imports, but not enough to improve the balance of payments to the extent required at that time. By the autumn of 1949 the pound was under pressure and the government was forced to devalue.

The government and the trade unions were now faced with an extremely difficult economic and political situation. Devaluation would create further inflationary pressures. Wage restraint would continue to be essential – and in a period when prices might be rising even more rapidly than in the past eighteen months. Moreover, the crisis had occurred when there was bound to be a general election within the next nine months. The continuation of a Labour government was at stake. Despite the industrial problems of imposing a further spell of wage restraint in the most difficult circumstances, the General Council supported the government by accepting what was in effect a wage freeze. It recommended that wage rates should be held stable for at least a year so long as the price index did not rise by more than 5 points. The Trades Union Congress in September called for abandonment of wage restraint, but the freeze recommended by the General Council held until after the election in February 1950. Wages in the 1949–50 round increased by only 2 per cent; prices rose by 2.5 per cent.

The policy of voluntary wage restraint adopted by the General Council in 1948 had been superimposed on its 1945 agreement (contrary to the views of Congress) to the continuation of Order 1305, which limited the right to strike and made provision for compulsory arbitration. The result of this was that there were no major official strikes, though one or two were threatened, but there were large numbers of unofficial strikes – a feature of the war years but now on a much increased scale. Militants in the unions were prepared to challenge the authority of trade union officers, particularly officers at national level, and the challenge increased following the onset of the 'cold war' and communist opposition to the Labour government. Significant numbers of trade union members were not persuaded that restrictions on collective bargaining and wage restraint were necessary and were ready to follow the lead of militants.

These conflicts within the trade union movement and the attitude of the government and trade union leaders towards such unofficial opposition to their agreed policies are well illustrated in the five dock strikes which took place between 1945 and 1950. These were the most damaging unofficial strikes of the period and, since they involved the Transport and General Workers Union, politically the most significant. In three strikes the government used its emergency powers to put in troops, action widely accepted as justifiable in the national interest. It was a clear move in support of the official leadership and policies of the union following its commitment to sustain the government. In a broadcast during a strike in 1948 Attlee stated that the government could not in any way recognise or deal with those leading an unofficial strike, since to do so would cut at the whole basis of collective bargaining. He blamed the disruption on 'a small nucleus who have been instructed for political reasons to take advantage of every little disturbance' – sentiments to be echoed by Harold Wilson during the seamen's strike in 1966.

In its attempts to maintain its wages policy the government in October 1950, for the first time since 1942, and again in February 1951, used the law to support Order 1305. The experience of these prosecutions, the reaction to them, political criticism of a law which was frequently broken and could not be effectively enforced and growing hostility within the trade unions, led in August 1951 to Order 1305 being replaced by the Industrial Disputes Order 1376. This provided that either side in a dispute could request reference to arbitration and on request the Minister of Labour could refer the dispute to an Industrial Disputes Tribunal (replacing the National Arbitration

Tribunal) without the agreement of the other side. An arbitration award by the Tribunal continued to be legally binding but there was no restriction on strikes (or lock-outs) after the award had been made. After eleven years there was a return to free collective bargaining with the additional procedure of unilateral recourse to arbitration.

Legacies of Coalition and Partnership, 1940–51

Between 1945 and 1951 there was a highly effective working partnership between the leading politicians in government and the most influential members of the General Council. On all major issues the leading personalities on each side of the labour movement supported each other. The support of the General Council extended to foreign policy issues when British foreign policy was still of major significance in the world and was particularly important for Bevin as Foreign Secretary after the beginning of the 'cold war' in 1947. The government could rely on wide support in the House of Commons, including that of the opposition, for most of its decisions, but policies which led to confrontation with the USSR and a firm alliance with the USA were disliked by a significant minority of the Parliamentary Labour Party and its supporters. Trade union support ensured that this minority opinion on the government side did not exercise effective influence. Any stab in the back of which Ernest Bevin might complain was unlikely to wound him or the government seriously.

The terms of the partnership were simple. The Labour government carried through a programme which gave effect to practically all the outstanding long-term objectives of the trade union movement. In return, Deakin, General Secretary of the TGWU, and his allies helped the government to meet the immediate post-war economic difficulties by self-imposed limitations on collective bargaining together with the acceptance of continuing legal restrictions on that process and on the right to strike. The partnership worked because of the personalities involved, past experience and the circumstances of the immediate post-war years. With Deakin, Williamson and Lawther committed to supporting Attlee and Bevin, the fact that the General Council had no effective formal authority over unions was relatively unimportant.

After 1945 governments committed themselves to 'managing' the economy to ensure full employment, economic growth, stable prices and a balance of payments which would protect the value of the pound. These commitments made it impossible for them to stand aside from the process of collective bargaining which determined the level of wage increases and influenced costs and prices. The extension of public ownership and the establishment of the 'mixed economy' further involved governments in the process of collective bargaining, though attempts were made to minimise this involvement. The war and continuing full employment after the war gave the unions greatly increased power in collective bargaining. The use of the power was restrained from 1940–51, but collective bargaining continued and was recognised by governments as the appropriate process for settling wages ('The best wages policy there is' to quote Godfrey Ince[6]). In spite of the restraint the 'annual' wage round was established and the annual wage increases were inflationary. The restraint 'imposed' from the top (by the government and General Council) created tensions within the trade unions and conflict between the leadership and militants and activists at lower levels. Continuing full employment reduced the influence of the leaders and increased the power of their opponents. The law and the commitment of the leadership meant an increase in unofficial strikes and other action not officially supported.

After 1951 there appeared two clear trends which can be regarded in part as a legacy of the years of 'coalition' between governments and the trade unions. All succeeding governments tried to restore some elements of the partnership of 1940–50, a desire which grew as they failed to achieve their economic objectives. This was met by an underlying reluctance in the trade unions to enter into such a partnership and an inability to make it effective. As government economic policies failed, the unions in time reverted to their traditional role of pressure groups in opposition to governments.

[6] Sir Godfrey Ince GCB, Permanent Secretary of the Ministry of Labour.

2 Free Collective Bargaining, Conciliation and Inflation, 1951-64

Industrial Peace, 1951-55

After the 1945 election the attitude of the Conservative Party towards
the trade unions was, not surprisingly, at first uncertain. The Party
had just experienced the worst election defeat since 1906, and by the
Labour Party, the political 'instrument' of the trade union movement.
To many Conservatives the trade unions, providing essential financial
and organisational support for the Labour Party, were primarily
political opponents. Opposition to the unions on the grounds of their
support for the Labour Party increased after 1945, following the rapid
growth in union membership and increase in union power during the
war years and the repeal in 1946 of the Trade Disputes and Trade
Union Act, 1927, which altered the terms of the political levy
unfavourably to the Conservative Party. There were, however,
equally good political arguments for co-operation. There was a danger
that the party might lose the votes of the many (millions it was
claimed) trade union members who voted Conservative, and whose
votes were necessary for a Conservative election victory, if a Conservative government took an unsympathetic or antagonistic attitude
to the unions. In 1945, moreover, an anti-trade union attitude
might be politically disadvantageous, as the standing of the trade
unions in the country was high as a result of their wartime role (though
it was to decline as a result of their association with policies of the
Attlee Government which were unpopular), and was in any case
difficult to justify when Churchill and others had worked so closely
with trade union leaders during the war. For a time after the 1945
election, however, hostility to the unions prevailed. The party opposed
the 1946 repeal of the Trade Disputes and Trade Union Act, 1927,
and in the *Industrial Charter* of May 1947 it proposed to reverse the

repeal at least to the extent of banning the closed shop in public employment and prohibiting civil service unions from supporting political parties.

By 1951 the position had changed. The proposal to reverse the 1946 repeal was put aside. Churchill was determined to avoid a return to the hostility which had existed between Conservative governments and the trade union movement from 1921–39. He had longer experience of dealings between governments and unions than any other politician or leading trade union figure – he had been directly involved in the industrial troubles before the First World War and those leading up to the General Strike of 1926 and had created the 'coalition' of 1940–45 – and more than anyone could argue for the benefits of co-operation with the unions as opposed to the political troubles and economic damage caused by conflict. In any case, in government after the 1951 election the Conservatives had to give priority to the unions as industrial rather than political organisations. The experience of the 1920s was a powerful reminder of the necessity of maintaining good relations and of the advantages of keeping government intervention in union affairs and in industrial relations to a minimum. Many of the more influential leaders of the Conservative Party had worked with union leaders during the war, knew them well and were, in any case, hopeful of being able to maintain good relations without undue sacrifice of Conservative principles. There was a reasonable basis for understanding and co-operation. The government was committed to the major objective of full employment and did not propose to reverse the more important social and industrial legislation of the Attlee Government (apart from denationalising steel).

Day to day responsibility for relations with the trade unions rested with Walter Monckton, Minister of Labour. Monckton was not a prominent politician in the Conservative Party. He aimed to present a non-party political image and to keep industrial relations out of politics. He did not, for example, speak at the Annual Conference of the Conservative Party. He explained his role: 'Winston's riding orders to me were that the Labour Party had foretold grave industrial troubles if the Conservatives were elected and he looked to me to do my best to preserve industrial peace',[1] adding later: 'I am a firm believer in government by consultation and consent and I shall do

---

[1] *See* Lord Birkenhead, *Walter Monckton* (Weidenfeld & Nicolson, London, 1969), p. 276.

everything I can to carry out that principle in the conduct of my ministry'.[2]

Much of the post-war machinery for consultation was maintained. There was continuing general discussion of the problems of wages, productivity, inflation and the economic situation on bodies such as the National Joint Advisory Council and the National Productivity Advisory Council for Industry. The proposals of interest to the unions, such as legislation to improve conditions of employment, which the Conservatives had included in their *Industrial Charter*, were discussed on the National Joint Advisory Council, but after an unenthusiastic reception by representatives of both the TUC and the employers were not pursued. On wages and industrial relations Monckton made it clear that the policy of the Ministry of Labour under Bevin and his successors, based on support of collective bargaining and insistence that collective bargaining machinery agreed between employers and unions should be used before the government would intervene, would remain unchanged. Intervention would again be limited to the use of conciliation, voluntary arbitration, courts of inquiry and other devices to settle disputes which could not be settled by negotiations; unions at official level would be supported and negotiations with unofficial representatives in any dispute, however serious, refused. The priority for the Churchill Government was industrial peace. The purpose of conciliation and arbitration was the settlement of disputes; the view of the Ministry of Labour that the best wages policy was collective bargaining was confirmed.

The General Council of the TUC was encouraging in its first reactions, indicating on its side also a wish to forget the twenties and thirties: 'It is our long-standing practice to work with whatever government is in power and through consultation jointly with Ministers and the other side of industry to find practical solutions to the social and economic problems facing the country'.[3]

The experience of the leading members of the General Council, together with political considerations, contributed to the willingness to co-operate. Leading General Council members had worked closely with governments for more than a decade and knew the country's problems and the difficulties facing any government in dealing with them. On the political side, the Conservative majority was small and the return of a Labour government seemed not unlikely. Rejection of

[2] Speech at Birmingham Union Festival Exhibition. 4 December 1951. *See* Lord Birkenhead, *op. cit.*, p. 283.

[3] Recorded in the General Council Report to the Trades Union Congress, 1952.

the Conservatives' approach and, even more, the use of industrial power to embarrass a government which had assumed a conciliatory attitude (and particularly one led by Churchill, still a 'national' figure) would be regarded as a political reaction which would alienate public opinion and damage the Labour Party. If the government stuck to its commitments and was ready to co-operate on issues affecting the industrial activities of the unions, particularly non-interference with collective bargaining, it could count on an attitude of 'friendly neutrality'.

There were some early temporary problems over wages. In October 1951 the government faced the problem of inflation caused in part by the Korean War and the increase in world commodity prices and in part by a rapid increase in wages following the end of the 1949–50 wage freeze and the pressure on the labour market caused by re-armament. Between mid-1950 and mid-1951 wages had risen by about 8 per cent and prices by about 9½ per cent; in the next twelve months wages rose by nearly 9 per cent and prices by about 10½ per cent. There was a serious balance of payments deficit. In May 1952 R. A. Butler, Chancellor of the Exchequer, expounded at a meeting of the National Joint Advisory Council the dangers of a wages-prices spiral and argued that wage increases should be linked to productivity, with a policy relating annual increases in the national wage bill to production. His views were not accepted by representatives of the General Council, who criticised the government's policy of reducing subsidies and increasing national insurance contributions. In July, Monckton, following the precedent set by George Isaacs, withheld approval for wage increases from twelve Wages Councils. The General Council protested to Churchill who, while emphasising the government's determination to strengthen the country's economic position, assured them that the proposals would be approved.

Fortunately for the government the threat of inflation and the problem of the balance of payments were eased by the ending of the Korean War and a fall in commodity prices. The rate of annual wage increases declined after 1952, though it continued to exceed increases in productivity. In these circumstances the Churchill-Monckton policy of support for free collective bargaining backed by conciliation could be continued without serious challenge. By late 1953, however, there were threats of industrial trouble and the policy came under attack.

The employers in the engineering and ship-building industries decided in late 1953 to reject a claim from the unions for a 15 per cent increase. The Engineering and Allied Employers National Federation twice appealed to Monckton not to intervene, arguing that a wage increase would be seriously inflationary, but after the unions had announced that they would impose an overtime and piecework ban Monckton set up a Court of Inquiry into the engineering dispute, with a parallel inquiry into the shipbuilding dispute. The Courts, under the same Chairman, recommended in favour of increases of the order of about 5 per cent, which were later agreed. Also at the end of 1953, the railway unions rejected a wage increase awarded by the Railway Staff National Tribunal. The Ministry of Labour intervened and the dispute was settled without a strike on the basis of an immediate increase as awarded by the Tribunal, a further increase within two months and a re-examination of the wage structure which, it was understood, would give further increases.

Twelve months later, the National Union of Railwaymen (NUR) rejected an offer of further increases arising out of the wage structure talks and again threatened a national strike. Monckton appointed a Court of Inquiry under Sir John Cameron, which led to a settlement on the basis of substantially larger increases than had originally been offered. The Report of the Court was criticised for its argument in defence of the increase on the grounds that it was based on 'comparability' and ignored 'ability to pay'. The Report had stated that since it was provided by statute that there should be a nationalised system of railway transport, the means had to be provided for the operation of this system: 'having willed the end the nation must will the means'. Employees in a nationalised concern should receive a fair and adequate wage and should be no worse off than comparable workers in comparable industries.

Criticisms of Monckton for his activities in these disputes and of the Courts of Inquiry extended to other institutions involved in industrial disputes, including the Industrial Disputes Tribunal, arbitration bodies and the conciliation activities of the Ministry of Labour. All were attacked as instruments of inflation – unreasonably perhaps, in view of their responsibilities and terms of reference to settle disputes, if necessary at the expense of inflationary wage settlements. At the same time, government policy on wages in the public sector was criticised by employers in the private sector as setting the pace and preventing private industry, which had to compete, from resisting inflationary demands.

In 1955 the Monckton approach ran into more serious difficulties. There were three national strikes of political significance, caused to a great extent by inter-union rivalries. In the docks a strike was called by the National Amalgamated Stevedores and Dockers (NASD), a London union competing (hopelessly) with the Transport and General Workers Union and demanding separate negotiating rights with employers. In the newspaper industry in London there was a strike by engineers and electricians against accepting pay settlements agreed in negotiations in which they were not represented. Most important in political terms, there was a strike by the Associated Society of Locomotive Engineers and Firemen (ASLEF) over differentials with other railwaymen and against the National Union of Railwaymen.

The ASLEF strike in May 1955 marked the end of the Monckton successes. It was the first national strike for over twenty years which seriously inconvenienced the public. Threatened immediately before, and started during, the election of May 1955, it continued into the early days of Anthony Eden's new government. Politics could not be kept out. The situation provoked the first important debate on industrial relations in the House of Commons for years and led to a meeting called by Eden with representatives of unions and employers and a series of discussions on the National Joint Advisory Council.

The industrial problems which Walter Monckton had handled from 1951–55 without serious challenge from his government colleagues and from the Conservative Party became from this time a source of disagreement and debate. The government's attitude towards the unions, wages and industrial relations changed. The central concern was, as from 1951–55, the avoidance of serious industrial trouble, but from now on this was coupled with concern to restrain the rate of wage increase as it became clear that the country was in a period of economic decline relative to its main industrial competitors. (Economic performance in terms of output, productivity, investment, exports and inflation was worse – and became increasingly worse.) The government's difficulty in pursuing its two objectives of industrial peace and wage restraint was compounded by its involvement in the public sector, where in some areas industrial trouble could cause serious economic damage. As in the 1920s, the trade unions became a political problem for Conservative governments seeking to control inflation.

The Search for Wage Restraint, 1955–59

Harold Macmillan, who had succeeded Butler as Chancellor of the

Exchequer in November 1955, and Eden, Churchill's successor as Prime Minister, began negotiations with the General Council in late 1955 in an attempt to secure support for the anti-inflation measures which were to be included in the 1956 budget and for some measure of wage restraint. Eden, with his experience of the wartime partnership between government and unions and his post-war support for Bevin on foreign policy, may have hoped for an understanding similar to that between the General Council and the Attlee Government in 1948.

The start of the operation by Eden and Macmillan was not promising. Faced with a deterioration in the balance of payments the government took mildly deflationary measures in late 1955 and early 1956 which were criticised by the General Council. On the other hand, the government obtained the co-operation of the British Employers Confederation, who persuaded a number of major companies to announce 'freezes' on their prices, usually for a period of six months. In March 1956 Eden, with the normal annual budget due in April, invited the General Council to discuss the economic situation. The General Council agreed that measures to reduce consumption and investment might be justified, but repeated its criticisms of the earlier deflationary measures. It argued for maintaining investment in schools, hospitals and housing, for increasing taxes on profits and higher incomes and reducing them on lower incomes, for lower taxes on fuel and essential items and for control of the import of less essential commodities.

The government published *The Economic Implications of Full Employment* (Cmd. 9725), restating the views it had put forward. A second meeting between Macmillan and the General Council following this made no progress, ending with the General Council stating that wage claims would continue to be pressed so long as the cost of living was rising. The budget, which was deflationary and met none of the points made by the TUC, was strongly criticised by the General Council. Further talks between Macmillan and the Economic Committee made no progress. Disagreement was registered publicly by Macmillan and Frank Cousins, who had recently become General Secretary of the Transport and General Workers Union. In a speech on 25 May 1956 Macmillan blamed rises in wages and salaries for price inflation and emphasised the dangers to exports and the consequent threat to the country's ability to import and to maintain full employment: 'Another general round of wage increases such as we have had cannot be repeated without disaster.' Cousins replied, accusing the government of creating unemployment to weaken the power of the unions.

Following this exchange Macmillan developed the policy to stabilise prices as a preliminary to a further approach to the General Council on wage restraint. The government announced a twelve-months' freeze on the prices of the nationalised industries and persuaded the Federation of British Industry and the British Employers Confederation to recommend that their members in the private sector take similar action. With this commitment to a 'price plateau', the government attempted to persuade the General Council to respond on wages, but with no success. After a meeting with representatives of the employers organisations, the nationalised industries and the General Council, the government suspended the talks on 1 August. At the Trades Union Congress in September, a resolution rejecting any form of wage restraint was approved unanimously:

> Congress asserts the right of labour to bargain on equal terms with capital, and to use its bargaining strength to protect workers from the dislocations of an unplanned economy. It rejects proposals to recover control by wage restraint, and by using the nationalised industries as a drag-anchor for the drifting national economy.[4]

The resolution was moved by Cousins who, in supporting it, announced that 'in a period of freedom for all, we are part of the all'.

There was, of course, no chance of a Conservative government establishing a relationship similar to that which had existed between the unions and the Attlee Government, which had been based on shared political aims and had reflected the political objectives of the General Council. A more limited understanding, for which Macmillan might have hoped, was ruled out by recent changes on the General Council, in particular the election of Frank Cousins as General Secretary of the TGWU, which widened the gap between the government and the trade union movement.

Cousins was out of sympathy with what he regarded as Arthur Deakin's excessively 'authoritarian' attitude as General Secretary and favoured a return to what he claimed was a more 'democratic' role, in which the overriding purpose of officers of unions, including himself, was to give effect to the immediate aims of the members as expressed by their more active and militant spokesmen. (The ban on communists holding office in the union, imposed in the late forties, was

[4] *TUC Annual Report*, 1956, p. 398; p. 528.

removed after Cousins became General Secretary.) The pursuit of the immediate interests of workers through collective bargaining was the essential purpose of trade unionism. Free collective bargaining was not irreconcilable with their longer term interests, including full employment: any failure to maintain full employment would be due to misconceived government policies. Cousins would not be prepared to accept the arguments put forward by Macmillan relating wages, inflation and full employment. In any event, as he supported the left wing of the Labour Party, an understanding with a Conservative government was unthinkable.

The rejection of wage restraint by the TUC and its refusal to respond to the promises of price stability appeared to leave the government in the 1956–57 wage round with no alternative to a policy of standing firm on wages at the risk of industrial conflict. The commitment to price stability was a powerful incentive to employers to resist wage demands. The Engineering Employers Federation (EEF), encouraged by an assurance it had received from the government that if it stood firm it would not be pressed by the government to settle (as had happened in 1954), and also the shipbuilding employers, refused to make any offer in response to trade union claims for increases at meetings over six months. A strike in shipbuilding began on 18 March 1957. In engineering, the unions decided to call out their members by stages from 23 March, so that there would be a total strike by June. There was the possibility also of a railway strike and a power workers dispute.

By the time this situation had developed events had brought about a change in the government's policy of resistance to inflationary claims. The failure of the Suez operation, followed by the resignation of Eden in January 1957, had damaged the standing of the government in the country and divided government supporters in the House of Commons. The Suez operation and American opposition to it had led to a serious run on the pound, which in March 1957 was still in difficulties. Oil supplies had been affected (petrol rationing had been introduced), resulting in higher transport charges which broke the policy of price stability.

In view of the threatened widespread industrial troubles, Macmillan, now Prime Minister, reviewed the government's emergency plans and organisation, but contemplated having to make use of them without enthusiasm. In his first public speech as Prime Minister, on 18 March 1957, he appealed for the settlement of industrial disputes by some form of arbitration rather than by 'self-destructive struggles'.

He followed this up by pressing Brian Robertson, Chairman of the British Rail Board, and the engineering and shipbuilding employers to settle the outstanding wage claims. The railway claim was settled with an offer of a 5 per cent increase. The shipbuilding employers also offered 5 per cent and the engineering employers, who were more determined, $3\frac{1}{2}$ per cent. These two offers were rejected and Iain Macleod, Minister of Labour since December 1955, appointed two Courts of Inquiry. The strikes were called off on 2 April 1957, the Courts of Inquiry recommending increases of 5 per cent. The EEF regarded itself as having been stabbed in the back and published a document criticising the government's reversal of policy.

The first serious attempts by a Conservative government to secure some degree of wage restraint, both through an understanding with the General Council and by readiness to accept industrial trouble, had failed. The first alternative, based on an offer of price stability, had not influenced the attitude of the General Council. The second, in spite of the early withdrawal by the government, had resulted in the days lost through strikes in 1957 being nearly $8\frac{1}{2}$ million – the highest figure since 1926. The operation as a whole was regarded by many Conservatives as proof that an understanding with the TUC was not possible on terms acceptable to a Conservative government and that the TUC attitude was determined by political hostility. The action of trade unions in calling strikes when the country was in serious economic difficulties and the government in even greater political difficulties after the Suez debacle confirmed this view. The retreat by the government meant that it would find it even more difficult to secure wage restraint in the future. It was left with the unpalatable alternative of taking deflationary measures to improve the balance of payments and protect the pound, measures which would lead to increased unemployment.

The weakness of the economy, the damage the unions could inflict on it and the political necessities of preparing for a general election in 1959 meant that it was not in fact until 1961 that any further serious attempt was made to contain inflation by some form of wage restraint. In 1957, however, the problem did not go away. The rate of inflation in the four years 1957–61 was relatively high in comparison with that of other industrial countries. There were recurrent balance of payments difficulties and the pound was from time to time under pressure. Government policies were mildly deflationary – except during the period immediately preceding the election in October 1959 – and this threatened the maintenance of full employment, at least at the level which had come to be regarded as normal in the ten years after the war.

From 1957 to 1961 there was discussion within the government, accompanied by public debate, about the need for wage restraint and possible means of achieving it. Arguments in favour of a 'wages policy' gained support, backed by a report from the Organisation for European Economic Co-operation (OEEC)[5] in 1958 and accounts of the success of wages policies in other countries, particularly Holland and Sweden. Some officials in the Treasury continued to press for a 'wages policy' and their influence increased. Officials in the Ministry of Labour, however, as during the war and after, continued to argue that the process of settling wages was too complex to be regulated by government policy and that there was no satisfactory alternative to the existing system of collective bargaining. The government was not ready to commit itself to another major initiative on wages, but some gestures were made in a further attempt to control increases. While these had no measurable effect in influencing the rate of wage increase, they caused some damage to the apparatus of collective bargaining, conciliation and arbitration.

The government appointed a Council on Productivity, Prices and Incomes in August 1957 to keep under review changes in prices, productivity and the level of incomes (including wages, salaries and profits) and to report on these from time to time. Such a council had been recommended by three Courts of Inquiry since 1955. The Council was independent and might, it was hoped, be an instrument to remove the wages issue from the political arena, partly by influencing arbitrators and Courts of Inquiry against what the critics of collective bargaining described as 'inflationary wage awards', though this could hardly be reconciled with the primary responsibility of arbitrators and Courts of Inquiry to settle the disputes referred to them. Whatever hopes the government had for the new body were effectively destroyed when the General Council rejected its first report as partisan and refused to co-operate with it.

The government made firm statements about wage restraint before the 1957–58 wage round following the adoption by the Trades Union Congress in September 1957 of a motion, moved by Cousins, rejecting wage restraint in any form. At the end of October, in a debate in the House of Commons on the economic situation, Peter Thorneycroft, Chancellor of the Exchequer, gave the government's reply: wage

[5] This later became the Organisation for Economic Co-operation and Development (OECD).

increases unrelated to, and going far beyond, the general growth of real wealth within the country were by far the greatest danger the country had to face; those who claimed, granted and adjudicated on, wages should bear this in mind. Iain Macleod followed this up by stating that the government, the largest employer, was determined not to finance inflationary awards, whether these were secured by negotiation or by arbitration. He emphasised the damage which industrial conflict might do to the economy and to the pound, but declared that the government would not hesitate to face such conflict. His statement was unconvincing in view of the government's retreat six months earlier and the fact that it was still anxious to avoid serious trouble which might threaten the pound. In the event, however, it succeeded in the latter aim while taking action which gave some temporary plausibility to its determination to stand firm and which was politically advantageous.

The government faced the most serious threat to the avoidance of industrial trouble on the railways, where the unions had rejected an offer of a wage increase of 3 per cent. Macmillan saw the unions and persuaded them to settle on the basis of 3 per cent, with the promise of the appointment of a 'comparability' committee to study the relative wages of railwaymen and comparable groups in industry, which the unions rightly considered would almost certainly result in substantial further increases. The committee was appointed with Guillebaud as chairman. The Prime Minister's proposal avoided an immediate dispute but caused problems with railway pay which were to continue to embarrass governments for ten years or more.

Like the establishment of the Council on Productivity, Prices and Incomes, the appointment of the Guillebaud Commission was an attempt to remove wages issues from politics, avoid direct confrontation between government and unions, relieve government of responsibility and avoid criticism from the private sector that government weakness in the public sector was the main cause of wage inflation. The move was criticised as showing the government's lack of resolution in standing on the line which ministers had proclaimed.

Accordingly, Macleod took the opportunity of showing the government's resolution in a less serious dispute. The Transport and General Workers Union had submitted a claim for an increase on behalf of London busmen in October 1957 and by January 1958 negotiations had failed. The government was not prepared to allow the Ministry of Labour to conciliate, but Macleod agreed that a committee should be appointed to do this. The agreement was withdrawn after the

Cabinet decided against it. Cousins was persuaded that the dispute should be referred to the Industrial Court, but made it clear that the union would not feel bound by an award of the Court. The award of about 4½ per cent was in fact rejected and a strike began on 5 May 1958. The government refused to take any further action and decided to sit out the strike, which ended after six weeks on 21 June with acceptance of the increase earlier awarded by the Industrial Court.

The strike and the settlement were relatively unimportant in the attempts to secure wage restraint, but the way in which the government dealt with the problem raised questions about the independence of the conciliation services of the Ministry of Labour and of arbitration and indicated a change of attitude in the Conservative Party towards the unions. The government, if not prepared for serious industrial conflict, seemed ready to weaken the apparatus of conciliation which might help to avoid it.

A further gesture was made to the advocates of wage restraint and critics of the industrial relations machinery when the post of Chief Industrial Commissioner in the Ministry of Labour and the Industrial Disputes Tribunal were abolished, the latter as a result of the government's decision to repeal all wartime defence regulations. Although the Tribunal had been criticised for making inflationary wage awards and for diminishing the responsibility of unions by removing an incentive to reach settlements by negotiation and agreement, reference to it had been helpful to trade union officers who were not able to agree a settlement or agree to arbitration because of pressure from their members but who could accept arbitration if a unilateral reference were made by the employer. On the whole, the Tribunal had been a useful device to prevent or at least postpone a strike.

Macleod offered permanent legislation in place of Defence Regulation 58AA, which had been the legal basis for the Industrial Disputes Order and hence for the Industrial Disputes Tribunal, in order to preserve the procedure of unilateral arbitration. The employers, however, rejected this, except for industries where both sides agreed to it – a reservation which made the legislation unnecessary. Continuation of the procedure might have been acceptable to many unions – though Cousins and others were increasingly critical of arbitration bodies on the grounds that they were no longer genuinely independent and that their awards were influenced by the government. The disappearance of the Tribunal marked the end of the machinery constructed by Bevin for dealing with wages and industrial relations within the process of collective bargaining.

By this time, however, concern within the government over inflation and wage restraint had been overlaid by the need for economic expansion and reduction of unemployment in preparation for the election which was likely within the next twelve months. The Chancellor, Peter Thorneycroft, and other Treasury Ministers had resigned in January 1958 on the grounds that government cuts in expenditure were not deflationary enough and would be inadequate to deal with the balance of payments problem and to protect the pound. The deflationary policies of 1956 and 1957, which had resulted in unemployment rising from 1.3 per cent to 2.2 per cent, were put into reverse. The general election followed in October 1959 and the government was returned with an increased majority.

One Nation, Incomes Policy and a Guiding Light, 1959–64

Relations between the government and the trade unions had deteriorated between 1955 and 1959, in part because of the government's concern about wages and the move to the left amongst trade union leaders. Macmillan had avoided serious industrial trouble, but some of his actions had been strongly criticised and he could not claim to have made progress in dealing with wages and inflation or the problems of industrial relations. There had been increasing public concern about these matters since the mid-fifties and they were now serious political issues. The theme of wage push inflation and the need for wages policies to check it had been taken up seriously by economists.[6] Government intervention in disputes had been criticised as inflationary. The *Economist* regularly attacked the Ministry of Labour as an instrument of inflation. Within the government after 1959 arguments for more effective measures of wage restraint were given increased support. The unions were blamed by the public for unofficial strikes, restrictive practices, overmanning and other activities damaging to the economy. There was talk of legislation to limit trade union power.[7] There was less concern amongst some in the Conservative Party about the political consequences of a conflict with the trade union movement. The unions were unpopular – the national credit they had built up during the war had gone – and a third

[6] For example, in the OEEC report mentioned on p. 30.

[7] *A Giant's Strength*, published in 1958 by the Inns of Court Conservative and Unionist Society, argued the case for legislation.

successive election which for the second time gave the Party an increased majority suggested that their political influence was declining.

The prospect of conflict with the trade union movement over wages or trade union power did not, however, appeal to Macmillan or fit in with the 'one nation' theme of the 1959 Conservative Party manifesto, which included an undertaking that the government would invite representatives of employers and unions to 'consider afresh the human and industrial problems that the next five years will bring'. He hoped to continue the conciliatory approach to the unions established in the Churchill–Monckton years in spite of the pressures for action on wages and industrial relations.

Edward Heath, appointed Minister of Labour in October 1959, followed up the manifesto commitment and revived the Joint Consultative Committee of the National Joint Advisory Council. A 'programme of work' was agreed, but before any action had been taken Heath was succeeded in July 1960 by John Hare, who continued the initiative. There were discussions which led to the Contracts of Employment Act and the preparation of a Redundancy Payments Bill.[8] The initiative was received without enthusiasm by the union representatives on the National Joint Advisory Council (they opposed the proposals on contracts of employment legislation). Their attitude was political (benefits of this kind were not welcome from a Conservative government)[9] but the proposals could not be regarded as anti-trade union and the argument between the unions and Hare on these issues caused inconvenience but no real conflict. On problems of industrial relations which prompted strong criticisms of the trade unions by the public and within the Conservative Party, Hare aimed to achieve improvement by agreement and outflank anti-trade union opinion, particularly proposals to restrict trade union power by legislation which were now being pressed by a number of employers and by a section of the Conservative Party.

Public concern about industrial relations centred on a limited number of industries, including the motor industry, shipbuilding, construction and the docks. Hare made what he described as a 'positive' approach to these industries.[10] In the motor industry he

[8] The Contracts of Employment Act was the beginning of the process of employment legislation which was continued by both Labour and Conservative governments into the 1970s, ending with the Employment Protection Act, 1975.

[9] The unions gave full support to legislation on redundancy pay introduced by the Labour government in 1965.

[10] This was a significant move. Traditionally Ministers of Labour acted only when there was a dispute.

persuaded both sides to agree to a joint statement in which they committed themselves to securing the observance of procedures for dealing with disputes, to making other reforms and to continuing the examination of the underlying problems which led to unofficial strikes. Meetings were held with representatives of employers and trade unions in the shipbuilding industry and the construction industry in an attempt to resolve problems. There were preliminary discussions about the possibility of further decasualisation in the docks. The activities led to no measurable improvements. They were, however, politically useful in offering, for a time, an apparently hopeful altern-ative to legislation to regulate trade union activities. They were relatively unimportant in influencing relations between govern-ment and unions in comparison with the measures the government took in response to the economic problems following the 1959 election.

Sterling came under serious pressure in early 1961. Arguments for a wages policy were pressed more strongly by the Treasury. The Ministry of Labour continued to argue against interference with col-lective bargaining. The Treasury finally won the argument by per-suading ministers that the consequences of continuing wage inflation were more serious than the political and industrial risks of interfering with collective bargaining and antagonising the unions.[11] Selwyn Lloyd introduced a deflationary budget in July 1961 and announced a pay pause without consulting the unions. The pause, he explained, would be imposed by the government in the public sector and, it was hoped, would be observed elsewhere. This was not all. He announced that the pause was to be followed by a permanent incomes policy.

Events following the announcement encouraged the government for a time. The pause was well-timed – it started at the beginning of a closed period for major wage negotiations and had no terminal date; union opposition was not, at first, troublesome. (The TGWU took a civil service case to the courts on grounds of breach of contract and lost.) Difficulties were not, however, long in arising. At the beginning of 1962 Harold Macmillan thought that 'everything turns on (a) holding on the wage pause for two or three months; (b) being able to slide into wage restraint; getting the machinery started for a long-

[11] This is an over-simplification. Some officials in the Treasury were not in favour of incomes policy (Sir Frank Lee, the Permanent Secretary, did not favour it) and some in the Ministry of Labour were not wholly committed to the defence of collective bargaining.

term policy',[12] but following a major breach of the policy in November 1961 in the electricity supply industry, where an agreement for a wage increase of 4 per cent was above the level authorised by the government and above the figure it had in mind for wage increases in the next stage of the policy, it was already obvious that the pause could not be maintained through the wage round.[13] The difficulty was that the government had not yet decided on the long-term policy to succeed it.

In spite of this dilemma Hare announced at the end of January that the pause would end on 31 March and be succeeded by the long-term policy. The Treasury had argued for a wages policy from time to time for twenty years and since 1958 had prepared detailed proposals. These, it now appeared, were not totally acceptable to ministers.[14] As a substitute the government produced an interim statement, *Incomes Policy: the Next Step* (Cmnd. 1626), published in February 1962, which provided for a 'guiding light' for wage increases of $2\frac{1}{2}$ per cent. Increases above this level would not be justified by arguments relating to the cost of living, comparability or increased profits. An increase in productivity would justify an increase above $2\frac{1}{2}$ per cent, but only if it had been achieved by acceptance of more exacting work, more onerous conditions or abandonment of restrictive practices. Insofar as there were some increases above $2\frac{1}{2}$ per cent, the increases in other cases should be less than $2\frac{1}{2}$ per cent – or to quote from the White Paper itself, in such cases 'considerations would point the other way'.

The 'guiding light', like the 'pay pause' revealed without consultation with the unions, was extinguished within three months by industrial and political troubles. There was a work-to-rule for a month by postmen – the first time they had taken industrial action; a threatened strike on the railways was avoided only after the railway unions again saw the Prime Minister and accepted an increase of 3 per cent; nurses organised a widespread protest campaign, which gained

[12] *See* Harold Macmillan, *At the End of the Day, 1961–1963* (Macmillan, London 1973), p. 49.

[13] The Prime Minister, thinking of Selwyn Lloyd and perhaps of those who criticised his flexibility as weakness, rebuked the Electricity Council (unconvincingly) in a statement in the House of Commons in November 1961. Privately, his reaction was that 'we have retreated ... from the one point in the line which it is in fact impossible to hold'.

[14] 'The Treasury are not very imaginative', wrote Harold Macmillan in mid-1962. *See* Harold Macmillan, *op. cit.*, p. 85.

considerable popular support, against an offer of 2½ per cent; the miners were offered an increase of over 3½ per cent, the Civil Service Arbitration Tribunal awarded 4 per cent to the Civil Service and the Industrial Court awarded 13 per cent to social workers in the National Health Service. A number of Wages Councils recommended increases of 8 per cent or more and stuck to their proposals after they had been referred back to Hare. The final blow to the policy came in the docks. Faced by a threatened national strike, the dock employers agreed to increases amounting to about 9 per cent. Macmillan commented in May 1962, 'this is a great blow to our incomes policy and makes it difficult to see where we go now'.[15]

At the same time the government faced an unpleasant economic and political situation. At the beginning of 1962 unemployment was rising and there was concern that a bad winter might put the figure above one million for the first time since 1947. The government was losing support in the country. Macleod, now Chairman of the Party, and Macmillan were convinced that the declining popularity was due to the incomes policy. Macleod reported on the defeat in the Orpington by-election: 'Incomparably the leading factor was the dislike of the pay policy and general dislike of the government which I suspect more than anything else is also connected with this'.[16] Macmillan reflected:

The pay pause – the government's policy – has offended dons, school masters, school teachers, civil servants, nurses, public utility workers, railwaymen and all the rest. But perhaps it is most resented by doctors, dons, nurses, etc. who feel that they are relatively ill-paid compared to the high wages which they hear about coming in to the ordinary artisan's household. And the Tories are very worried. Anyway it is a portent.[17]

Macmillan decided to withdraw from what he had earlier described as the 'decisive wage battle' – but he needed to cover the withdrawal and produce the promised permanent policy. This was finally revealed in an economic debate in July 1962: there was to be a National Incomes Commission (NIC).

The establishment of a National Incomes Commission had been under consideration for some time. In the early stages it had been proposed that the Commission should deal with important pay claims

[15] Harold Macmillan, *op, cit.*, p. 66.
[16] Report from Iáin Macleod to Harold Macmillan. *See* Harold Macmillan, *op. cit.*, p. 63.
[17] Harold Macmillan, *op. cit.*, p. 59.

referred by either party concerned or referred by the government on the grounds that settlement of the claim was important in the national interest. The Commission was thus conceived as a revised version of Bevin's National Arbitration Tribunal, adapted for the purposes of incomes policy. In addition the Commission was to be superior to other arbitration bodies and able to override their decisions or remove references from them. Macmillan was, however, no longer prepared to accept the industrial and political consequences of intervening in collective bargaining on this scale. When he announced the establishment of the NIC its task was confined to examining pay settlements and commenting on the effects of these on the economy. The Commission was not to interfere in the process of collective bargaining until settlements – damaging or not – had been reached. The Commission was, thus, little more than a revised version of the Council on Productivity, Prices and Incomes. The government had moved back to a policy of education and exhortation. Macmillan explained the retreat: 'That phase of the battle [the pay pause] is over. We have achieved a sound basis for growth and we must confirm that and move to a new phase ... an incomes policy is therefore necessary as a permanent feature of our economic life'.[18]

In spite of the limits on the activities of the Commission, the TUC refused co-operation. They would not nominate members and would not appear before it. They took up the position they had taken towards the Council on Productivity, Prices and Incomes, but on this occasion without waiting for the first report. Macmillan's statement in July, whatever his private view, represented the end of his attempt – the first attempt by a government since the war – to impose an incomes policy. It had survived for twelve months. In political terms it had been expensive.

The policies of deflation, announced in July 1961, the pay pause and wage restraint were accompanied by proposals, inspired by the current admiration for the apparent success of 'indicative' planning in France, to set up a new body which would encourage a higher rate of economic growth. Whatever promises they offered for the future, they were, not surprisingly in the circumstances, received without enthusiasm by the General Council. Selwyn Lloyd offered alternatives – a completely independent body or a body under government chairmanship which would include government members, representatives of the General Council and employers and some independent

[18] Debate on an opposition motion of censure in the House of Commons, 26 July 1962.

members. The TUC expressed no preference and the second alternative was chosen.

The government proposals were in accordance with past trade union thinking and George Woodcock, now General Secretary of the TUC, favoured co-operation. On the other side, Frank Cousins and others on the General Council were reluctant to collaborate with a Conservative government and the 'pay pause' and incomes policy had inspired union animosity. There were, however, negotiations over the details of the form and the terms of reference of the new body in which most of the points put forward by the General Council were accepted and the General Council finally agreed to co-operate and to nominate representatives to what became the National Economic Development Council (NEDC). The TUC insisted that the Council should not be concerned with wages and other issues covered by collective bargaining – an obvious defeat for the government, which had decided that an incomes policy and some form of control of collective bargaining was essential for the management of the economy and had devised the Council as a means of examining ways in which the economy could be managed more effectively than in the past. The Council could hardly have begun its work in more discouraging circumstances.

By early 1963 incomes policy was no longer stressed as a main feature of the government's approach to the economy. The emphasis was by then on economic expansion and growth. Selwyn Lloyd had been replaced by Reginald Maudling as Chancellor of the Exchequer in the extensive reorganisation of the Cabinet in July 1962. Preparations were made for reflation and were launched by Maudling in his budget of April 1963. In the debate on his budget he made clear the government's policy: 'expansion without inflation' by means of a 'real partnership between government, employers and trade unions'. He emphasised that the budget changes in income tax allowances were the equivalent – for a married man with two children earning £15 per week – to a rise in wages of 2½ per cent without addition to costs. Economic growth might, after all, he seemed to suggest, be a substitute for incomes policy. It would certainly be a great deal more popular, particularly if it could be secured through tax reduction.

Although the government could hardly abandon the cause of incomes policy and wage restraint entirely, in practice the cause was deserted during its last year in office. The remnants of the permanent policy promised in 1961 were in the hands of the NIC, which examined and reported on the implications of a handful of wage settlements. The rate of wage increase again accelerated in the wage round of 1963–64 and in the autumn of 1964. Faced by a threatened electricity strike in the spring of 1964, the government resorted to the traditional device of appointing a Court of Inquiry, which led to what supporters of incomes policy no doubt regarded as an inflationary wage settlement. Pursuit of the cause was postponed until after the general election. At the same time, the initiatives taken by Hare to improve industrial relations petered out. A Contracts of Employment Act was passed but the possibility of redundancy payments legislation was not pursued. There was no evidence that Hare's other activities had made any contribution to improving industrial relations.

In the thirteen years of Conservative administration, from 1951–64, the Churchill–Monckton policy of treating organised labour 'with circumspection'[19] had, overall, prevailed. Although for short periods in 1956 and 1961 policies which threatened serious trouble with the unions had been adopted, the government had withdrawn on each occasion. As well as being concerned to avoid conflict the government had made positive attempts to further government-union co-operation. The establishment of the National Economic Development Council to increase the rate of economic growth was a recognition that the achievement of this aim depended on trade union co-operation. Exclusion of wages from the NEDC and the negative reaction of the trade unions to other moves indicated the limits they would impose on co-operation with a Conservative government.

In 1964 the relationship between the unions and the government may not have seemed much different from what it had been in 1955. In fact, it had been changed significantly by government policies and failures in the three years up to 1964. The promises of economic growth, a permanent incomes policy and improved industrial relations were to dominate the relationship between unions and the governments of Wilson and Heath.

The Early 1960s: a Summary of the Position

After 1961 both political parties promised a higher rate of economic growth. Both emphasised the importance of the problem of wage inflation and accepted that the rate of wage increase produced by

[19] *See* Michael Foot, *Aneurin Bevan, 1945–1960* (David-Poynter Ltd, London, 1973), p. 350.

free collective bargaining since 1945 threatened the maintenance of full employment. The Wilson and Heath Governments were to seek wage restraint and to interfere with, and at times prevent, the process of free collective bargaining. Both were to attempt to reform industrial relations. In doing so they challenged the manner in which trade unions had exercised their industrial power since 1945 and eventually tried to limit that power.

In 1961 the unions did not seem to be in a strong position to resist any such challenge. They were unpopular. Their leaders were blamed for being too weak to prevent their members going on unofficial strikes and maintaining practices which reduced industrial efficiency and damaged the economy, and for being too powerful in pressing their wage claims and causing inflation.[20] The General Council appeared less effective than before 1955. There was no dominating group and Cousins provoked as much opposition as support. There were signs that the self-confidence evident between 1940 and 1950 had gone. Some union leaders accepted the need for wage restraint and recognised the problem of reconciling this with collective bargaining – though they would, of course, put on a show of unanimity with others against the interference with collective bargaining by a Conservative government. Some members of the General Council were even prepared to admit publicly that not all trade union activities were above criticism. There had been an abortive inquiry by the TUC into unofficial strikes; George Woodcock had asked, 'what are we here for?', and had persuaded Congress in 1962 to institute an inquiry into trade union organisation and structure.[21] If the basis of unity – opposition to a Conservative government – were to be removed by the return of a Labour government, the General Council might well find it difficult to present a united front.

On the other hand, the events of 1961 had confirmed the importance of trade union power. The government may have interfered in collective bargaining without forewarning; it had not been prepared to push the intervention too far nor to maintain it. It had, furthermore, sought union co-operation for 'expansion without inflation'. In the discussions over the NEDC the unions had established for the first time since 1951 a recognised 'bargaining position' with a Conservative government and had used it effectively. They

[20] The exposure of communist ballot-rigging in the ETU was particularly damaging to their reputation.

[21] In 1964 he went further and was ready to agree to the appointment of a Royal Commission.

had made no concessions and had excluded wages and collective bargaining from the terms of reference of the Council. The government's incomes policy and plans for economic growth had provided one answer to George Woodcock's question: the unions were there to oppose governments and to bargain about the terms on which they might co-operate.

If the standing of the unions in the country and their political influence had greatly declined since 1951, the criticism they attracted and the attitude of the government were evidence that their industrial power was certainly no less and that their political influence might be reviving. For the first time since the war, membership of unions affiliated to the TUC was beginning to increase substantially and, partly in reaction to the pay pause and incomes policy, their influence extended to groups of workers where it had so far been relatively weak. The incomes policy generated some identity of interest among professional groups, public servants, white-collar workers and others and between them and the groups traditionally powerful within the TUC.

This was the position at the outset of the period in which governments began to interfere with the central union activity of collective bargaining and eventually sought a way of reducing union industrial power. In spite of the problems caused by collective bargaining, it is possible that neither major party left to its own devices would have chosen to deal with the latter issue by questioning the legal framework within which the trade unions operated. It was hardly conceivable that the Labour Party would willingly choose to do so. Opinion amongst Conservatives had become increasingly anti-trade union but their behaviour in office since 1951 and the terms of their manifesto suggested that they too would be unlikely to choose willingly a policy which could lead to general conflict with a united trade union movement. Neither party was, however, able to avoid the issue. A decision of the Courts, as in the Taff Vale case of 1901, compelled the politicians to consider the legal basis on which trade union power had developed.

In the case of *Rookes* v. *Barnard* in 1963 the House of Lords ruled that Rookes, a non-unionist who had been sacked because the union had threatened to strike in support of the closed shop, was entitled to damages from the union. The decision made it clear that the Trade Disputes Act, 1906 did not give union activities all the protection assumed by the unions to have existed for sixty years. Woodcock pressed Joseph Godber, Minister of Labour since October 1963, for a Bill to restore the protection the unions thought they had, offering in return to accept the appointment of a Royal Commission. In view of opinion in the Conservative Party and the prevailing general unpopularity of the trade unions, the Conservative government insisted that the implications of *Rookes* v. *Barnard* would need to be examined as part of a general inquiry. An inter-departmental committee of officials was asked to report on possible changes in the law affecting trade unions and industrial relations and a commitment to a public inquiry was made in the Conservative election manifesto. The political consequences of *Rookes* v. *Barnard* were (indirectly) to be comparable with those of Taff Vale.

PART II

Harold Wilson, 1964–70 – 'The New Britain'

Harold Wilson became Prime Minister in October 1964, offering hopes of a partnership between trade unions and government similar to that which had existed during the Attlee Government. Central features of the partnership were to be a national economic plan to provide a higher and sustained rate of economic growth and an agreed policy for 'planned growth of incomes' to curb inflation. When it came into office, the government had, however, to face the problems arising from an adverse balance of payments, which continued until late 1969 and had a decisive influence on its economic policies and its relationship with the trade unions. By 1969 the partnership had collapsed: 'what we are talking about', said Wilson, 'is a deep and fundamental split between the two wings of the movement'.

The years of the Wilson Governments, during which the relationship between government and unions changed so completely, can be divided into four periods. There was a period of partnership between government and unions from October 1964 to July 1966. An incomes policy was agreed within six months and a national plan formulated in less than a year; first moves were made to 'reform' industrial relations. The government, however, changed the principles of the agreed incomes policy within twelve months and, following the most damaging national strike since the 1920s, in May 1966, economic growth and the national economic plan were pushed aside by deflationary measures. The partnership was broken and the basis for it destroyed.

The second period, which might be described as one of co-existence, lasted until late 1967. The unions accepted the consequences of the deflation of July 1966, including a wage freeze and statutory incomes policy. While they continued to support the government, they became increasingly critical and prepared their own alternative policies for economic growth and incomes. The government's attempts to improve industrial relations had no effect. There were serious strikes in 1967, at a time when the pound was in trouble, and the government was forced to devalue.

The third period, following the devaluation of October 1967, was one of disagreement, leading to the 'deep and fundamental split' over *In Place of Strife*. Facing increasing union opposition to its statutory incomes policy, the government decided to relax on wage restraint but to legislate on industrial relations. The government's proposals for legislation, opposed by the unions, were abandoned.

In the fourth period, leading up to the election of May 1970, the government gave priority to restoring relations with the unions. It retreated from policies it had presented as essential for economic success, and, while doing so, finally achieved its objective of a favourable balance of payments.

3 Partnership: The First Phase, October 1964– September 1965

The Hopes and Promises of the Wilson Government, October 1964

The economic record of Conservative governments since 1951 – 'the thirteen wasted years' – and the need for a higher and sustained rate of economic growth were major issues in the 1964 election. *Signposts for the Sixties*, adopted by acclamation at the Labour Party Conference in 1961, put economic growth and planning first in a list of five major issues. The 1964 Labour Party manifesto, *Let's go with Labour for the New Britain*, emphasised the need for economic growth, innovation and efficiency. It criticised the economic planning of Conservative governments, their policies of 'stop-go' and the continuing inflation; it promised more effective planning to achieve a higher rate of economic growth and a 'technological revolution'. An incomes policy was proposed as one of the measures to control inflation: the growth of incomes would be broadly related to the annual growth of production and this would be achieved by the government's entering into 'urgent consultations with the unions' and employers' organisations concerned'. The manifesto also promised general improvements in the social services and education, emphasising that these depended on success in increasing the rate of economic growth.

On planning, economic growth and incomes policy, the Labour Party shared common ground with the Conservatives, who had committed themselves to 'indicative planning' in 1961. Labour politicians might, however, claim more credibility for their promises. They had always believed in planning, while the Conservatives had destroyed the planning apparatus after 1951 and had only ten years later become unconvincing converts. The Labour Party had not, during these years, carried the disadvantage of responsibility for deflation to protect the pound and was free to attack 'stop-go'. Labour politicians could argue also that their proposals for an incomes policy were more than a development of Conservative policy – their opposition to the latter, indeed, made this necessary. A Labour government's policy would be accompanied by social and tax measures which would make it fairer and more acceptable and, most important, it would be agreed with, and supported by, the trade unions. A higher rate of growth and the curbing of inflation would make possible improvements in the welfare state with minimum pain to the mini-mum number – and bring about the gradual transformation to socialism. The journey towards Bevans's Mecca could be resumed.[1]

The reference in the manifesto to incomes policy meant that, if elected, the next Labour government would be the only one since the war to take office committed to a policy which questioned the working of the free collective bargaining system. The general increase in wages was to be 'planned'. Since the late fifties economists had stressed the importance of wage-push inflation created by collective bargaining in a situation of full employment and had argued for a wages policy. The Macmillan Government had been converted. Nevertheless, the persuasions of economists identified with the Labour Party might be thought to have exercised a surprising influence on Labour politicians and an even more surprising one on their trade union partners. There were, however, respectable precedents for wages policy amongst politicians in the Party, dating back to 1947, and the manifesto had been worded to gain the widest possible support from the unions. At the Labour Party Conference in 1963 Frank Cousins had spoken in favour of 'planned growth of wages', while at the same time opposing wage restraint. This was interpreted as an offer to co-operate in an incomes policy which implied some restraint in collective bargaining if a Labour government adopted a policy for economic growth, controlled dividends and profits, reformed the tax system and took measures to raise the incomes of the poorer members of the community. His speech could be interpreted differently. Cousins might have meant that the politicians were to ensure a more rapid increase in real wages while the unions continued to secure the highest money increases they could through free collective bargaining. If this interpretation existed at the time, it did not become an obstacle to agreement for the purposes of an election manifesto.

On industrial relations and 'the trade union problem' the manifesto was, not surprisingly, silent, except for a declared intention to reverse

[1] Aneurin Bevan, *see* page xii.

the judgement in the case of *Rookes* v. *Barnard*. Harold Wilson did not, however, disregard the public concern which had led the Conservatives to promise an inquiry into trade unions and industrial relations. At the Trades Union Congress in 1964, on this occasion, as on others, a pre-election rally, he promised to reverse the decision in *Rookes* v. *Barnard*, but criticised the trade unions over restrictive practices and other problems. He reminded Congress of its pledge to support an incomes policy.

During the election campaign the Party did its best to avoid the topic of industrial relations and the unions officially did their best to help. Negotiations on wage claims in the docks and steel industry, which might have led to industrial trouble during the campaign, were extended. But official union efforts were not wholly successful. In the first week of the campaign there was an unofficial strike at Hardy Spicer which threatened large-scale lay-offs in the motor industry and, in the last week, a strike on the London underground. Wilson reacted to the first strike with a diversionary suggestion for an inquiry into whether strikes at election times were deliberately fomented on behalf of the Conservative Party, mentioning strikes at British Oxygen in 1955 and 1959. The London underground strike was rapidly condemned by both Wilson and Ray Gunter. The strikes were commonplace enough, but they might cost votes and this was irritating during a close election. The industrial wing of the movement did not always give the help a politician could hope for during his most important political activity.

In office, memories of the Attlee Government set the pattern. This was the only precedent of political success for the labour movement: in partnership with the unions the government had established full employment, the mixed economy and the welfare state. In it Wilson had started his progress towards becoming Prime Minister, as a junior minister and later as President of the Board of Trade. The situation of the Wilson Government in 1964 was, however, very different from that of the Attlee Government in terms of governmental experience, public attitude to its policies and its trade union partners and the relationship between trade union leaders and their members.

The more important figures in the Attlee Cabinet had long and immediate experience of government; the government had an overall majority of 146 and could claim a clear mandate in favour of radical change; the sense of national unity generated by the war continued for a time to influence public judgement of its policies; some major features of its programme – full employment, the Beveridge Plan, the

National Health Service – were consensus policies inherited from the war-time Coalition Government; it had been a normal practice for the General Council and unions to work closely with government during the war and Attlee inherited the advantages of this well-established process; the national standing of the unions in 1945 meant that their considerable and open political influence did not reflect adversely on the government. The position of the Attlee Government had been helped also by the set-up on the General Council, where the leaders of the four or five most important unions on most issues involving political considerations – including industrial activities which might affect the position of the government – shared the same views as, and consistently gave support to, the Attlee-Bevin axis within the Cabinet. On major issues they carried with them a majority of the General Council and could rely on substantial backing amongst trade union members for support for the government. Their authority and influence over their members was partly an inheritance of the position they had assumed during the war and partly reflected fears of a return to the unemployment of the thirties and the priority given by trade union members (and the country as a whole) to achieving and maintaining full employment. It was this which enabled them to support with determination and consistency the first government ever to give priority to full employment as a political objective – and to achieve the objective.

The Attlee Government thus started with wide support in the country and a strong parliamentary position. A firm basis for effective and close collaboration was ensured by the powerful representation of the trade unions in the government, particularly by the presence of Ernest Bevin, the final guarantee that the partnership between the Trades Union Congress and the Parliamentary Labour Party and between the unions and the government would not be broken.

Wilson's position was very different. The more important members of his Cabinet had little or no experience of government and had been in opposition for thirteen years. A majority of only five in the House of Commons was reduced to three within two months. The prospective short life of the government meant that priority had to be given to winning the next election, in the hope that a larger majority would then provide a basis for carrying through its long-term programme. The timetable of politics would not enable the promised benefits of economic planning and planned growth of incomes to be enjoyed before the next election. Nevertheless, the 'national economic plan' and 'national incomes policy' depended on long-term commitments from the trade unions. Some trade union leaders were bound to have reservations about making such commitments, given the possibility of an early election and the return of yet another Conservative government.

The close working relationship between governments and the General Council which had existed from 1940–50 had disappeared during the thirteen years of Conservative government. The Conservatives, it is true, had tried to rebuild a relationship in the last two or three years, but a return to the situation prevailing between 1945 and 1950 would need positive efforts by both government and unions. The links that existed between the two wings of the movement when in opposition would not be enough. The public standing of the unions had also changed since 1950. The prestige and respect they had enjoyed following the war had disappeared and a partnership which gave the impression of trade union domination of the government and the Parliamentary Labour Party could well be electorally damaging. The balance of influence within the Labour Party, which had so concerned MacDonald, had not been a serious political problem for Attlee, at any rate in his years as Prime Minister. (It was Harold Laski, not trade unionists, who embarrassed Attlee in the 1945 election![2]) The problem had reappeared by the time Wilson became Prime Minister. The influence of trade union leaders over their members was by 1964 much less than it had been in 1945–50. Strikes in breach of national agreements and unofficial strikes not supported, and at times opposed, by unions at the centre rather than the exercise of trade union power nationally had become the major issue of industrial relations. The leading figures on the General Council no longer gave as united a lead on political and related industrial issues as they had done between 1940 and 1955. Cousins' political alignment and trade union philosophy differed from those of other leading members of the Council such as Williamson, Cooper and Carron. Political differences between trade union leaders reflected antagonisms within the Labour Party. For the politicians the trade unions were, by 1964, not only partners but a political problem.

On coming into office, Wilson included in his cabinet much the same proportion of ministers with trade union background as had Attlee. Cousins, like Bevin in 1940, entered the government without previous parliamentary experience. In spite of his personal qualities, for the reasons already given he could hardly be expected to repeat

[2] Harold Laski, Chairman of the Labour Party 1945–46 and at that time Professor of Political Science in the University of London.

Bevin's performance in sustaining the prestige of the government with the public or in guaranteeing an effective partnership with the General Council. Within the government the main responsibility for maintaining the partnership was to rest on Wilson himself, George Brown, Secretary of State of the new Department of Economic Affairs, responsible for economic planning and incomes policy, and Ray Gunter, Minister of Labour, responsible for industrial relations. The basis of the partnership was relatively frail compared with 1945.

While some union leaders might hesitate about giving long-term commitments to what might be a short-lived government, the possibility of an early election meant that the government could hope for support in the immediate future to lay the basis for another Labour victory. The politically more moderate leaders – Carron, Cooper, Greene, Ford and others – could be counted on. Cousins, who might have been less helpful, had entered the government and might exercise his influence on its behalf. At the least, as a minister his influence in the General Council would be less and his instinctive trade union reactions might be modified. George Woodcock, whose view of politicians, including Labour politicians, was reserved (at the Trades Union Congress in 1964 he had 'hoped there will be a Labour Government because ... if the present Government were to be returned they would be insufferable'), favoured trade union involvement with governments in economic planning and accepted incomes policy as a necessary part of the exercise.

The Wilson Government thus took office committed to an ambitious programme which could not be carried through without support from a General Council whose members were not united on major issues and who were without experience of working closely with government. It also faced the problems of an adverse balance of payments and serious pressure on the pound resulting from the pre-election reflation of the last government.

The Response to Current Difficulties
The reaction of Conservative governments in similar economic situations had been deflation. In late 1964 adequate deflationary measures would, necessarily, have been severe. For the Wilson Government they would have been an immediate contradiction of declared intentions on economic growth. Devaluation was an alternative favoured by some ministers and advisors, but this would make the commitment to curb inflation more difficult to achieve and

would not, in any case, rule out the need for deflation. There were strong political and historical arguments against it: it would damage belief in the ability of a Labour government to manage the economy more efficiently than the Conservatives and Labour might be branded as the party of devaluation.[3] Either course of action – deflation or devaluation – would reduce the possibility of the government's being returned at the next election with an increased majority.

In the event, the decision was postponed. In a paper, *The Economic Situation: a Statement by Her Majesty's Government*, published on 26 October, the government announced emergency measures, including a surcharge on imports, discussions with the International Monetary Fund and a re-examination of the economic viability of the Concorde project. Publication of the paper was made the occasion for the first public display of the partnership between the government and the TUC. The full General Council met the Prime Minister and announced its support for the measures in the paper, particularly for the surcharge on imports. At the same meeting they agreed to begin discussions on incomes policy and the preparation of the national plan.

James Callaghan, Chancellor of the Exchequer, introduced an emergency budget on 11 November, which the government presented as a first move to meet its promises on social justice and economic growth and as including deflationary measures to protect the pound. Not surprisingly, an all-purpose exercise of this kind was not regarded abroad as adequate. The pound came under severe pressure. Wilson rejected proposals for deflation, including cuts in public expenditure pressed for by the Bank of England, and pressed the Bank to raise a loan in support of the pound. In the event of this being unsuccessful, he made plans to float the pound and prepare for another election to be fought on the issue of a 'banker's ramp'. The shade of Attlee had been present when Wilson was forming his government a month earlier; the spectre of MacDonald and the 1931 crisis might now be summoned to support the Labour government's cause. The plans were not, in the event, put to the test. The Bank organised loans, the pressure on sterling eased and decisions on devaluation and deflation were further postponed.

The balance of payments and the pound continued to be the all-important economic problems for the government until 1970 and its reactions to them were to have a decisive and damaging effect on

[3] In the last forty years the pound had been devalued only under MacDonald and Attlee.

relations with the trade unions. Meanwhile, however, there was time for the government to embark on its long-term economic policies for growth and incomes. Success in this enterprise would remove the need for politically unpalatable decisions on deflation or devaluation. The responsibility rested with George Brown and the new Department of Economic Affairs.

Preparing for an Agreed Voluntary Incomes Policy and a National Plan

The central responsibilities of the new Department of Economic Affairs (DEA) were to plan the future of the economy and develop an incomes policy, but its powers were limited. The main responsibility for government policies crucial to the first – on taxation and public expenditure – remained with the Treasury, while responsibility for dealing with problems of collective bargaining, which would influence the second, remained with the Ministry of Labour.

Despite these limitations, the DEA under Brown became the central link between government and TUC. This suited Woodcock: the Treasury, after all, was concerned with problems on which the views of the trade unions were not the most influential and he regarded the Ministry of Labour as relatively unimportant. The Ministry had been a politically inspired creation of the First World War to provide a link between the government and the trade unions. It had survived – though at times only just – in the inter-war period. It had, during the Second World War, with responsibility for manpower policies, been a department of first importance and the main link with the trade unions, but by 1964, apart from its involvement in industrial relations, its marginal responsibilities for some of the employment consequences of government economic policies were of limited concern to the TUC. Woodcock attached first importance to involvement in major economic decisions and regarded the DEA as the best instrument to achieve this. The creation of the new department inevitably generated some confusion and friction within government and weakened other contacts between government and TUC.

While the government was reacting to the immediate problems of the pound, Brown made his first moves for the preparation of the 'national economic plan' and the development of a 'national incomes policy'. Economic staff were transferred from the National Economic Development Office to his department to work on the plan and he had early discussions with Woodcock on incomes policy. There were differences of approach between them. The TUC commitment to incomes policy assumed that the policy would complement a national plan and would develop as part of the government's long-term policy for economic growth. If Cousins and others had accepted an incomes policy which would change the process of collective bargaining, it was within this context. Any policy would be a voluntary one, agreed between the TUC and the government. Collective bargaining would continue and the purpose of the policy would be to influence the process. In Woodcock's view the TUC would be the major instrument for this purpose, though other devices might be used in support. The policy required a fundamental change in the attitude of trade unions and their members and would take time to produce results. The government had a different time-scale. Under the pressure of the problems of the balance of payments and the pound, it wanted early action to reduce the rate of wage increases and inflation.

The only action on wages which might have helped immediately was a freeze for a limited period during which the longer-term policy could be agreed. The General Council might have accepted a freeze for political reasons, but there would have been difficult industrial problems. Important wage negotiations for the 1964–65 wage round were already in progress with settlements of around 8 or 9 per cent in prospect. A temporary freeze would have seriously dislocated the collective bargaining cycle and made the prospects of a long-term permanent incomes policy a good deal worse. It would also have looked remarkably like the Selwyn Lloyd pay pause as a preliminary to 'the next step'. The possibility of a freeze was, therefore, rejected. The only contribution Brown could make to the immediate situation was to announce in a statement on 4 November his intention to open discussions on incomes policy and to emphasise the importance of bringing the policy within the framework of a national plan for economic expansion.

It was, perhaps, just as well. The government was in much the same position as the Macmillan Government had been in 1962: there was to be a permanent incomes policy based on agreement with the unions (and other interests), but no firm ideas about the form it might take had yet been developed.

Given this and the ambiguities in the attitude of some trade union leaders, it might have been expected that discussions with the General Council and the detailed working out of the policy would take some time (Macmillan's more modest efforts in pursuit of wage restraint in 1955–56 had extended over many months). Brown and Woodcock, however, made rapid progress. The policy and the machinery to apply it were established within six months. It was the most ambitious attempt so far to solve the problem of maintaining full employment and controlling wage-push inflation.

Brown proposed an operation in three stages: agreement first on objectives and principles, secondly, on the machinery to operate the policy and thirdly, on the details of the policy. The first stage was completed with agreement on the *Joint Statement of Intent on Productivity, Prices and Incomes* and its signing on 9 December – with maximum publicity – at a ceremony at Lancaster House by representatives of the government, TUC and employers' organisations.

The Lancaster House ceremony was typical of the atmosphere surrounding incomes policy in 1964 and later. Brown exaggerated the contribution an incomes policy could make to solving the problems of the economy and attached to it an element of drama which surrounded few, if any, other domestic issues. The drama continued with Barbara Castle and reached new peaks with the 'confrontations' of the Heath and Callaghan Governments and the elections of February 1974 and May 1979. The drama was not simply created by George Brown (and other politicians); it was in part inherent in the nature of the policy and the events which flowed from it. The policy was bound to bring trade unions into conflict with government as well as employers and since resolution of the conflicts necessarily took place in public, the results became the subjects of political argument in which the government was judged to have won or lost. Since 1964 the 'drama' has reflected the reality of social and industrial tensions and, since governments have been directly involved, the political tensions created by attempts to impose wage restraint in a period of accelerating inflation. These manifestations of the policy, as well as the policy itself, have had significant political consequences for governments and trade unions. As strikes against government policies continued and governments were defeated it became politically impossible for ministers to ignore the issue of trade union power.

In 1964, however, Brown's style and performance suited the government admirably. The first step in convincing the country that the Labour Party could govern as effectively as the Conservatives in a situation where it was impossible to put through long-term policies was to show activity and, in the euphoria of 1964, Brown was the most active of politicians.

Much of the *Joint Statement of Intent* might have formed part of any election manifesto and it echoed the pronouncements of governments both before and since. There was a declaration of the government's economic and social objectives – the achievement and maintenance of a rapid increase in output and real incomes combined with full employment and the distribution of the benefits of faster growth in a way consistent with the claims of social need and justice – and a reference to the immediate problems which could frustrate the achievement of these objectives: the adverse balance of payments, lack of competitiveness and low productivity. The government proposed machinery to keep a continuous watch on the general movement of prices and money incomes of all kinds and to examine particular cases. The other signatories – representatives of the Trades Union Congress, the Federation of British Industries, the British Employers' Confederation, the National Association of British Manufacturers and the Association of British Chambers of Commerce – committed themselves to aid in the achievement of the general objectives. The content of the *Joint Statement* was a good deal less impressive than its presentation. 'The setting, in the gilded salon of Lancaster House, was appropriate to an international disarmament treaty, but it was an historic occasion. The test was to be its implementation.'[4]

The Development of the Prices and Incomes Policy

After the *Joint Statement of Intent* Brown was anxious to press on with discussions about the new machinery for the incomes policy. Woodcock and other members of the General Council had reservations while there was still talk of the need for further deflationary measures and fear that the government might succumb to pressure from financial interests and end the prospect of economic growth. There was concern also, since Labour had lost the first by-election of the parliament, which reduced its majority to 3, that the government would not survive long enough 'to prepare and implement' a national plan. Against this background, a TUC commitment to a long-term incomes policy might be unwise. The political argument could, however, be put the other way: since the government was in difficulties it should be given greater support.

Alternatives to immediate discussions on the second stage were considered by the General Council. There was debate about whether the next stage of discussion should be about the machinery for the policy or the substance of the policy – that is, the terms of reference

[4] Harold Wilson, *The Labour Government 1964–1970* (Weidenfeld & Nicolson and Michael Joseph, London, 1971), pp. 63–4.

to which the machinery would work. Logic pointed to the second, and Woodcock favoured this. The General Council, however, decided to consider the machinery in advance of the 'terms of reference', explaining later that they were 'mainly influenced by the consideration that the Minister for Economic Affairs was anxious that investigations into price increases should begin as quickly as possible and that for such investigations no complex terms of reference were needed'.[5] This provided convenient justification for the procedure, which suited Brown: agreement on machinery would be easier than agreement on substance, he could maintain the momentum of discussions and there would be less risk of exposing any serious difference of view between government and unions which might affect foreign opinion and the pound and weaken the government's political position.

A White Paper setting out the machinery of the policy, *Machinery of Prices and Incomes Policy* (Cmnd. 2577), was published on 11 February 1965. It proposed the setting up of a tripartite National Board for Prices and Incomes (NBPI) to examine particular cases and advise on whether or not the behaviour of prices and money incomes was in the national interest as defined by the government after consultation with management and unions. Emphasis was laid on the voluntary nature of the policy: its success would depend on the extent to which unions and employers applied it in practice. The effectiveness of the machinery would depend on the willingness of those concerned to accept investigation of proposed individual price increases and wage claims and settlements. Collective bargaining would continue, but in cases which seemed likely to affect the national interest adversely the influence of the new independent expert body could be brought to bear.

Responsibility for review of the general movement of prices and incomes was given to the NEDC. In the light of its review of reports submitted to it, the government, managements and unions would be expected to take any required action in their respective spheres of responsibility. This provision met Woodcock's aim of formalising the involvement of the TUC in judgement of the national interest and the consequences for the development of the policy, matters which otherwise would be for the government alone to interpret. It was, naturally, welcome also to other interests on the NEDC, as it promised an extension of their potential influence – a significant

[5] *Productivity, Prices and Incomes: Report of a Conference of Executive Committees of Affiliated Organisations, 30 April 1965* (TUC, London, 1965), p. 11.

development of the tripartite concept. The hopes were disappointed. Political and economic events were to make it little more than another statement of intent of little importance.

The voluntary nature of the new policy was underlined by the fact that the NBPI was to be appointed as a standing Royal Commission and would have no legal powers to compel parties to appear before it to give evidence or produce information and facts. This was at the time an essential issue for the General Council, who opposed any element of compulsory interference with free collective bargaining. Although the policy was based on consent, the White Paper made it clear that control of the operation of the machinery was to be in the hands of the government, which would retain direct responsibility for all references, though some might arise from complaints on prices or, in the case of wages, at the request of one or both of the parties concerned. The right of the government to make a direct reference was stressed and the hope expressed that the parties concerned would co-operate in such cases. (This form of government interventionism was to be repeated some years later in the proposals made for dealing with 'unofficial' strikes in *In Place of Strife* and contrasted with the position taken by the Heath Government in its legislation on both industrial relations and prices and incomes.)

Even at this early stage, however, the government had reservations about the effectiveness of a voluntary policy. The White Paper made it clear that although the government intended to give the voluntary method every chance of proving that it could be made to work, it would have to consider giving the NBPI statutory authority 'if experience shows this is necessary'.

Following publication of the White Paper Brown appointed members of the NBPI and started discussions with the General Council and employers' organisations on the principles which were to be the guide for the interests concerned and which would provide criteria for investigation of particular cases by the Board. These were set out in the White Paper, *Prices and Incomes Policy* (Cmnd. 2639), published on 8 April 1965. The central principle, at any rate for Brown and the government, was the fixing of a 'norm' for wage and price increases. The norm finally agreed for the opening phase of the policy was set at $3-3\frac{1}{2}$ per cent – a figure based on what the politicians might regard as a modestly optimistic view of the early effects on the rate of growth which would flow from the national plan, the policies they would introduce to support it and the commitment of the interests concerned to increase productivity.

Though optimistic, the figure was, however, sufficiently low to present serious industrial difficulties since, in the current wage round (1964–65), increases were averaging around 7 per cent. Woodcock warned against expecting an early reduction in the level of wage settlements to anything like the norm and argued that an early failure would damage the prospects for success of a permanent policy. Brown accepted that there would be serious difficulties. The norm could have no effect during the last stages of the current wage round. The best hope was that it would be observed from autumn 1965 or, failing this, that it would by then at least have some influence on negotiators and put a brake on the recent acceleration in the annual rate of increase. In any case, the pound was still under pressure and a declaration of a $3-3\frac{1}{2}$ per cent norm might persuade foreign opinion that the government and the unions were determined to reduce the rate of inflation.

The majority of the General Council – many of whom represented unions which had recently settled for wage increases at a higher level and would not be negotiating again for six months or more – supported the government and accepted the norm. Their decision was made easier as the White Paper provided for exceptions for productivity, movement of labour, low pay and relativities. Given these opportunities to exploit in bargaining, the policy was not too restricting in spite of the general qualification that increases above the norm should be confined to cases in which special treatment could be shown to be in the national interest.

The curtain came down on the first act of partnership between government and unions at a Conference of Executives on 30 April. The basis for the partnership was explained in a report from the General Council on the discussions with the government from November 1964 to April 1965 which had resulted in the *Statement of Intent* and the two White Papers, and in speeches from Brown and Woodcock. The report from the General Council emphasised that the incomes policy was a part of the promised national plan and Brown developed this theme. He reiterated the main objectives set out in the *Statement of Intent*, emphasised the importance of the national plan and stressed the voluntary nature of the NBPI, which was intended to work alongside the machinery of collective bargaining, not to take its place. The productivity, prices and incomes policy, said Brown, had 'nothing in common with the wage restraint policies of previous Conservative governments'; it was an attempt to bring together the industrial objectives of the trade unions as wage bargainers with their wider political aims. He ended on an evangelical note:

> I was always brought up from the very earliest days in the trade
> union Movement to believe that in the end we are more than
> wage bargainers. Our people aim higher than the mere satisfaction
> of their basic fodder requirement. Our people want to play a bigger
> role in society and take more decisions as citizens, and to live in a
> society of which they can feel proud, because it is fair, because it
> is decent, because it is egalitarian. The policies we are collectively
> offering you I believe will help us to make a great, an enormous,
> breakthrough in the achievement of the age-old and historic aim
> of our movement.[6]

Woodcock spoke in support of the policy in rather more realistic
terms, drawing attention to the difficulties as well as the promise.
He pointed to the possibility of conflicts between all governments and
the trade union movement, in spite of the partnership of the labour
movement and the links between the political and industrial objectives of the trade unions. He welcomed the moves made by the government and took credit for dissuading it from imposing a wage freeze
and for persuading it to work for a 'more flexible and sensible and
more permanent policy', towards which it was now making the 'first
cautious tentative step'. His speech ended in prophetic vein: if the
unions were not prepared to work with governments to make it
possible – or not impossible – for them to fulfil their economic and
social obligations, either governments would renege on their obligations and no longer accept the duty to maintain full employment or
they would make moves to restrict the activities of unions by trying
to restrain free collective bargaining and perhaps even by trying to
limit the right to strike.[7] (In the event it was not to be a question of
'either/or': governments of both parties did both.)

The report of the General Council was adopted by a majority of
4,800,000 votes, but with 1,800,000 votes against, including the votes
of the Transport and General Workers Union. The 'first tentative
step' of the voluntary productivity, prices and incomes policy had
been endorsed by the trade union movement, but with the TGWU,
which had members over a wider spread of industry than any other
union, voting against it, with other unions opposed to it and in an
economic situation which, while temporarily at least not critical for
the government, was still serious.

---

[6] Conference of Executive Committees, *op. cit.*, p. 30.
[7] 'Statement for the General Council', Conference of Executive Committees, *op. cit.*,
pp. 31–40.

Brown ensured that the National Board for Prices and Incomes went into business without delay. In May and June he made seven references each on prices and pay, ensuring that the Board started work with a satisfying symmetry. Reports from the Board started to appear in June.

During the first six months the government–trade union partnership could hardly, it seemed, have done better: the need for the prices and incomes policy and the principles of the policy had been agreed; machinery to supplement the process of collective bargaining in applying the policy had been established and had started to operate. The centrepiece of the policy – the national plan – was still in the wings, but construction was going ahead rapidly so that it could be moved to the centre of the stage by the autumn before the major wage negotiations for 1965–66, or in time for an autumn election. The curtain could then rise on the hopeful drama of sustained rate of economic growth with 'planned growth of incomes' without inflation.

The National Plan (Cmnd. 2764), published in September 1965, was a hasty construction. It was regarded by many as setting out impossible productivity targets and as containing little explanation of how these and other objectives would be realised. It set out to achieve a 25 per cent increase in total national output by 1970, which required productivity to rise at a rate of 3.4 per cent per annum (as compared with a rise of 2.8 per cent per annum since 1960) and exports to rise by about 5.25 per cent per annum (compared with the average of about 3 per cent per annum over the last 10 years). To achieve these objectives there would have to be fundamental changes in attitudes and policies towards industrial efficiency and use of manpower. There would have to be an average increase in manufacturing investment of about 7 per cent per annum between 1964 and 1970 and, unless there were changes in manpower policies, there would be a gap of almost half a million workers between manpower requirements and available supply by 1970.

In the event, the lack of realism of the National Plan was to be of little practical significance. Events and the government reaction to them after April 1965 had already raised serious doubts about the prospects for economic growth and about the government commitment to a voluntary incomes policy by the time the Plan was published in September. By that time the basis of the government–union partnership had already been undermined.

The Government Changes the Rules

The possibility that the long-term voluntary policy might not be adequate had been discussed as early as November 1964, and though the government had committed itself to a voluntary policy, it had reserved its position in the White Paper in February 1965. It quickly became clear that the reservation was more important than the commitment. The pound continued to be in difficulties and it was necessary to continue borrowing. The government had to give evidence that more effective measures were being taken to reduce the rate of inflation, either by deflation or by slowing down the rate of rise in costs, particularly wages, or by doing both. Wages and salaries were rising at about 7 per cent a year and prices at around 4 per cent. It had been accepted by the government that the prices and incomes policy could not be expected to lead to a quick reduction, but the public commitment to a norm of $3\frac{1}{2}$ per cent now highlighted an apparent failure.

In seeking further loans the government announced some limited deflationary measures in July 1965 and, under pressure to take more effective action on wages, again considered, but rejected, the possibility of a wages freeze. By August, however, it had reached the point of deciding to consider legislation taking powers to require early notice of wage claims and prospective price increases, to refer a wage claim or proposed price increase to the NBPI (without agreement of the parties), to delay implementation of any case referred until the Board had reported and to make the Board a statutory body with powers to require information and evidence. It was hoped that announcement of this intention might reassure foreign opinion.

The intention was in direct contradiction to the basic principle of the understanding on which the TUC had agreed to the existing policy, but it was important for economic and political reasons that it should not oppose the new proposals. Its opposition would weaken foreign confidence in the determination of the government either to introduce the new measures or to make them effective; a break in the government–trade union partnership before the continuously imminent next election – and as autumn approached an election seemed increasingly likely – would be politically damaging.

An urgent exercise in persuasion of members of the General Council was necessary as Congress was due to meet on 3 September and was undertaken by George Brown. He informed Council members of the negotiations for a further loan, the pressure from the United States and other countries for more effective measures against wage inflation and the ideas of the government for legislation. He asked them to agree to the proposed legislation and to act at once as though it was in force since it could not be introduced until Parliament re-assembled in the autumn. He failed to obtain agreement following a discussion in which George Woodcock repeated points which had been argued by the unions in the discussions between November and April: the policy had been intended as long-term and related to economic growth; the government was wrong to expect immediate results and to use it to meet immediate problems; the norm of $3-3\frac{1}{2}$ per cent had been unrealistic in relation to the current level of wage settlements; the proposal of the government for legislation would be unacceptable to a very large number of trade union members and would make the prospects of a successful voluntary policy more unlikely. The General Council was divided, the majority taking Woodcock's view. The government, nevertheless, decided to proceed with the legislation, taking the first step on a course which was to destroy its partnership with the unions.

The immediate response of the General Council, however, was to change its view at a later meeting with Brown on 2 September. There had been talks with individual members of the Council between the meetings and in any case the responsibility now facing them was reduced: they were being asked to accept a decision, not to agree before the decision had been taken, and the onus of preserving or breaking the partnership with the government now rested on them. A compromise was reached: the government would introduce the legislation, with provisions for early warning, reference and delay in implementation during consideration by the NBPI, but would bring the law into operation only if there was clear evidence that the voluntary system was failing. Meanwhile the latter would be reinforced by the establishment of a 'wage-vetting' system within the TUC, a device which, the TUC argued, would make the statutory early warning unnecessary.

At the Congress, the General Council recommended acceptance of the legislation on these terms and the establishment of 'wage-vetting' machinery by the TUC. Woodcock presented the different views, arguing in favour of accepting the proposals but putting greater emphasis on the establishment of a TUC Incomes Policy Committee (the wage-vetting device) and the need for the policy to be run by the TUC, insisting that if the TUC could not run an incomes policy, nobody could. He echoed his own words at the Conference of Executives on 30 April: if the TUC did not contribute towards an incomes policy, either the government would attempt 'greater direction' of the unions or it would give up the task of maintaining full employment and economic growth.[8]

The Congress approved the motion by 5.3 million to 3.3 million votes, a majority for the revised policy much smaller than that supporting the General Council at the Conference of Executives, though still large in view of what the unions were being asked to swallow. The smaller majority might be explained in part by the fact that Congress was more likely than a Conference of Executives to be concerned about wage bargaining and less influenced by the politics of the relationship between the General Council and a Labour government. The reduced support reflected, however, a deep, instinctive suspicion of interference with collective bargaining by government and the law which the pressure for an urgent decision had left little time to remove, and was a reaction to the basic change in the policy which the proposals for legislation represented. The government was no longer seeking to influence collective bargaining: it was now preparing to interfere with the process and to prevent work people securing wage increases which employers might be willing to give.

The government had now committed itself to a statutory incomes policy, a proposition opposed successfully by the unions throughout the war and the post-war period. The compromise on the TUC wage-vetting scheme provided some safeguard, but the large minority vote was also against this. This may have been due in part to the terms of the motion, but many of those at Congress, members of unions throughout the country and the executives of many unions may well have regarded intervention by the TUC as an equally unacceptable interference with their collective bargaining activities.

The government's commitment to legislation and the apparent intention of the TUC itself to ensure restraint in wage increases so that the legislation would prove unnecessary helped the government to borrow to support the pound. The expected autumn election, which may have influenced some members of the General Council in deciding to accept the government's proposal, did not take place. The government had now to provide evidence that the new policies were reducing the rate of wage increase and inflation.

[8] *See TUC Annual Report,* 1965, p. 472.

Industrial Relations

The negotiations between the government and the General Council over the prices and incomes policy dominated their relationship for the twelve months after October 1964, but there were other issues of direct and immediate importance to individual unions and general issues of importance to the trade union movement as a whole in which the government was involved and which were the responsibility of Ray Gunter at the Ministry of Labour.

On taking office in October 1964 Gunter's immediate problem was a threatened dock strike. Negotiations on a claim for a wage increase had been going on during the summer while the Conservative Government was in office and had been extended because of the impending general election. With the election over, the unions gave six weeks notice of intention to strike – a reasonable, even generous, period of time for government intervention. A national dock strike would have been extremely serious in the existing economic situation and Gunter immediately appointed a Committee of Inquiry under Lord Devlin. The Committee was asked to report urgently on the dispute about pay and then to examine other matters concerning the port transport industry – the decasualisation scheme, causes of dissension in the docks and other matters affecting the efficiency of dockwork. It was hoped that the report would provide a basis for further legislation to make improvements on Bevin's decasualisation scheme incorporated in the Dock Workers (Regulation of Employment) Act, 1946.

The pay issue was settled following the Committee's report before the strike was due to take place. The extension of the terms of reference beyond the immediate issue of the strike was unusual, but concern about labour relations in the docks was of long standing and it was early evidence of the government's intention to deal with the industrial relations issues which it had sought to avoid during the election. The reference to efficiency reflected the emphasis the government placed on the need to improve productivity as an element in its policies for economic growth. It was the last major inquiry appointed to examine a wages issue without the complications of a formal incomes policy and the existence of the National Board for Prices and Incomes. The members of the Committee included Hugh Clegg and Jack Scamp, appointed for the first time to a government inquiry of this kind. Both were to become important figures in the evolution of the government's policies on incomes and industrial relations. The second report of the Committee was to have unfortunate consequences for the government in 1967.

The most important industrial relations issue so far as the unions were concerned was the reversal of the judgement in the case of *Rookes* v. *Barnard*. The election commitment to legislate was repeated by the government in the Queen's Speech. With public concern frequently stirred up by reports of strikes and threatened strikes, the government could not, however, ignore wider industrial relations issues. Woodcock had declared himself ready to accept an inquiry into industrial relations under the previous government provided that the decision in *Rookes* v. *Barnard* was reversed, and the idea had attractions for the Labour government. The appointment of a Royal Commission might take the issue of industrial relations and trade union power out of politics for two or three years, and certainly for the period until the next general election. There was, also, always a hope that a Commission might eventually put forward proposals which would improve industrial relations, satisfy public opinion and be acceptable to the trade unions.

Gunter obtained the formal agreement of the General Council to the appointment of a Royal Commission and announced that the government would institute a 'high level and searching inquiry into the role of both the trade unions' and the employers' organisations in a modern society'. There was argument with Woodcock about membership of the Royal Commission, Woodcock insisting successfully that the trade union members should be nominated by the General Council and not selected by the government and – contrary to Gunter's wishes – nominating himself as a member of the Commission. As a member he was in a far more effective position to influence the outcome and inject his personal views than he would have been had he merely given evidence on behalf of the General Council. The Commission, with Lord Donovan as Chairman, was appointed on 2 February 1965 and the Trade Disputes Bill to deal with *Rookes* v. *Barnard* published on 3 February.

The government also picked up without delay the plan for redundancy pay which had been one of the items in the Conservatives' promised 'charter of rights for all employees' but which they had dropped before the election. It was hoped that provision for redundancy pay would remove one of the causes of industrial trouble, minimise resistance to changes needed to increase industrial efficiency, reduce over-manning and encourage labour mobility. The terms which the Conservatives had had in mind were improved, proposals were sent to the TUC and the British Employers' Confederation and a Redundancy Payments Bill was published on 1 April 1965. The Trade Disputes Act, 1965 and the Redundancy Payments Act, 1965 received the Royal Assent on 5 August. The second report of the Devlin Committee of Inquiry was published on the same day and was followed up by the appointment of a Docks Modernisation Committee under the chairmanship of Wilfred Brown (a Labour peer and advocate of radical reform of collective bargaining) to preside over negotiations between port employers and unions to give effect to the Devlin recommendations.

In September 1965 Harold Wilson himself decided to make a move to improve industrial relations in the motor industry by calling a conference of representatives of employers and trade unions. Wilson was amiably described by Gunter on one occasion as a 'real star turn' and his intervention in the motor industry diverted attention from Brown, who had again been holding the centre of the stage with his incomes policy negotiations. It was evidence, too, that while the government was anxious to secure the co-operation of the trade unions, it did not take an entirely uncritical view of their activities. Industrial relations in the motor industry were generally regarded as a serious national problem: unofficial strikes were affecting production in an important export industry. The Conservative government had attempted to improve the situation by political intervention at a lower level, but had failed. In general, unofficial strikes were a major cause of the lack of foreign confidence in the British economy and a main symptom of 'the British disease' – and they were politically damaging to the Labour Party. The fact that the problems were being examined by the Donovan Commission did not satisfy critics of the government and the unions. These were arguments for an intervention by the Prime Minister. Wilson recorded with some satisfaction that his involvement was described as 'a dramatic move, unparalleled in peacetime'.[9]

Suggestions which had been current for some time were put forward at the meetings with employer and union representatives. Gunter suggested that the unions should discipline shop stewards and unofficial leaders involved in strikes in breach of procedure agreements. In return, employers should accept the principle of the closed shop and a check-off system for union dues. The employers argued that legislation was necessary to impose discipline and suggested that they might be empowered to deduct fines from wages, which would be

[9] Harold Wilson, *op. cit.*, p. 135.

paid into a special fund for research and training in industrial relations. The unions rejected any system of discipline and penalties. In
the light of existing trade union membership in the motor industry,
the compensatory offer of a closed shop had, after all, little attraction.
Wilson finally suggested the special appointment of an industrial
relations 'trouble-shooter' for the industry, and it was agreed that
there should be a Motor Industry Joint Labour Council with his
'trouble-shooter' as independent chairman. The Council would inquire into particular disputes and examine longer term measures to
improve labour relations. The proposition was a development of John
Hare's original suggestions and a variant of the Devlin Committee
approach on the docks. Gunter appointed Scamp as chairman.

With Wilson's intervention government activity in response to the
problems of industrial relations almost equalled that on incomes: it
had appointed the first Royal Commission for sixty years, passed two
Acts, averted the recurrent threat of a dock strike and now offered
a hope of permanent improvement in both the docks and the motor
industry.

The End of the First Period of Partnership
The change in the principles of the agreed incomes policy altered
the basis of the government's partnership with the unions. The fact
was that the voluntary prices and incomes policy agreed after six
months discussion between the General Council and the government
had come to an end within four months of the agreement. In supporting the new proposals the majority of the General Council had given
priority to the political objectives of the movement. It was doubtful
whether this position could be reconciled with the industrial objectives
of unions and their members and whether the new weakened partnership could continue to be effective.

Wilson's intervention in the motor industry and the setting up of
the Motor Industry Joint Labour Council had wider implications
than the special problem of labour relations in that particular
industry. Intervention by the Prime Minister emphasised the political
importance of industrial relations. Jack Scamp was soon to become,
for a time, the best known conciliator and arbitrator in the country
(he was chairman of ten Courts of Inquiry outside the motor industry
between 1965 and 1970), inquiring into nine disputes in the motor
industry in 1966, three in 1967 and two in 1968. As with all industrial
arbitrators, the confidence of the parties in him declined as some

of his awards failed to satisfy one or the other side. He was unable to persuade the employers and unions to agree to changes in their negotiating arrangements which (he thought) might improve relations. The Council decided to dispense with the services of an independent chairman and in his final report in February 1968 Scamp made his own recommendations. These were not discussed by the industry. The record of disputes did not improve over the period. The failure of Wilson's initiative was to influence later reactions to the report of the Donovan Commission and the reform of industrial relations.

4 Partnership: the Second Phase, September 1965– July 1966

Incomes Policy and the Railways

Harold Wilson's initiative in the motor industry was, immediately, little more than a temporary diversion from the major pre-occupation shared by the government and the unions – the follow up of the September revised version of the incomes policy. They had now to give effect to the proposals approved by Congress in September. The government published a White Paper, *Prices and Incomes Policy: an Early Warning System* (Cmnd. 2808), on 11 November. At the end of the year George Brown had meetings to discuss the proposed legislation and a Bill was published in February 1966. The TUC established its Incomes Policy Committee to examine claims by affiliated unions – the 'wage-vetting' procedure. By April it had examined more than 250 claims.

While this activity showed good intentions, it was more important that the policy should show some success in securing wage restraint. Stricter observance of the norm and criteria agreed in April was the first requirement. The early reports on pay by the NBPI had been conciliatory. A report on the printing industry where, for all practical purposes, the Board was considering a settlement which was not likely to be changed (rather in the manner of the National Incomes Commission) made suggestions which, it was thought, would improve productivity in the future. On the pay of white-collar workers in electricity supply – referred against a background of selective strikes – the report justified increases above the norm on the grounds that, following changes in the pay level of manual and technical workers, the employees concerned felt 'a sense of disturbance' and the increases were needed to restore a balanced pay structure.

After the events of August and September the tone became more severe – a report on the pay of bank staff in November recommended a standstill until early in 1967. Five new references on pay were made, four in the public sector, in spite of earlier assurances that, unlike the Macmillan Government, the government would not discriminate in this way. All four public sector references, moreover, cut across established procedures for settling pay – the fair wages principle in government industrial establishments, a special exercise on comparability for pay in the armed forces, a recommendation of a standing advisory committee in the higher civil service and the principles of the Guillebaud Report and arbitration by the Railway Staff National Tribunal in the railways. Interference with collective bargaining was well under way.

The politics of pay on the railways, important under the Churchill and Macmillan Governments, had not changed with a change of government and the reference of railway pay to the NBPI was far the most significant in the new phase of the incomes policy and for the standing of the Board with the trade unions. The railway unions had rejected the offer of a two year agreement for increases of 3½ per cent, in line with the incomes policy norm, and had decided to refer their claims (which, they argued, were based on the principles of comparability established by the Guillebaud Report) to the Railway Staff National Tribunal. The general rate of wage increases since October 1964 had been well above 3½ per cent. If the Tribunal were influenced by arguments based on Guillebaud it would award higher, perhaps substantially higher, increases than those offered. If this were to happen in the public sector, where it might be thought the government could exercise effective influence and where it certainly had financial responsibilities, serious doubts would be cast within weeks on its determination and ability to secure a reasonable degree of wage restraint and a question mark would be placed against the usefulness of the policy and the role of the Board.

Two of the railway unions had voted in favour of accepting the government's proposals at the Trades Union Congress in September 1965. They were now persuaded by George Brown to accept a reference to the Prices and Incomes Board on the understanding that the 3½ per cent offer would be implemented immediately. The Board would examine the case for additional increases and report by the end of the year. The unions would retain their right to go to the Railway Staff National Tribunal after that. The understanding suggested that the government might have difficulties later.

The NBPI reported in January 1966. The report referred to the statement in the White Paper, *Prices and Incomes Policy* (Cmnd. 2639), that less weight than hitherto should be given to comparability and other factors and more weight to the norm and recommended that the unions should drop the practice of basing their claims on the comparability formula of the Guillebaud Report. It rejected the claims for increases above $3\frac{1}{2}$ per cent for the staff represented by the NUR and ASLEF, though it recommended that the date of the second $3\frac{1}{2}$ per cent increase should be brought forward from October to July 1966. It recommended an additional $1\frac{1}{2}$ per cent from 1 January 1966 for clerical staff represented by the TSSA, together with proposals for increased mechanisation and flexibility of working. Most important, it recommended abolition of negotiating arrangements which had existed with little change since 1921 and the substitution of national joint pay and productivity councils. It suggested that these councils could, by October 1966, agree on programmes to increase efficiency, improve the use of manpower and reduce overtime. Such changes would make possible wage increases above the norm of $3\frac{1}{2}$ per cent, but in accordance with the criteria of the incomes policy. It recommended – going rather beyond its terms of reference – that the government should announce an annual target to reduce the working deficit of the railways and instruct the Railways Board to act on a commercial basis.

This was the most ambitious and important report so far produced by the Board. It was the first on a major wage claim applying with some rigour the norm and criteria of the policy and supporting the apparent government determination since September to secure a rapid reduction in the rate of wage increases. Apart from the rejection of the claims for increases above $3\frac{1}{2}$ per cent, the recommendations were bound to provoke an adverse reaction from the unions. The proposal that the railways should run on a commercial basis might be in line with the *Statement of Intent* and the government's emphasis on efficiency and productivity, but it was contrary to long held views in the unions about the position of the railways as a public service and the purpose of nationalisation. It appeared to be in direct contradiction to the statement in the Cameron Report, 1954 – as the unions interpreted it – that 'the government having willed the end must will the means'.

The attack on the Guillebaud principles destroyed the basis of previous negotiations and discredited the unions' arguments. Not surprisingly, the NUR Executive rejected the report. Efforts by Brown and Gunter to persuade it to accept ended in failure and the

Executive announced a national strike to start on 14 February.

In spite of an incomes policy agreed with the TUC, the Wilson Government had not avoided the dilemma of earlier governments – the choice of standing by a policy of wage restraint at the cost of a damaging strike. Its position was, however, more difficult. On the one hand, the prices and incomes policy was formalised and had been presented as a crucial element in the policy for economic growth. An open breach at such an early stage would discredit the government in the country and overseas and the effect on the pound might be damaging. On the other hand, a railway strike might be equally damaging to the pound and to opinion in the country. It would certainly weaken the claim that the government could achieve its economic objectives through partnership with unions. In any case, there was no guarantee that determination in facing a strike would lead to a settlement not in breach of the policy. The dilemma was, moreover, presented at a time when it might do the maximum political damage, as Wilson had now decided on an early general election.

Wilson saw members of the NUR Executive and impressed on them the damaging political consequences of a strike at that particular time. They were persuaded to reverse the strike decision and to accept the offer with a promise of early productivity talks which would open, if they wished, under Wilson's chairmanship. Apart from the political arguments, the change of decision was due in part, no doubt, to recognition that the Prime Minister's refusal to improve on the offer was final (Macmillan had been similarly persuasive in 1958). Also, his offer of personal involvement in productivity talks promised more immediate benefits than the machinery proposed by the NBPI and could leave their negotiating machinery undisturbed.

The credibility of the government–trade union partnership and the prices and incomes policy was preserved. The NBPI was not publicly deserted, though from this early date politicians were bound to have misgivings about the dangers of an independent body expressing views on issues of political and trade union sensitivity. An early collapse of the incomes policy had, however, been averted only by government intervention at the highest level and in political circumstances most favourable for securing trade union acquiescence. It was a warning – or, as Harold Macmillan might have said, a 'portent' – that an attempt to apply the policy to secure a rapid reduction in the rate of wage increases would cause serious industrial troubles.

The Economic Situation and the Election of March 1966

It was clearly doubtful by the early months of 1966 whether the incomes policy and machinery agreed to achieve the long-term policy were adequate for the new and more urgent purpose of securing the degree of wage restraint which the government thought necessary to prevent a further decline in foreign confidence. Wage rates since September 1965 had been rising at around 5 per cent per annum. The attitude of the NUR showed that support of Congress for the policy in September 1965 would not prevent individual unions, including those who had voted in favour, from pressing for wage increases beyond the norm, or employers, under pressure, giving such increases. Not all might be justified by the criteria of the policy – though 'productivity agreements' were rapidly becoming fashionable. The wage-vetting machinery of the TUC was so far ineffective in terms of government objectives. The operations and influence of the NBPI were limited. Its authority, moreover, was already being questioned. The Transport and General Workers' Union, which in September had voted against government policy, was refusing to co-operate with the Board on pay references. The proposed legislation for early warning, published in February 1966, had not been followed up: it was not clear that the government could pass the legislation because of left wing opposition and the possibility that the trade unions opposed to it would put pressure on backbenchers. Within the government, Frank Cousins shared the views of his union on the proposed legislation and there was already talk of his resignation.

All these difficulties became, however, problems for the future and a new political situation. Following the railway settlement, 'the lines', said Harold Wilson, 'were cleared for the next election'. This was to take place on 31 March. In the circumstances one might take a rather negative view, as did Richard Crossman – in private: 'The cost of living is still rising; the incomes policy isn't working; we haven't held back inflation; we haven't got production moving. We are going to the country now because ... we shall need a bigger majority with which to handle them.'[1]

The case for the government could, for election purposes, however, be put in a more encouraging light. It asked for a larger majority to carry through the policies put forward in 1964, including 'the weapon specially fashioned for ... attack' on the rising cost of living – the

[1] Richard Crossman, *The Diaries of a Cabinet Minister*, Volume One 1964–66 (Hamish Hamilton & Jonathan Cape, London, 1975) p. 461.

policy for productivity, prices and incomes 'which forms an essential part of the National Plan'. The policy would be developed with increased emphasis on productivity (a Prime Minister's conference was promised) which would also 'form part of an effort to stimulate industrial democracy'.[2]

The government was returned with an overall majority of 97. In parliamentary terms Wilson was now placed to pursue the long-term strategy of 1964 and to repeat the success of the Attlee Government. In reality, however, he faced immediate economic difficulties, which had to be surmounted if the long-term policies were to have time to work. The deficit on the balance of payments in 1966 seemed likely to be higher than in 1965 and to continue well into 1967. Renewals of loans and credits would be needed to maintain the rate of the pound. Further deflationary measures, which the United States and others had pressed for in the summer of 1965, would be required, in contradiction to the pre-election budget forecast. Renewed efforts would be needed to secure effective wage restraint through the prices and incomes policy: the government had to proceed with the Prices and Incomes Bill published in February. The decision, announced in the Queen's Speech, was still opposed by Cousins and his resignation, already threatened, would put strain on the partnership between the government and trade unions over the prices and incomes policy and possibly cause a breach. Wilson foresaw enforcement of the policy as meaning 'a long hot summer'.

There was a re-shuffle of ministerial responsibilities. Brown retained general responsibility for prices and incomes policy, but departmental ministers would handle individual price and wage questions. The Minister of Labour 'would be at the centre of the stage when needed in wage negotiations'. The re-organisation suggested that while the government might be determined to maintain the policy, the possibility of conciliation and flexibility was not ruled out if it gave rise to serious industrial trouble.

The Seamen's Strike, Economic 'Crisis' and TUC Support

Industrial trouble and a major threat to the incomes policy came quickly after the election. On 14 April the National Union of Seamen (NUS), which had been negotiating on a claim (which was estimated would increase wage costs by around 30 per cent) since November 1965, rejected an offer from the Merchant Shipping Federation and

[2] Labour Party manifesto, 1966, *Time for Decision.*

called a national strike to start on 16 May. The employers offered improvements to extend over three years, well below the claim but above the 3½ per cent norm. After the rejection of the offer and the announcement of the strike, Gunter met officers of the union and the union negotiating committee on several occasions. He tried to persuade them to accept the employers' offer together with the appointment of a Court of Inquiry into their conditions of employment, including the effect on these of the special provisions in the Merchant Shipping Act, 1894. These suggestions were rejected, as was a direct approach by Wilson himself, and the strike began on 16 May.

Discussion within the government about whether it should stand firm in defence of the incomes policy (already breached by the employers' offer) or conciliate to prevent a strike was largely irrelevant. The causes of the strike went far beyond the simple issue of the level of any future wage settlement. For some years there had been growing dissatisfaction with the failure of union officials to secure changes in the Merchant Shipping Act, which limited industrial action by seamen, and growing suspicion of the relationship of national officers with the employers. This had resulted in the election of left wing representatives to the union Executive, who by 1966 had obtained effective control of the negotiating committee. From this position they were able to reject all offers and persuade the Executive to support their line and call a strike. (The politics of some of the militants meant, of course, that breaking the incomes policy was a desirable objective to be added to defeat of the employers, the moderates and the union bureaucracy.) In private talks union officers who favoured a settlement assured Gunter that there would be a strike even if the claim were met in full because of the situation in the union, which, in a sense, was an extreme, and in some ways special, case of a general trend in many trade unions since the mid-1950s.

After his first intervention Wilson continued to be closely involved, handling the situation with zest and continuous activity. This Prime Ministerial involvement was criticised, but it was justified by the situation. Wilson had three objectives: first, to show the government's determination to stand by the incomes policy (and to show his personal commitment to the policy, which had at times been questioned); secondly, to keep the General Council on the side of the government and avert sympathetic action which might be damaging, particularly in the docks; and thirdly, to persuade the full Executive of the union to overrule the negotiating committee.

A declaration of the government's firmness on wages might perhaps help the pound, which would certainly suffer as a result of the strike. In an early broadcast Wilson emphasised the economic damage the strike would cause, saying that acceptance of the seamen's demands would 'breach the dykes' and mean higher and higher living costs and the country's being priced out of the export market. He had, he said, recognised in January that a confrontation of this kind would have to be faced; 'the tragedy was that it had to be done in an industry where a strike was so damaging to the nation'.[3]

It was extremely important that there should be no sympathetic action in support of the strike. Seamen went on strike only if their ships were already in British ports or as their ships arrived in British ports. Exports would be immediately reduced but imported supplies of food and other essentials, including raw materials for industry, would not be seriously affected for some time, unless the seamen could persuade dockers and other transport workers to support them. When the union made appeals to the dockers and foreign transport unions, the government declared a State of Emergency so that powers could be taken to deal with the problems which might result. At the same time a Court of Inquiry under the chairmanship of Lord Pearson was appointed to inquire, first, into the wages issue and then, later, to review the Merchant Shipping Act, 1894 – a conciliatory move which made it easier for other unions to refuse support. (Use of the NBPI was not appropriate and was not seriously considered, but a bow was made to it, and to incomes policy, by appointing Clegg, a member of the Board, to the Commission and requiring the Commission to have regard to national interest.)

An interim report on 9 June (Cmnd. 2025) recommended improvements on the employers offer. Despite efforts by the TUC and the government the union rejected the report and in doing so reduced its chances of obtaining sympathetic action. The TUC and the TGWU informed the International Confederation of Free Trade Unions and the International Transport Workers Federation that the TUC was not supporting the strike. Attempts by militants to secure unofficial support in the London docks failed. Further meetings by the government with the TUC, the NUS and the shipping Federation made no progress and by the end of the fifth week of the strike, Wilson – after some thought – re-affirmed that the government could not agree to a settlement which went beyond the Court of Inquiry report except

[3] *See* Harold Wilson, *op. cit.*, p. 230 for the text of the speech, delivered in a television broadcast.

in return for 'copper-bottomed' improvements in productivity. The TUC pressed the NUS to negotiate further. The union refused, the General Secretary, William Hogarth, announcing: 'The TUC can do nothing for us. The position is wide open. We are going to ask for some positive support, not just sympathy. This is a fight with the Government, not with the ship-owners.'[4]

On 20 June, the government announced a renewal of the State of Emergency and arrangements to use the armed services on a limited scale. In announcing this Wilson referred to the political aspects of the strike, blaming a 'tightly knit group of politically motivated men' for endangering the security of industry and the economic welfare of the nation and for forcing great hardship on members of the union and their families.[5] He followed this with a further statement on 28 June about the activities of the militants on the negotiating committee and Executive and their links with the Communist Party. The statements recalled Clement Attlee's broadcast during the dock strike of 1948. They were, however, given a relatively sceptical reception, which perhaps reflected the shift in political influence and sympathies within the trade union movement and the evaporation of the 'cold war' anti-communist spirit.

Meanwhile Pearson was meeting the union and Shipping Federation to follow up Wilson's suggestions on productivity, while Wilson and the TUC continued to put pressure on moderates on the Executive Committee. By this time it was clear that the union would be in such serious financial difficulties if the strike continued that its future as an independent organisation would be jeopardised. The Executive finally voted to call off the strike, which ended on 3 July after 47 days. Wilson, with support from the General Council, had succeeded in limiting the effects of the strike, but he had failed to shorten it and the final settlement was beyond the limits of the incomes policy. This was the most damaging national strike since 1926 and preceded, though it was not the only cause of, the most serious crisis for the pound since November 1964.

The Prices and Incomes Standstill, a Statutory Incomes Policy and the End of the Partnership

On 4 July 1966 the government finally decided to re-introduce the

[4] Statement made on 17 June after TUC leaders tried to persuade the NUS to resume negotiations. *See* Harold Wilson, *op. cit.*, p. 235.

[5] Harold Wilson, *op. cit.*, pp. 235–9.

Prices and Incomes Bill. Following the decision, Cousins resigned from the government. The re-introduction of the Bill – born in the 'crisis' of the autumn of 1965 – was overtaken by events and the economic situation, which was far more serious than it had been nine months earlier. The second reading was moved by Brown on 14 July, immediately after a statement on the economy by Wilson. The bank rate was raised, other measures were taken to restrict credit and the government's intention to take further deflationary measures in the near future announced. The further measures were not yet agreed. Some ministers thought the pound should be devalued or floated and time was needed for ministers to accept particular public expenditure cuts affecting their policies and departments. There was agreement on the need to tighten the prices and incomes policy to secure more effective wage restraint, but not on how this should be done.

The delay led to increased pressure on the pound so that decisions had to be brought forward. On 20 July Wilson announced that indirect taxes and surtax were to be increased, hire purchase restrictions and building controls tightened and public expenditure cut; there was to be a six-month standstill on incomes, to be followed by a further six months of 'severe restraint', and a price freeze for twelve months, with limited exceptions to take account of increases in import prices.

There had been debate within the government about the standstill on incomes and alternatives, including a norm of $3\frac{1}{2}$ per cent (or lower) without exceptions and a zero-norm with exceptions, were considered. There were arguments for trying to preserve some threads of the original agreed policy, but the seriousness of the situation, the need for a simple policy with no scope for evasion, the probability of industrial trouble if there was room for collective bargaining and the relative success of the Selwyn Lloyd pay pause were arguments in favour of a freeze.

Wilson's announcement on 20 July had been made earlier than intended and, as a result, like Selwyn Lloyd's pay pause, the standstill on wages was imposed without consultation with the General Council. In the haste and attendant political difficulties all that could be done for the General Council was for Wilson to inform some members of the contents of his statement an hour or so before it was made. The CBI was informed by telephone.

Cousins reacted immediately by saying that the Transport and General Workers' Union would not observe a wages freeze. Other trade union leaders supported him or expressed doubts about whether a freeze would work. There were moves to avert a direct clash with the General Council, due to meet on 27 July. At a meeting with Wilson, members of the Economic Committee attacked the standstill and the decision not to devalue. The Prime Minister defended both, saying that devaluation would not provide an easy way out and that there was, in fact, no alternative to the standstill: without it the government's measures would have to be more deflationary and this would mean a bigger increase in unemployment.[6]

The General Council was faced with a government decision to go ahead with the freeze, whatever its views. Though Woodcock and others thought the freeze might be unworkable, the majority of its members were, in the end, as in August 1965, prepared to support the government. The government's policy was accepted, the General Council insisting that it should operate to promote social equity and should not inhibit productivity.

The government published its fourth White Paper on prices and incomes policy, *Prices and Incomes Standstill* (Cmnd. 3073), on 29 July, announcing its intention to legislate. A new Part IV was added to the Prices and Incomes Bill already before Parliament, containing temporary provisions which would continue for 12 months and give the government power to make orders directing that specified prices, charges or rates of remuneration should not be increased without ministerial consent and power to reverse unjustified price or pay increases. The powers could be taken only by Orders in Council. In debates on the Bill and in discussions with the General Council (and CBI) the government stressed that the policy depended on voluntary co-operation. The powers would be held in reserve and not invoked unless this was necessary to deter the selfish minority who would not co-operate. In September the Trades Union Congress endorsed the decision of the General Council to give 'reluctant acquiescence' to the wage freeze and the legislation, but with a majority of only 344,000.

The sterling crisis provoked by the seamen's strike, leading to the deflationary measures announced on 20 July, marked the end of the 'partnership' between the unions and the Wilson Government. Circumstances now compelled the government to give priority to the balance of payments. The National Plan, more rapid growth and planned growth of incomes were pushed aside. The agreed voluntary

[6] *See* Harold Wilson, *op. cit.*, p. 261. Wilson says that one right-wing union leader 'almost plaintively' commented, 'you asked us for voluntary restraint to avoid a freeze, and we agreed. Now you are asking us for a freeze to avoid unemployment.'

policy was replaced by the first statutory incomes policy, imposing the most severe wage restraint, since 1948. The deflationary measures appeared to be the most serious departure since the war from the commitment to full employment – and by a Labour government. Trade union support for the government, as measured by votes at Congress, had only just survived. Support from the General Council – the acceptance of policies which were the reverse of those hoped for in 1964 – now rested entirely on political considerations. The partnership between the government and the unions, which was to repeat the achievements of the Attlee Government and reconcile the political and industrial objectives of the labour movement, was dead – though the government held out hopes of resuscitation.

On the government side the wake had already taken place when George Brown was appointed Foreign Secretary in place of Michael Stewart, who moved to the Department of Economic Affairs in Brown's place on 14 August.

Co-existence:
July 1966–
December 1967

A 'Temporary Interruption' of the Partnership

In 1966 the government published two White Papers on incomes policy which set out the criteria to govern wage negotiations until mid-1967. *Prices and Incomes Standstill* (Cmnd. 3073), published on 29 July, laid down that until the end of 1966 the standstill was to apply to prices of all goods and services (with certain exceptions) and to all increases in pay and reductions in working hours – the operative dates of any increases already agreed were to be postponed for six months. New agreements could be reached during the period but increases could not take effect before 1 January 1967 at the earliest and there was a warning that they might not be allowed to come into effect under the stringent criteria intended for the period of severe restraint, when there would be no scope for general wage increases and any criteria would apply against the background of a zero norm.

The White Paper, *Prices and Incomes Standstill: Period of Severe Restraint* (Cmnd. 3150), published in November, proposed only very limited relaxation for the second period of the standstill. The exceptions for price increases were widened very slightly. Wage increases under earlier agreements, due to be paid during the freeze but halted, could now be paid, but with a six months delay on their original date; similar increases due in the period of severe restraint were to be deferred until at least 1 July, unless they satisfied the criteria in the White Paper. The criteria on pay agreed between government, management and unions in April 1965 would continue in abeyance: no general increases were justifiable and the norm was zero. Strictly limited exceptions to this general freeze were allowed – for agreements designed to increase productivity and efficiency and for the lowest paid workers. Pay increases on grounds of comparability and to attract or retain manpower were ruled out. Proposed price and wage increases would be subject to scrutiny by the government through an early warning system.

The government undertaking that the statutory powers in the Prices and Incomes Act, 1966 would not be invoked unless absolutely necessary had a short life, Part IV of the Act was activated on 5 October and during the twelve months of standstill and severe restraint 14 orders were made stopping pay increases, including increases due under the national three-year agreement in the engineering industry and under cost-of-living agreements. The standstill was reasonably effective, with wage rates increasing by about 4 per cent and prices by about 2 per cent between July 1966 and July 1967.

The July 'crisis' measures were presented by the government as an interruption of their original long-term policies: the powers in Part IV of the Prices and Incomes Act, 1966 were 'purely temporary provisions' which would lapse automatically in twelve months and which would not be renewed. The Department of Economic Affairs, which had responsibility for economic growth and the long-term prices and incomes policy, and the National Board for Prices and Incomes continued in being.

The government picked up remnants of the policies of 1964–65. With the policies for growth, full employment and voluntary incomes policy in suspense, Harold Wilson turned his attention to productivity, a subject which at national level at least could be discussed without great controversy. It had been a theme in the *Statement of Intent*, the NBPI was advocating 'productivity bargaining' as a method of justifying pay increases above whatever norm was likely in any foreseeable incomes policy and it was a subject well suited for discussion on the NEDC, which also had to adjust to the disappearance of economic growth and the agreed incomes policy. Wilson developed the theme in his speech to the Trades Union Congress in September 1966 and took the chair at a national conference on productivity held – yet again – at Lancaster House. There was a productivity conference working party of the NEDC and eventually a joint CBI/TUC statement on productivity which repeated the admirable intentions of the *Statement of Intent*. The NBPI produced a report, *Productivity and Pay During the Period of Severe Restraint* (Cmnd. 3167). The government asked the Board to examine seven productivity agreements and to report on them in time for the return to the longer-term prices and incomes policy.

Ministers reiterated hopes for a return to a long-term incomes policy on the basis of agreement with the unions and employers. In the Chancellor's annual speech at the Mansion House James Callaghan said that there could be no return to a free-for-all after the standstill and asked employers and trade unions to find methods for voluntary regulation of a prices and incomes policy which they could administer themselves. Ray Gunter, in a speech on economic affairs in the House of Commons, said that it would be disastrous to return to the situation which had existed before July. A permanent policy to follow the standstill would need to be worked out with the TUC and the CBI. The extent of government interference in collective bargaining should, he said, be reduced, but the policy must ensure regard to the public interest in the process of bargaining.

The hopes were unrealistic. The chances of a return to an agreed prices and incomes policy and restoration of the early partnership between the government and the trade unions were poor. In response to a government suggestion that the TUC and CBI should join with it in setting up a tripartite body to supervise wage and price increases during the period, the TUC Economic Committee informed the government that it preferred to strengthen its own 'wage-vetting' activities and rejected the suggestion. The period of divergence of view between the TUC and the government over incomes policy and general economic policy had begun and was to end in open conflict.

A Second Unilateral Statement on Incomes Policy

George Woodcock still favoured a long-term incomes policy and still hoped to increase the influence of the TUC over its affiliated unions to develop such a policy. It did not follow from this, however, that he favoured a further agreement with the government on a policy. There was, of course, the possibility that the government might, for political reasons, propose a policy after the standstill which a majority of the General Council would wish to support for political reasons. It was unlikely, however, that any such policy would be endorsed by a conference or that it would genuinely influence the attitude of affiliated unions. Following the return of Frank Cousins to the General Council, the government certainly could not hope to get effective agreement to a policy which included any statutory element. A voluntary policy and free collective bargaining could, however, mean a return to the rate of wage increase and inflation between 1964 and 1966, which had been one of the causes of the July 'crisis'. Given the balance of payments position and the continuing weakness of the pound, this was not something the government could contemplate.

In any case, the General Council had adopted a plan in December 1966 under which there would be a TUC incomes policy after the standstill. The General Council would produce a report on the economic situation each autumn, with a recommendation for a norm for wage increases during the next twelve months, and this report and recommendation would then be put to a Conference of Executives. The plan, for what was to become the annual *Economic Review*, was to be put to a Conference of Executives in March 1967 and, if approved, would operate from the autumn of that year. Inspired by Woodcock, the plan was to lead in time to the disastrous 'social contract' policy of the TUC in 1974–75. Immediately its consequences were not so serious. It meant, however, that the most the government could now hope for after the standstill and period of severe restraint was acquiescence by the unions in a further stage of incomes policy during which it would again have to take unilateral responsibility and rely on statutory powers. This was not necessarily too daunting a situation: the exercise of statutory powers during the standstill had gone surprisingly smoothly and Woodcock's gloomy warnings of July had proved unfounded.

There was still no promise of a continuing surplus on the balance of payments in early 1967 and any doubt about the government's intentions on wage restraint after July would damage confidence in the pound. The fact that the TUC was unwilling to co-operate with the government would receive full publicity at the Conference of Executives in March and scepticism about whether the government would persist with a policy of wage restraint in face of trade union opposition would grow. The government had, therefore, to make its position clear well before the end of July and show determination that there was to be no return to a wages free-for-all. Any decision to continue with a statutory policy would, however, present political and other difficulties. Some members of the Cabinet would not be happy with such a policy, some members of the Parliamentary Labour Party would oppose it and, more important, the General Council might not, this time, acquiesce in it.

The government had to judge how far it might go in terms of restraint and decide on the nature of the powers to give restraint statutory backing. Michael Stewart had discussions with representatives of the General Council and the CBI in January, but no final decision could be taken until after the Conference of Executives in March. It would be unwise after the failure to consult in July 1966 for the government to come to decisions without waiting for the views of the conference. On its side, with the conference due, the General Council could not react definitively to government proposals. Anyway, there was a risk that if the government made its intentions known the conference would reject them and perhaps tie the hands of the General Council.

When the conference met in early March, the report from the General Council stated (reflecting Woodcock's views) that it accepted the need for an incomes policy but only in the context of an economic and social plan to improve real incomes and redress inequalities. The General Council believed the Labour Government also supported this concept of an incomes policy as a long-term objective. The disagreement with the government stemmed, it believed, from different perspectives and time-scales: the General Council considered incomes policy as a long-term instrument of planning, while the government regarded it primarily as a short-term regulator of incomes and costs with restraint as the most important objective. The General Council's view was that an incomes policy could not be enforced by legislation and that the government should not renew or introduce any reserve powers over prices and incomes after the standstill.

The report then argued that for the purposes of a planned long-term incomes policy the TUC should have more powers and influence over individual unions, through an economic report which would include views on the appropriate general level of increase in wages and salaries and on the circumstances that would justify deviations from the general level. The 'authority' of the TUC would derive from the Conference of Executives which would receive the report. It might be possible to have regular consultations with the CBI; it might also be possible for unions concerned with major pay claims to submit and negotiate them simultaneously after consultations with the TUC. The existing 'wage vetting' process would, in any case, continue and might be developed. The policy statement from the General Council was overwhelmingly approved by more than $7\frac{1}{2}$ million votes to 963,000.[1]

Wilson reacted to the conference by expressing hopes for a return to an agreed policy. Government, unions and employers should, he said, agree on a 'national dividend' for distribution between all forms of income. It would then be for the trade union movement, through the machinery it was developing, to ensure that what was distributed was related to the workers' share and did not run ahead of the amount

[1] *Incomes Policy: Report of a Conference of Executive Committees of Affiliated Organisations, 2 March 1967* (TUC, London, 1967), pp. 5–12.

earned by production. (All this was, of course, to be on the basis of steadily rising incomes.) This, he stated, would be 'a new concept, unique in a democracy in this or any other country'.

This was rather an exaggeration. The concept was neither new nor unique. It was little more than a proposition for a return to the agreement of April 1965, with the TUC possibly exercising more effective influence over affiliated unions. Though the experience of the policy of 1965 had been as unsatisfactory to Woodcock as to the government, it had been so for different reasons and Woodcock's reaction to Wilson's 'new concept' was discouraging. A proposal from the CBI in May – there had been monthly meetings between the TUC and the CBI since January – that there should be a joint declaration on incomes policy was rejected. The possibility of converting the proposed new long-term policy of the TUC into Wilson's 'new concept' was not promising.

The immediate concern of the government was to make its own position on wages clear for the period after the end of June. This was done in the White Paper, *Prices and Incomes Policy after 30th June 1967* (Cmnd. 3235), published on 22 March. This was another unilateral declaration by the government and the most it could claim on this occasion was that it was 'common ground' with the TUC and the CBI that decisions about prices and incomes should be related to the interests of the community as a whole and that there would be a need for continued moderation during the twelve months following June 1967 to provide a sound basis for the resumption of sustained economic growth.

The White Paper was an attempt by the government to move back towards the situation in 1965. It reaffirmed the objective of returning to the policies of 1964 and 1965 – to create conditions favourable to sustained economic growth and to work towards the operation of an effective policy on a voluntary basis in agreement with the CBI and the TUC. The criteria for price and pay increases were those set out in the White Paper on prices and incomes policy published in 1965 (Cmnd. 3150) and the arrangements for early warning were to be those set out in the complementary White Paper published at the same time, *White Paper on Prices and Incomes Policy: An Early Warning System* (Cmnd. 2808). The major difference from 1965 on the pay side was that the norm was zero: it was emphasised that there was no justification for returning to the norm of $3-3\frac{1}{2}$ per cent, which had in practice been regarded as the minimum increase which everyone expected to receive.

The government had difficulty in deciding about the statutory powers to back the policy. Various possibilities had been considered while Stewart was having his earlier discussions with the General Council, including a suggestion that, whatever powers were taken, they should be permanent, unlike those in the 1966 Act. Since this would have implied permanent rejection of free collective bargaining, it was hardly more than a proposition to be conceded in discussions with the General Council. The government statement in the White Paper reflected its indecision, but, in the light of probable reactions within the Parliamentary Labour Party, it was finally decided to strengthen the Part II powers by extending the delaying period on reference of a proposed price or wage increase to the NBPI from three to seven months. A Prices and Incomes (No 2) Act became law on 14 July and the strengthened Part II was activated on 28 July. The General Council did not offer to this further stage of government policy backed with statutory powers the 'reluctant acquiescence' it had given to the standstill, but immediate outright opposition was avoided. Woodcock said that a rigid interpretation of the White Paper would result in inflexibility and unfairness, but described the powers in the Prices and Incomes Act, 1967 as 'innocuous'.

Industrial Relations and Devaluation

The first requirement for a return to the policies of 1964 and 1965 and a renewal of the partnership between government and trade unions was a continuing balance of payments surplus. The White Paper in March 1967 had been hopeful. It claimed considerable success for the July 1966 measures: exports had increased and the trade gap had narrowed; the balance of payments had improved and was in surplus in the fourth quarter of 1966; sterling had been strengthened and some short-term debt had been repaid. In the budget debate in April, James Callaghan had expressed satisfaction with the past twelve months and hope for the future with his message, 'steady as she goes'. Following the budget there were minor moves towards reflation. By the end of August – with the Trades Union Congress and Labour Party Conference due in the next few weeks – Wilson offered further signs of hope: hire purchase controls were relaxed, social security benefits increased and investment grants accelerated. There were ministerial changes. Michael Stewart, responsible for prices and incomes policy during the standstill and the period of severe restraint, the zero norm for general wage increases and the departure of the trade unions to pursue their own policy, moved from the Department of Economic Affairs to become Lord Privy Seal. Harold Wilson himself took on oversight of the Department and the chairmanship of the NEDC. He might, it seemed, be about to take the road back to 1965.

These moves had little effect on the Trades Union Congress in September. A motion criticising government economic policy, including intervention in collective bargaining, was passed by 4,883,000 to 1,380,000 and a motion supporting the government's prices and incomes policy was rejected. For the first time since November 1964 supporters of the government on the General Council were not backed by a majority of Congress. Wilson had a minor consolation when the subsequent Labour Party Conference passed a motion in support of government policy by a narrow majority and rejected a motion opposing government prices and incomes policy.

Wilson's pre-conference optimism was hardly justified by economic developments. The improvements in the balance of payments were minor and fluctuating. The standstill, though effective, had been a wasted effort. Foreign confidence was affected by the relaxation of the prices and incomes policy and the rejection of the policy by the unions. The minor reflationary measures and Wilson's own optimism added to doubts about the government's intention to control inflation. International economic difficulties following the Six Day War and the closure of the Suez Canal inevitably caused renewed pressure on the pound. A difficult economic situation worsened as two industrial problems – legacies of government activity in the hopeful days of 1964–66 – came to a head.

The first source of trouble was in the docks. The Docks and Harbours Act, 1966, which gave effect to the Devlin Committee Report, had become law in August 1966 and discussions had proceeded on decasualisation, though it would not be possible to give the necessary wage increases during the standstill. Progress was slow: in spite of the efforts of the Docks Modernisation Committee, three inquiries and prolonged negotiations (together with unofficial but not serious strikes in London in the summer), there was, a year later, still no agreement on all points between the employers and the two unions concerned – the TGWU and the NASD.

Gunter finally made an Order introducing the new decasualisation scheme from 18 September. There was an immediate unofficial strike in Liverpool, followed by unofficial strikes in London which closed down most of the port, and by minor troubles in other ports. The government was reluctant to depart from the changes decided upon for the introduction of decasualisation, particularly in the rates of wages, and it was not until mid-October, after four weeks of strikes, that it decided to intervene.

In the Liverpool strike, Gunter appointed Scamp to conciliate and Jack Jones, Assistant General Secretary of the TGWU, took over from his local officials and negotiated on behalf of the leaders of the unofficial strikers. Wilson joined in the exercise, keeping in close touch with Jones, a long-standing political 'ally'. After a continuous 48-hour session by Scamp and the parties and an all-night interventionist vigil by Wilson, agreement was reached between the employers and Jones and between Jones and the unofficial strike committee. The agreement, at first rejected by the dockers, was finally accepted and the port reopened on 30 October, after being closed for six weeks. Cousins and Jones then attempted to end the unofficial strike in London, but in spite of their efforts and appeals by Callaghan and Gunter and agreements at national level between the TGWU and the NASD officials, it was a month before there was a full return to work.

There was trouble also on the railways, where the British Railways Board and the National Union of Railwaymen had been negotiating for twelve months over productivity bonuses as a follow-up to Wilson's pre-election railway settlement of February 1966. The Board and the unions failed to agree, the NUR imposed a ban on 'second man' duties on 11 September and some guards took unofficial action which threatened to stop the railways if it became widespread. The report of a Court of Inquiry which recommended changes in the productivity proposals put forward by the Board was rejected by the union. The government prepared to declare a State of Emergency if the situation worsened. The dispute was finally settled on 30 October after a meeting with Gunter – on terms which were to cause trouble later with ASLEF.

The strikes in the docks and on the railways were accompanied in the later months of 1967 by other labour troubles which received full publicity and stimulated criticism of unions and government. Industrial relations became a major political issue.

Two unofficial strikes on large construction sites in London, marked by violence, were the subject of a Court of Inquiry. This reported in September (Cmnd. 3396), describing the activities of a communist-backed London Building Sites Liaison Committee, blaming bad organisation and ineffective consultation by management and criticising the failure of union officials to control their members. The report was followed by a union recommendation to return to work, which pickets tried to prevent. Four pickets were arrested and charged. Frank Chapple, General Secretary of the Electrical Trades Union (ETU), was physically attacked at the union headquarters and union officials were prevented from speaking at the building sites. Leslie Cannon, President of the ETU, requested the TUC to investigate the violence in the industry but the Finance and General Purposes Committee decided that no special investigation was necessary. It was not until later in November that work was resumed on both sites.

A prolonged strike over recognition (it had begun in November 1966) took place at Roberts Arundel in Stockport, with violent demonstrations and picketing. Attempts at mediation – by the EEF, the TUC and, during the more general troubles of September and October, by the Ministry of Labour, failed and the company finally closed down operations at the end of the year. (Only the fact that Roberts Arundel was in Stockport and not London made the strike a less serious political and public issue than the Grunwick dispute in 1977.)

The strikes in the docks, the troubles on the railways and the other industrial disputes gave the impression, not unfairly, that the government was not able to deal with industrial troubles and that two of its most powerful trade union partners, the TGWU and the NUR, were not particularly effective in dealing with their members. The industrial troubles coincided with a rapid deterioration in the position of the pound during September and October. John Davies of the CBI described the country as 'bleeding to death'. The results of three by-elections registered dissatisfaction and doubt about the government's capacity. The closing of the Suez Canal and the dock strikes would result in a series of adverse trade figures and abroad some thought devaluation inevitable. The French openly recommended it.

The pound was devalued by 14.3 per cent on 18 November. There were immediate deflationary measures.[2] It was announced that there would be further measures to reduce public and private spending in the new year but that there was no intention of reintroducing a wage or price freeze. Ministerial changes followed devaluation:

[2] The bank rate was raised to 8 per cent; restrictions on hire purchase, which had been relaxed a very short time earlier, were strengthened; the premium due under the selective employment tax was limited to development areas; corporation tax was increased from 40 to 42 per cent.

Callaghan moved from the Treasury to the Home Office and Roy Jenkins was appointed Chancellor of the Exchequer.

The government's failure and the disappearance of Wilson's short-lived 'promise' of a return to economic growth and the policies of 1965 coincided with the public birth of the TUC's own policy for economic growth and incomes which had been planned earlier in the year. The Economic Committee of the General Council met in accordance with the decision of the Conference of Executives, discussed its report on the economy and set a norm for wages in 1968. The report 'forecast' a growth in the gross national product of 6 per cent, on the basis of which wage increases between $3\frac{1}{2}$ and 4 per cent were thought possible without causing inflation.

At the time of preparation of the report, the recommended general increase diverged from the policy set out in *Prices and Incomes Policy after 30th June 1967* (Cmnd. 3235) when the government view of the situation had been rather more hopeful. After devaluation there was an unbridgeable gap between the TUC forecasts and the economic prospects for 1968. The TUC, while it made no move to revise the report, suggested when it was presented to Wilson in December that a nil norm might be accepted until the summer of 1968, the date up to which the policy set out in *Prices and Incomes Policy after 30th June 1967* was to run, and a general increase allowed only after that. Wilson's earlier optimism was not to be so soon revived and the dangers in giving the impression that he was even thinking of embarking on a policy of economic expansion led to the DEA's insisting in reply that the TUC forecast was too optimistic, its proposals unacceptable and that the nil norm must continue.

Industrial trouble continued in the concluding months of the year. In November ASLEF protested against one of the consequences of the agreement which had settled the troubles amongst NUR members in October. As a contribution towards productivity, the NUR had agreed that brakevans should be eliminated from certain trains and that the guard should be in the rear cab of the locomotive – a preserve of ASLEF. ASLEF argued that this was in breach of a 1965 manning agreement. The normal attempts at negotiation, intervention by Scamp, conciliation by the Ministry of Labour and a broadcast by Gunter, in which he described the dispute as 'the silliest in the decade', failed to settle the matter. The removal of the guard's van on 4 December was accompanied by a work-to-rule by ASLEF members and a refusal to allow guards in the engine cab. After talks with Wilson ASLEF accepted removal of the vans on the understanding that there would be discussions on train-manning, recruitment and promotion. At the end of the year Scamp published his second annual report on labour relations in the motor industry. His first report in 1966 had been discouraging: his view had been that union members in many cases had shown disregard for procedure agreements, in opposition to the wishes of their full-time officials. Twelve months later, at the end of 1967, he reported no improvement and felt that some union leaders were obstructing examination of changes in procedures.

Industrial Relations: the Donovan Commission and Conservative Proposals for Reform

Against this background of the failure of government economic policies, public concern and increasing government involvement at the highest level in labour troubles, the Royal Commission on Trades Unions and Employers' Associations had been making what in the circumstances appeared to be relatively slow progress. It had certainly failed to take the problems of the trade unions and industrial relations out of politics. Though appointed in early 1965, it was not until November 1966 that the TUC evidence was submitted. This argued that any improvements in union organisation and collective bargaining must come from within. It stressed the importance of the voluntary principle and opposed change in the law, was against extension of government interference in collective bargaining and favoured the re-establishment of compulsory arbitration which could be put into effect at the request of one party, on the lines of the post-war Industrial Disputes Tribunal abolished by Iain Macleod.

Before the Commission could report Robert Carr outlined the plans of the Conservative Party to reform industrial relations at the Conservative Party Conference on 20 October. He proposed legislation which would include compulsory registration of unions and employers' associations, a new system of industrial courts to deal with industrial disputes, legal enforcement of collective agreements and a legal duty on employers to recognise and negotiate with trade unions, provided this was desired by over half the employees concerned. Individual workers would have the right of appeal to the industrial courts against unjust dismissal or coercive action from any quarter – presumably the trade unions – and the Ministry of Labour would have powers to order a 60-day cooling-off period to delay strikes threatening the national interest. The National Board for Prices and Incomes would no longer be concerned with pay but would be reconstituted as a Productivity Board to investigate restrictive practices.

In Parliament the opposition pressed for more effective government action in some of the current strikes and for the early introduction of legislation to deal with unofficial strikes. Gunter replied that the government would not rush into action before the Donovan Commission had reported, but as pressures continued he asked the Commission to speed up its work. In December 1967 the CBI gave further evidence to the commission, influenced by the current state of industrial relations and the public reactions to them. It said that since submitting its written evidence in November 1965 industrial opinion had hardened in favour of penalising individuals who took 'unconstitutional' action in the form of unofficial strikes, pressed that the legal enforcement of procedures should be seriously considered and suggested that a new registrar of trade unions might be given power to take proceedings against unofficial strikers.

The Donovan Report was eventually published in June 1968. An understanding of the further deterioration in the relations between the government and the unions which followed the publication of the Report and led to the 'deep and fundamental split' of 1969 might be helped by an assessment of the views which government and unions could reasonably take of each other at the end of 1967.

The Positions of Government and Unions, Late 1967

By the end of 1967 the government's economic policies had failed and its standing in the country was low. For months after devaluation there was speculation about Harold Wilson's replacement, the prospect of a coalition government and even talk of a 'government of businessmen'. By-elections were lost; public opinion polls were adverse. The two leading economic ministers in the government had left as failures the jobs they had taken in 1964[3] – and it was not possible to ignore the more obvious contributions of the trade unions to their failures. The rate of wage increases flowing from collective bargaining in 1965–66 – well above the norm of the agreed incomes policy – and the seamen's strike had contributed to the 1966 'crisis'. The withdrawal of trade union support for the government's policies at the Congress in September 1967, the strikes provoked by the attempts to improve working conditions and labour relations in the docks, together with other industrial troubles, had accompanied the 1967 devalu-

[3] George Brown and James Callaghan.

ation. The initiatives on industrial relations taken by the government had shown no results.

Industrial troubles in the difficult months since July had highlighted what some people regarded as the defects of the trade unions. First, trade union officers were unable to 'exercise authority' over their members: in the Liverpool docks, local officers of the TGWU had been ineffective, and in London, little better. The activity of the NASD in Liverpool (under the TUC rules it was entitled to operate in London only) was evidence of the failure of the TUC to exercise authority. Secondly, inter-union competition caused trouble: the dock strikes had been due in part to rivalry between the NASD and the TGWU and the trouble on the railways had been caused by antagonism between the NUR and ASLEF. Inter-union rivalry was a background to industrial trouble in the motor industry, where it arose in part from the expansionist policies of the TGWU.

The view of some ministers of the role played by the unions was not made more favourable by the resignation of Cousins to return to the union leading the opposition to their policies and by the fact that in the most difficult economic situation since 1964 the TUC was promoting an economic policy and a prices and incomes policy which in their eyes were completely unrealistic. What was regarded by some as a non-constructive attitude in the evidence of the TUC to the Donovan Commission was a further source of dissatisfaction.

The government was aware that foreign commentators and many of the public at home related their economic failures to trade union militancy in pressing for inflationary wage increases and to bad labour relations. Conservative promises of reform were attracting public support, as a general proposition if not in detail. The Labour Party's close links with the trade unions thus carried serious liabilities. The 'trade union problem' which had been slipped to the Donovan Commission in April 1965 was now a major political issue too embarrassing to be neutralised by the Royal Commission process of research, evidence and detached deliberation. A solution to it seemed one of the measures necessary for the success of the government's economic policy, for the restoration of its standing in the country and for countering Conservative promises to produce a solution. Gunter had responded to Conservative pressures for immediate action by saying that action must wait for the Donovan Report, but there were ministers who would have liked to see legislation without the delay that involved – though no specific ideas were advanced or considered.

Such 'anti-trade union' views were no doubt influenced by the depressing political atmosphere of late 1967 and were not entirely fair. They ignored the help the General Council and individual unions had given to the government and the difficulties this had caused national officers within their own unions. The TUC had agreed a voluntary incomes policy on the assumption that the government would respond with a national plan for economic growth. Within four months of the voluntary agreement the government had introduced a statutory element, which the General Council had accepted. The NUR had settled for a wage increase below the going rate to avoid damaging the government's prospects in the 1966 election. It was hardly its responsibility that promises within the agreement were to lead to difficulties for the government at an even worse time. The General Council and unions closely concerned had refused comfort to the NUS and thereby reduced the damage done by the seamen's strike. Following the strike they had accepted the imposition of a wage freeze and the collapse of the National Plan.

At national level the unions had supported 'their' government on policies contrary to the immediate interests of their members and, in some cases, contrary to their political convictions. They were now sharing the odium for economic failure with the politicians – and might well feel they were receiving an unfair share of it. If the standing of the government had fallen greatly and opinion of it in the press and other media was almost universally critical, there was corresponding criticism of the trade unions. Many national officers were also under increasing attack from activists and militants and aware of growing dissatisfaction amongst their members.

As a result, trade union officers at national level – and the General Council – were moving towards greater industrial militancy and politically towards the left. There were a number of explanations of this: belief that the unions should resume their central activity of collective bargaining without interference from the government, judgement of opinion amongst their members, disillusionment with the results of the agreed policies of 1964–65 and the acceptance of the policies of 1965–66, dissatisfaction with the government's general economic and social policies of which these were a part, suspicion that the government had surrendered to the city and foreign bankers and conviction that the government should pursue alternative 'socialist' policies – all played a part. Those leaders who believed that priority should be given to their traditional industrial objectives and the immediate claims of their members rather than to the politics of support for their 'misguided' government increased their influence.

Cousins had left the government and rejoined the General Council in part because he took this same view of proper union priorities.

During Cousins' period in office, his deputy, Jack Jones, had emerged as a national figure. Jones was a convinced and powerful advocate of his own version of trade union democracy, believing that the first duty of a national officer was to represent the views of the local spokesmen for his members. He was a committed supporter of the left wing of the Labour Party and a believer in 'socialist policies'. Cousins' views and political alignment were very much the same as those of Jones, but his period in government may have given him some doubts about the immediate practibility of some 'socialist policies' and moderated the vigour with which he pressed for policies which might seriously damage the government's standing. Over the next twelve months he was to allow Jones to take the lead.

Changes were also taking place in other unions. William Carron, whose views on industrial and political issues differed from those of Cousins and Jones, was due to retire as President of the AEU at the end of 1967 and would be followed by Hugh Scanlon. Scanlon was politically left wing, with views similar to those of Jones and Cousins on industrial issues, though this comradely identity of view could be obscured by competition and conflict between their unions and by personal rivalry. Unlike Carron, Scanlon had limited experience of relations between trade unions and government at the national and political level. These changes at the top of the two biggest unions on the General Council were of major significance (their votes could be crucial in the distribution of offices held by members of the Council and in the election of those hoping to become members) and they were followed by similar changes amongst the national officers and in the executives of other unions.

There were changes in the government, too, which significantly affected relations with the unions. Brown and Callaghan, the two senior ministers with trade union antecedents, had now left the jobs in which they had been responsible for those government activities of closest concern to the unions. Their successors, Roy Jenkins and Michael Stewart (and later Peter Shore), had no similar trade union background. Gunter, the third of the senior 'trade union' ministers, was moved from the Ministry of Labour in April 1968. Brown and Gunter had resigned from the government before the end of 1968.

6 Deflation and Disagreement, 1968

Incomes Policy: Firmness and Flexibility

The Conference of Executives on 28 February 1968 endorsed the report presented by the General Council (the *Economic Review*), which largely repeated the proposals approved by the Economic Committee and already rejected by the government. The *Review* argued for the expansion of the economy by 6 per cent for the year from July 1968, based on the assumption of an increase in productivity of about 5 per cent. It accepted that some incomes policy was necessary and suggested that in the July 1968–69 period an average increase in incomes of 5 per cent would be consistent with stable labour costs. On the basis of these assumptions the General Council suggested that the average increase in wage rates should be around $3\frac{1}{2}$ per cent and that on top of that there should be a further $1\frac{1}{2}$ per cent to allow for wage drift and local bargaining. Priority should be given to low pay, productivity and labour shortages and sympathy should be shown to claims for equal pay.

There was reason for doubting whether the realities of collective bargaining would be influenced by the TUC policy. Although the conference had endorsed the *Review*, it had done so by a narrow majority of 4,620,000 votes to 4,084,000 and the unions against the policy included the AEU and the TGWU. In any case, it could not possibly be accepted by the government in the circumstances following devaluation. The government had to show its determination to keep wages under control, though a government policy of wage restraint more severe than that adopted by the conference, which had itself been opposed by major unions, carried a high risk of conflict with individual unions and the breach with the TUC meant that the position of the government in the event of any such conflict would be seriously weakened.

In his budget speech in March, Roy Jenkins announced that the government would seek new reserve statutory powers over prices and incomes to replace those due to expire in August 1968. A White

Paper – the seventh on incomes policy since 1965 – *Productivity, Prices and Incomes Policy in 1968 and 1969* (Cmnd. 3590), was published on 3 April.

The policy had to combine restraint to satisfy foreign opinion and meet what the government judged to be the requirements of economic policy with flexibility to avoid industrial trouble. Flexibility was essential: the prospect of facing an official strike as damaging as that of the seamen but without the support of the General Council or an unofficial strike as damaging as that of the dockers but without being able to count on trade union help was not something the government could contemplate without anxiety. How to be firm and how firm to be were difficult problems.

A return to the almost complete inhibition on collective bargaining imposed by the freeze and the period of severe restraint was out of the question. The political credit with the unions which had secured acceptance of the standstill was exhausted. A freeze would almost certainly lead to damaging strikes, both official and unofficial, and the open collapse of the policy. This, following the economic failures and industrial troubles of 1966 and 1967 at a time when the standing of the government was extremely low, would have been a most serious threat to Wilson and his government. The 'fifth stage' of the policy had to allow collective bargaining to continue while aiming to reverse the trend in wage increases which had followed its resumption in July 1967.[1]

To be both firm and flexible was not easy but, for presentational purposes at least, the White Paper achieved the combination with some ingenuity. Determination to maintain wage restraint was shown by the announcement that the government intended to extend its powers to delay wage or price increases on reference to the NBPI from seven to twelve months and that it would seek these strengthened powers for a period of eighteen months and not for twelve months as in previous stages of the policy. The 'continued moderation' required after 30 June 1967[2] now became the objective of 'substantial restraint' involving even a fall in real incomes. There would be a ceiling of 3½ per cent on wage, salary and dividend increases. (If the government hoped that the coincidence of the 3½ per cent ceiling with the 'norm' for wage increases of the TUC policy would moderate the opposition of the trade unions in resolutions and debates, it was quite

---

[1] It was already clear that collective bargaining was producing increases beyond the limits of the policy set out in *Prices and Incomes Policy after 30th June 1967* (Cmnd. 3235).

[2] See *Prices and Incomes Policy after 30th June 1967* (Cmnd. 3235).

unlikely to influence the force with which they pressed their claims for increases above the figure or to affect the final outcome of negotiations.)

The flexibility needed was provided by the criteria justifying wage increases, which had been the same since 1965, though different comments and glosses had been made on them from time to time. They could be used, as they had been before July 1966 and since June 1967, to justify increases for almost all groups. The most important element was provided by a reiteration of the theme of increased productivity and efficiency which Harold Wilson had developed after the 1966 'crisis' and which had become the centrepiece of the reports of the NBPI: the government wished 'to encourage agreements which genuinely raise productivity and efficiency' and the policy provided for exceptions to the $3\frac{1}{2}$ per cent ceiling for such agreements.

For this stage of its policy the government could no longer, as in 1967, make even the modest claim of sharing common ground with the TUC and the CBI. It appealed for support on a voluntary basis, 'to enable us to seize the opportunities in the new situation after devaluation and so ensure the basis for a lasting improvement in living standards for the whole community'. The assurances made since 1966, that the statutory powers the government proposed to take would be held in reserve, were repeated.

The new policy was accompanied by changes within the government. Gunter was moved from the Ministry of Labour in April, responsibility for prices and incomes policy was transferred from the Department of Economic Affairs to the ministry which was to become the Department of Employment and Productivity and Barbara Castle was appointed First Secretary of State for Employment and Productivity.

A New Department and a New Minister
The transfer of responsibility for prices and incomes policy to the Department of Employment and Productivity (DEP) had both advantages and disadvantages. On the side of wage restraint, it could be argued that it would contain the conciliation activities of the Ministry of Labour within a policy for which the new Department was responsible – conciliators would no longer be the engineers of inflationary wage settlements. In other circumstances it could ensure flexibility: if the government decided that priority must be given to avoiding or settling a damaging strike, the new Department would have the

capacity to produce a compromise – within the limits of the policy, it was to be hoped, but failing this a compromise which would do the least possible damage to the policy. The contradictions inherent in reconciling more severe wage restraint and flexibility to avoid industrial trouble would, anyway, be the responsibility of one minister and department. The change had at least one serious disadvantage. It more or less destroyed the remnants of any claim the Ministry of Labour still had to provide an 'independent' and acceptable conciliation service.

Unlike Ray Gunter, Barbara Castle had no trade union background. She was, however, a politician from the left of the Labour Party with political views, which, it might be assumed, were close to those of Jack Jones and Hugh Scanlon and their supporters. This might improve relations with the unions. Certainly she was closer to Jones and Scanlon politically than was Gunter, who was on the right of the Party and politically out of sympathy with them. Gunter's relations with the trade unions were by this time strained. He was sceptical about the TUC incomes policy and promises of voluntary restraint in collective bargaining and his personal relations with Woodcock were poor. After more than three years' involvement in disputes over wages he had inevitably attracted disfavour from many union leaders. His attempt to improve industrial relations had caused trouble in the docks and had failed in the motor industry. Industrial relations were becoming worse and were being exploited politically by the Conservatives.

It might also have been thought that Castle would have a better chance than Gunter of persuading the left wing of the Parliamentary Labour Party to accept a statutory incomes policy. A declaration to Jones that 'incomes policy is socialism' may have been an exaggerated simplification of her position, but she appeared committed to prices and incomes policy, aiming to restore the partnership between the government and unions in the operation of the policy as a step to advance the cause of socialism and to promote the well-being of the Party and the movement.

Industrial and Political Difficulties

Barbara Castle spoke with energy and rhetorical conviction in defence of the government's incomes policy at annual conferences of trade unions throughout the spring and summer, making it clear that full advantage should be taken of the flexibility for productivity and efficiency provided in the White Paper. To help in this she set up a new manpower productivity service in her department. She made new appointments to the NBPI, including James Mortimer of the Draughtsmen's and Allied Technicians' Association, a trade unionist on the left of the Labour Party and a critic of statutory incomes policies.

Her political alignment and these activities were not markedly successful in producing results. Yet another Prices and Incomes Act became law on 10 July, but the government majority was smaller than expected and 35 left wing members abstained on the second reading. Resolutions against the government's incomes policy were passed at all important trade union conferences and at the Trades Union Congress in September a resolution calling for repeal of the legislation was passed by over 7 million votes to 1 million. The continuing breach between trade unions and the government extended to criticism of the government's attitude towards the National Economic Development Council and some talk of withdrawal from it: the General Council Report to Congress complained that the Council was used as a sounding-board for government policies and not as a forum for developing an agreed programme for economic growth.[3]

Collective bargaining proceeded against a background of general trade union opposition to the government's policy. The criteria in the White Paper were used to justify wage increases for practically all groups and extensive use was made of the opportunity for increases above the $3\frac{1}{2}$ per cent ceiling through productivity agreements. Between April 1968 and April 1969 wage rates increased by around 5 per cent and earnings by around 7 per cent. The incomes policy may have had some effect in securing some restraint in wage increases, but there was no doubt that it meant a series of interventions in wage negotiations which brought Castle and the government into conflict with practically all important unions, including the TGWU and the AEU, and that the efforts to impose some degree of wage restraint were accompanied by an increase in the number of strikes. Castle was involved in wage negotiations in engineering, construction, road passenger transport, the railways and at Fords, among others. There were strikes, threatened strikes and other action in these disputes and also by air pilots, in television, newspapers, the London docks and the banks.

The negotiations in engineering and road passenger transport were of particular significance. A national engineering strike would have

[3] *See TUC Annual Report*, 1968, p. 374, para. 354.

been disastrous for the government and damaging to the economy and the pound – more so than in the 1950s. Fortunately the unions concerned were not united and the more moderate leaders were unwilling to line up behind Scanlon. A strike was avoided after months of negotiation and days of conciliation. The final settlement was, however, in breach of the policy and contrary to recommendations in a report by the NBPI. The difficulties in road passenger transport arose from a direct conflict between the Transport and General Workers's Union and the government over the wages of municipal busmen. In January 1968 the government delayed the payment of a nationally agreed wage increase by referring the agreement to the NBPI, using its powers under Part II of the Prices and Incomes Act, 1966, and then imposed a further delay after the Board had reported adversely by using its powers under the Prices and Incomes Act, 1968. The TGWU reacted by authorising a strike from 12 August. The government in turn reacted by saying that the law would be applied (thus threatening the union with prosecution under the Act). Following negotiations between Castle and Jones, however, the union announced that it was calling off the strike and proposed to negotiate local agreements with individual councils.

The economic consequences of a busmen's strike could have been tolerated (even in the summer of 1968!) but it would have provided distressing evidence of the limited value of the political links between Castle and Jones and of the failure of the Cabinet changes to improve relations between unions and the government. It would also have strengthened the opposition to a statutory policy in the left wing of the Parliamentary Labour Party and might have exposed the practical difficulties of enforcing the law. The political ties between unions and the Party were still, fortunately, strong enough to avoid these consequences.

Castle's activities in other disputes stirred up a good deal of excitement and some opposition. She had a difficult twelve months, which she got through with considerable skill. The elements of flexibility in the White Paper and the ability of the Department, unions and employers to exploit them enabled the government to avoid any strikes as damaging as those of 1966 and 1967. Nevertheless, by the end of 1968 it was difficult to see how the balancing act of defending the policy without provoking a serious strike could be continued. It could, perhaps, be maintained with diminishing severity until the end of the 1968–69 wage round. It was, however, due to run until the end of 1969 and the prospects of its continuing effectively until then without serious industrial troubles were slight. Moreover, it was clear by this time that attention would have to be given to the political difficulties the policy was creating within the labour movement. An election was highly probable some time in 1970 and a continuing procession of unions entering the DEP during the next twelve months to be irritated by Castle's exhortations in defence of incomes policy was an unattractive prospect. It was highly desirable to re-establish the partnership between the government and the trade unions before the election and to avoid a repetition of trade union opposition to government policies at their conferences in the spring and summer of 1969 and at the Trades Union Congress in September.

It was to be hoped that by 1970 the government's policies would have secured a favourable balance of payments so that there could be some relaxation of the incomes policy as part of a reward for the 'two years hard slog'.[4] Unhappily for the government, at the beginning of 1969 the policies were not yet working and the pound was not strong. Evidence of a retreat on wage restraint might lead to loss of confidence and the failure of the economic policy adopted after November 1967. The situation required another moderately severe budget and, in logic, a reaffirmation of determination to continue wage restraint until the end of 1969 and beyond. The government was in a dilemma. By March 1969 it thought it had found the solution: to relax on incomes policy but retain foreign confidence by dealing directly with industrial relations and the 'trade union problem'. It had, in any event, to produce a policy on these issues, since the Donovan Report had been published in June 1968.

[4] 'These measures are in themselves severe. In the short term, as I told the House on 17th January, we must have a stiff Budget followed by two years hard slog.' Roy Jenkins, Budget Speech, 19 March 1968.

7 'A Deep and Fundamental Split', 1969

The Donovan Report

The Donovan Report was in form unanimous, though it recorded a division of opinion on the only two suggested changes in the law directly relevant to collective bargaining and was accompanied by a series of notes which, taken together, questioned the basis on which the Report was written and the value of its recommendations.

The basis of the Report was Chapter 3, 'The System of Industrial Relations', which was calculated to minimise the part government could and should play in industrial relations and to minimise also the importance of trade unions and employers' associations at national level, the only level at which in general government could exercise any effective influence. The chapter explained that 'Britain has two systems of industrial relations': the formal system, operating at industry-wide level, in which collective bargaining took place in accordance with certain agreed rules, and an informal system, operating at company, factory or shop floor level, in which collective bargaining proceeded often without agreed rules, and which settled many of the more important issues. This informal system had been developed since 1940, encouraged by the situation of full employment since then. The two 'systems' were in conflict. The second was the more important and more powerful.

The informal system of industrial relations could, the Report argued, be made more orderly only by those involved in it – management and the immediate representatives of the work people concerned. 'Self-reform' was the watchword and the responsibility for this attached principally to management. The employers' associations and trade unions could help with advice and assistance and should develop their organisations to do this. Government, too, might encourage, advise and assist the process of self-reform. The second 'system' was, however, so anarchic – 'largely informal, largely fragmented and largely autonomous' – that reform through legislation was quite impracticable.

On the part the government might play in the reform of industrial relations, the Report recommended legislation to require companies to register their procedure agreements, or, if they had none, to state why, and also proposed the establishment by the government of a Commission on Industrial Relations which would 'on reference from the Department of Employment and Productivity investigate and report on cases and problems arising out of the registration of agreements'. The Commission should operate on a voluntary basis: 'there would be no penalties for non-compliance with the Commission's recommendations though this question would have to be reviewed in the light of experience'. It was argued that these limited requirements would compel boards of companies to give more attention to labour relations and take steps to improve them.

Two possible changes to the Trade Disputes Act, 1906, which provided the basic legal protection for the exercise of trade union power in collective bargaining, were referred to in the main part of the Report. Section 3 of the 1906 Act provided that 'an act done by a person in contemplation or furtherance of a trade dispute shall not be actionable on the ground only that it induces some other person to break a contract of employment'. The Commission pointed out that this gave protection not only to trade unions and persons acting on behalf of unions but also to 'unofficial bodies such as those in the construction industry and in the docks'. Seven members – a majority – of the Commission, including the Chairman, thought that this immunity should cease and apply only to registered trade unions. The two trade unionists, George Woodcock and Harold Collison, and the two academics, Hugh Clegg and Otto Kahn-Freund, opposed this change. The Commission also considered the limitation of protection to those inducing others to break a contract of employment. A minority recommended deletion of the words 'of employment'. The majority repeated their view that, whether the section was changed or not, the protection should apply only to registered trade unions.

There were other recommendations in the Report. There should be legislation to protect workers against unfair dismissal (a majority favoured extending this to cases involving refusal to join a trade union), to make void any prohibition of trade union membership in a contract of employment, to re-introduce compulsory unilateral arbitration, to lay down certain requirements on trade union rules relating to admission, discipline, disputes between a union and a member, elections and shop stewards and for the establishment of an independent review body to hear appeals from members against refusal of admission to a union and expulsion from a union and complaints of breach of trade union rules or violation of natural justice. The Report specifically rejected major proposals current at the time, including legal enforcement of collective agreements, cooling-off periods and compulsory ballots in strikes of major national interest and a tribunal to deal with restrictive labour practices.

Except for the proposals on trade union rules and the independent review body, the Report might have been tailor-made to provide the government with a programme for the 'reform' of industrial relations which would avoid adverse reaction from the trade unions to add to the difficulties already arising from incomes policy. Donovan had given first priority to avoiding a minority report signed by Woodcock and the three other members almost certain to support him. A majority report unacceptable to Woodcock and his allies might well have been unacceptable to a Labour government or, if accepted, might have been unworkable in the face of trade union resistance.

The impression of unanimity was, however, severely damaged by an addendum from Lord Donovan himself, a note of reservation from Andrew Shonfield, which questioned the assumptions of the Report, and by supplementary notes from four members. In his addendum Lord Donovan, while accepting the analysis in the main part of the Report and the proposals for 'reform', expressed doubts, on the grounds that progress on this basis was certain to be slow. He added, 'in the circumstances I have been reluctant to trust entirely to the expected effect of better procedure agreements and have sought some interim remedy which would be both workable and just. I have found it very elusive'. He made no recommendations. The supplementary notes suggested that the Secretary of State for Employment should be given power to order compliance with recommendations from the Commission on Industrial Relations where persuasion failed, and that the Commission should be given power to deregister any union or employers' association which failed to comply with its own rules or which frequently or gravely breached its registered agreements. Deregistration should remove legal immunity and leave a trade union open to civil actions for damages.

Andrew Shonfield in his note of reservation attacked the analysis on which the Commission's recommendations were based, saying that it was no longer possible to accept the traditional notion of the individual workplace as a separate and largely autonomous estate, where employers and employees were able to conduct their quarrels with little or no regard to the effects of what they did on other work-places. One of the obligations upon trade unions was, he stated, to conduct their industrial relations in such a way as not to hold back improvements in the standard of living of the community as a whole. He thought the Report understated the role that government should play in securing reform: the non-interventionist philosophy set out in Chapter 3 of the Report was out of date and not justified in the light of the intervention that the government had embarked on since the early sixties.

On the strength of this quite different analysis he recommended increased protection under the law against damage to persons or property caused by strikes, powers of intervention, backed by monetary penalities, for the Commission on Industrial Relations to deal with inter-union disputes, an independent 'judicial' function for the Commission so that it was not so dependent on references from the Department of Employment, power for the Commission to order parties under pain of financial penalties to bargain to extend the scope of their agreements where these were inadequate, similar powers in respect of restrictive practices and a change in the law so that collective agreements took on the character of normal undertakings in which each party had a claim for redress if the other failed to keep to the bargain. In general, he argued for intervention in industrial relations and for a legislative framework within which they should operate.

Shonfield's note of reservation was, in effect, a minority report which highlighted the narrowness of the analysis of the subject in Chapter 3 and the limitations this had imposed on the main Report. The latter had concerned itself almost exclusively with relations between managements and workpeople and had more or less ignored the wider economic and political consequences of collective bargain-ing and the use of trade union power in the process of bargaining. By raising these wider issues, Shonfield drew attention to the responsi-bilities of government (whether Labour or Conservative) in its role as representative of the interests of the community and the implications of these for its relationship with the unions. Taken with Lord Donovan's hesitation, his views made it difficult to regard the Report as offering the only possible contribution towards the objective given the Commission in its terms of reference – 'to consider the role of trade unions and employers' associations in promoting the interests of their members and in accelerating the social and economic advance of the nation'.

Reactions to the Donovan Report

The Donovan Report was published two years too late for its advocacy of 'voluntary self-reform' to be acceptable to many. Experience of both incomes policy and industrial relations justified scepticism on the part of politicians and others about the likely results. So far as incomes policy was concerned, the voluntary policy of 1965–66 had not worked, while legal intervention on wages – the most important issue of collective bargaining – had been effective in 1966–67 and seemed to be working in June 1968. Woodcock's explanation that the voluntary policy had not been given time, however true, was discounted by those who felt that the country might not be in a position to give time for self-reform of industrial relations. In any case, an experiment in industrial relations had been launched by Wilson himself in the motor industry – the sector where unofficial strikes and other difficulties attracted the most publicity – but Scamp had reported no real improvement and, with the move to the left in some of the unions concerned, his patient, experienced, but fruitless exercise in advice and persuasion had come to an end. Generally, the number of unofficial strikes and the damage they caused were increasing. The damage done by the seamen's strike in 1966, the docks strike in 1967 and other events since the Donovan Commission had been appointed lent support for the widespread view that trade union activity had contributed to economic failure – and persuaded many that Andrew Shonfield was right in arguing that the law should concern itself with 'the activities of mighty subjects'.

Political considerations influenced the government's reactions to the Report. The Conservative Party, inclined at one point to wait for Donovan, had anticipated the line which would be taken by the Commission and had published *Fair Deal at Work* in April 1968, arguing in favour of legislation. In the circumstances of mid-1968 the Conservative promise to legislate seemed politically more attractive than the 'laissez-faire' approach of the Commission. Moreover, reform of ageing 19th century institutions by government action was in fashion: the government was committed to making changes in the civil service and local government. To those ready to accept neither the theoretical expertise of the academic members of the Commission nor the practical experience but not unbiased views of the trade union members, there seemed no reason to exclude trade unions from his process.

Personalities also influenced the government response. The Commission reported after Gunter's succession by Castle. Gunter was concerned about the state of industrial relations, highly critical of the trade unions and anxious to find remedies. His first reaction may well have been to regard the Report as inadequate, but his knowledge of the trade unions and his temperament would have made him cautious about taking measures not endorsed by the trade union nominees and their allies on the Commission. His final, regretful, reaction might well have been the same as that of Donovan. Castle, however, was not a politician with reservations about the desirability of government intervention or doubts about such intervention having the consequences intended. As Secretary of State she had dealt with the trade unions, mainly over incomes policy, for a relatively short time, but had been given a close view of the processes of collective bargaining. It had been an experience which supported her temperamental disinclination to stand aside and rely on self-reform.

Castle accepted the analysis and philosophy of the main report, expressing this rather more succinctly in the phrase 'power has passed to the shopfloor', but thought the recommendations inadequate. The state of industrial relations, particularly the increase in unofficial strikes, was bad for the standing of the government, which towards the end of 1968 was at its nadir, bad for the Labour Party and damaging to the economic position of the country. She judged that the industrial activities of the trade unions and the manner in which they were carried out were serious obstacles in the pursuit of the social objectives of the party which they supported. Harmony between the trade union movement and the Party was essential, but it must be constructive. The Donovan Commission's proposals for government action were too negative; the process of self-reform would be too slow. She wanted measures which would deal with the worst situations while self-reform proceeded. While she reflected on possible measures, the TUC, the CBI and other interests were asked for their views.

The interim reactions of the TUC were given in *Action on Donovan*, published in November 1968. The TUC welcomed many of the recommendations in the Report, particularly the rejection of legal intervention for making collective agreements enforceable, of cooling-off periods and of strike ballots. Not surprisingly, however, it thought that the Report underrated the importance of collective bargaining at industry-wide level and made proposals for strengthening and developing this through joint industrial councils. There were reservations about the proposal for registration of agreements with the DEP and about the way in which the Commission on Industrial Relations would function solely by references from the Department. The establishment of an independent review body to 'protect' the interests of trade union members was opposed. In general, the TUC wanted to reduce the very limited degree of government intervention recommended by the Donovan Commission.

In the light of these reactions there is little doubt that if the government had accepted the main Report and had entered into full consultation with the TUC the difficulties would not have been serious, though the TUC would have insisted on concessions and urged the government not to proceed with the establishment of the independent review body.

The Government's Proposals: *In Place of Strife*[1]

In considering alternatives to Donovan, the choices open to Castle were limited. The proposals in Andrew Shonfield's note of reservation could not be accepted. The degree of legal intervention would have provoked determined opposition from the trade unions. Shonfield had proposed giving considerable powers to the quasi-independent Commission on Industrial Relations – the centrepiece of the main Report – inspired by, or modelled on, the National Board for Prices and Incomes of which Hugh Clegg was a member. By the second half of 1968, however, Castle and the government had reservations about the Board. An independent body concerned with matters of close interest to the trade unions and laying down principles by which it bound itself in examining particular issues, it had been at times embarrassing and even unhelpful to the government. (Harold Wilson was particularly irritated in December 1968 by a report on the pay of university teachers.[2]) If there were to be legislation, the Commission should be under the control of a minister, a member of the labour movement who could co-operate with the trade unions in helping to solve their difficulties.

At some points also Shonfield's note too much resembled the proposals in *Fair Deal at Work*. These were, of course, unacceptable and not only because of their political origin. They threatened to change the Trade Disputes Act, 1906. Though in the intervening sixty-odd years circumstances had greatly changed and union power had greatly

[1] For a blow-by-blow account of the government's attempt to reform industrial relations, *see* Peter Jenkins, *The Battle of Downing Street* (Charles Knight and Co. Ltd., London, 1970).

[2] Cmnd. 3866.

increased, it was unthinkable that the Labour Party should backtrack towards Taff Vale. The problem for Castle was how to go further than the Donovan Report and give the government a more positive role without causing serious conflict with the trade unions.

Castle's decision on how to proceed was set out in *In Place of Strife: A Policy for Industrial Relations* (Cmnd. 3888), published in January 1969. The tone of the White Paper was very different from that of the Donovan Report. It conveyed a sense of urgency, gave more weight to wider economic and social considerations and, because it was a statement of government intentions, centred on the actions to be taken by the government. Despite this emphasis on the need for government intervention, practically all the proposals of the Donovan Report were accepted and some further action was proposed to give support to the unions. The Secretary of State would have powers to require an employer to recognise and negotiate with a union and, if he did not, the union would be able to take him unilaterally to arbitration and the award would be legally binding; there would be legal backing for the hope expressed in the Donovan Report that systematic information should be available to workers' representatives for the purpose of collective bargaining. On worker participation at Board level, the White Paper went further than the proposals supported by the majority on the Donovan Commission and backed the line taken by Woodcock, Collison and Kahn-Freund, that there might be workers' representatives appointed to the Boards of companies. It also went further in its recommendations for 'modernising' the trade union movement, proposing that the Commission on Industrial Relations should have money for a 'trade union development scheme' – a proposition much favoured by Wedgwood Benn as a trade union equivalent of the Industrial Reorganisation Corporation.[3]

It was hoped that these proposals, intended to be attractive to the unions, would help to secure their acceptance of the White Paper as a whole, including three proposals for government intervention with legal powers which departed radically from Donovan. The proposals concerned unconstitutional strikes, certain official strikes and inter-union disputes over recognition.

On unconstitutional strikes the proposal was that the Secretary of State would have power to impose a 'conciliation pause'. This would require those involved to desist from a strike for up to 28 days and require the employer meanwhile to observe specified terms and con-

[3] The IRC was set up by George Brown in 1966 to help with mergers and the restructuring of industries and companies.

ditions. The 28 days would give an opportunity to settle the dispute by conciliation, inquiry or other procedure. The power would be used only where the unconstitutional strike was likely to have serious consequences for other workpeople or the economy. In a proposed official strike which would involve a serious threat to the economy or public interest, or where there was doubt that a strike commanded the support of those concerned, it was proposed that the Secretary of State would have power to require the union or unions involved to hold a ballot. This power would be used only after consultation with the unions concerned and only if they were not prepared to consult their members and did not have valid reasons for this. Where inter-union disputes arose over recognition the proposal was that the Secretary of State would, in addition to the power to require an employer to recognise and negotiate, have power to make an Order excluding one or more unions from recognition.

The three proposals could be presented as relatively modest departures from the Donovan Report, particularly when compared with those of Shonfield and *Fair Deal at Work*. In proceeding with them the government might outflank the Conservatives politically and at the same time protect the unions from the menace of the legislation threatened by the opposition. The provision for a conciliation pause was, after all, very like the powers taken in 1940 enabling the Minister of Labour to require 21 days' notice before strike action so that he could conciliate or, if necessary, refer a dispute to the National Arbitration Tribunal and the 28 days period was short compared with the delays on wage increases which could be imposed under the Prices and Incomes Act. The strike ballot – favoured by Wilson himself – existed in the United States and elsewhere and would be used only in circumstances of national emergency and after consultation with the unions – and some unions, anyway, made use of strike ballots. The powers in inter-union disputes would be used only after attempts to settle the difficulty on a voluntary basis by the TUC and CIR had failed: they would be there as a last resort to support the objectives of the TUC in settling inter-union disputes.

Sanctions to support the powers would, of course, be necessary. Workers who went on strike in defiance of an order for a conciliation pause would be fined and refusal to pay could lead to contempt and prison. The 'taint of criminality', as Feather described the proposal, could not be expunged. The prospect became increasingly distressing to politicians as discussions on the White Paper proceeded. The Lord Chancellor and others sought for devices, such as attachment of wages, to avoid the possibility of 'martyrdom', but without success. (Castle realised that if only the unions instead of the individual could be fined the problem would not exist, but the nature of the proposal made this impossible. The Conservatives later thought that they had avoided this trap but the Court of Appeal decided otherwise.) A union which acted in defiance of an order on recognition (or which refused to conduct a ballot) could also be fined, but the possibility of martyrdom through contempt in these circumstances gave less concern.

The Reactions of the General Council to *In Place of Strife*

However modest the three proposals, it was obvious from *Action on Donovan* that they would be opposed by the trade unions. The issue was how serious and determined the opposition would be. Castle had reasons to hope that it would not be pushed too far: the proposals were part of a larger package favourable to the unions, much of it already accepted; there had been similar sanctions in the prices and incomes legislation, but so far there had been no need to use them; there were some trade union leaders who at times gave the impression that they would welcome support in persuading their members to observe agreements and some who thought that the TUC procedures for dealing with inter-union disputes did not invariably work successfully (one union leader thought the government had 'got it made: it's just what we wanted'); and, of course, there were leaders of some unions who had very recently balloted their members during the engineering dispute.

Any optimism needed to be heavily qualified, for the reaction to be expected from others, particularly Jones and Scanlon, would be very different. They would regard the proposals for a conciliation pause as prejudging the right of their members to go on strike – something they would hesitate to regard as proper for a trade union national officer, still less the government. A conciliation pause would coerce their members into observing procedure agreements and it was unjustified, they would think, to assume that all procedure agreements were right and all action in breach of them wrong. Moreover, an order imposing a conciliation pause might not be observed and in this event the sanctions were highly objectionable. The proposal was, anyway, in their view, likely to be unworkable.

As national officers representing the two largest unions, Jones and Scanlon would see no virtue either in the proposal that government should intervene in inter-union disputes. The argument that the powers would be used only where the TUC had failed would not be attractive to them: powerful unions seeking additional members could not be expected to welcome obstacles that might be put in the way of their expansion. A strike ballot imposed from outside would also be regarded by most union leaders as unjustified interference with the normal procedures of their unions and a reflection on the 'democracy' of these procedures.

On each of the three issues, then, there were likely to be substantial numbers on the General Council who would offer determined opposition, though the numbers might vary with the issue and opposition be pursued with varying degrees of enthusiasm. Even moderates such as Sidney Greene of the NUR, however, already objected to the Donovan Commission's proposal for an independent review body as unjustified interference with the internal business of trade unions. The powers now proposed would be permanent and opposition was thus likely to be more sustained than that to the legislation on prices and incomes, which had given the government only temporary powers.

Castle's qualified early optimism about the likely reception of the White Paper, however misguided, was encouraged by Woodcock's reactions. Woodcock wanted, was offered and accepted the chairmanship of the new Commission on Industrial Relations (CIR), which was to be established as a Royal Commission so that an early start could be made in giving effect to the 'radical changes needed in our system of industrial relations'. The early establishment of the Commission was evidence of Castle's sense of urgency; the appointment of Woodcock as Chairman proof of her determination to work with the trade unions.

In response to a request by Woodcock, the draft White Paper was shown 'in confidence' to the General Council before it was put to the Cabinet. Cousins argued for rejecting the White Paper as a whole on grounds of principle. The General Council, however, finally adopted a statement put forward by Woodcock and published on 17 January 1969. In this it was accepted that some of the proposals in the White Paper could help to improve industrial relations and promote trade union objectives. There was opposition to other proposals, and this was set out: the General Council did not exclude the possibility that the government might add its weight to recommendations by the CIR but was convinced that sanctions with financial penalties would 'militate against finding a general solution of this problem', it was unenthusiastic about the trade union development fund, it regarded compulsory strike ballots as 'completely misguided and quite un-acceptable' and the conciliation pause as 'neither practicable nor desirable'. It hoped that the government would reconsider these points. At best the statement did not threaten immediate and total opposition.

By this stage, however, the proposals were already causing trouble within the government. The White Paper had been agreed between Harold Wilson and Barbara Castle and supported by Roy Jenkins. Other ministers were consulted after the General Council and, in consequence, after the proposals had leaked. In part for these reasons, but also because of disagreement, some ministers, including Callaghan, opposed the proposals. It was only after long argument that it was agreed that the White Paper should be published, with some of the critics persuaded that they were not committed to a final decision. There would be lengthy consultations with the unions and other interests; only after these would they need to decide on legislation for the next session.

Following the difficulties within the Cabinet, and perhaps influenced by his view of some of the opponents to Castle, Wilson strongly supported the White Paper publicly, explaining that he and Castle had worked on the proposals together. In face of growing opposition, Castle planned to speak at trade union conferences in the spring and summer in defence of her industrial relations policy, as she had done in 1968 in defence of the prices and incomes policy. Consultations with representatives of the General Council and other interests went ahead in preparation for an Industrial Relations Bill to be ready for the 1969–70 parliamentary session.

Events in the next three months changed the generally expected programme and Castle's plans. The opponents of her proposals within the government and on the General Council encouraged each other. When she opened discussions with Feather and members of the General Council it was clear that any optimism based on Woodcock's reaction and the first statement from the General Council was misleading and that there would be sustained opposition from a considerable majority of the General Council.

Political Reactions to *In Place of Strife*
Before discussing the political difficulties provoked by *In Place of Strife* it is worth making reference to Victor Feather, who was closely involved with both trade union and political opposition to the govern-

ment and was later to make a major contribution to the political failure of Edward Heath's dealings with the unions in 1972. As Woodcock was going off to the CIR, Feather was now Acting General Secretary of the TUC.

Castle and other politicians had been impatient with Woodcock. Though he had consistently argued for changes in the trade union movement and for incomes policy, he was prepared to accept a pace which politicians regarded as too slow; he did not share their time scale and sense of urgency. Politicians at times not only gave the impression of thinking he rode the TUC horse but of misunderstanding the relative importance of rider and animal. While Castle had a low opinion of Feather's 'principles', she, and Wilson, thought he might be an operator more likely to get things done and more likely to goad the TUC to react more quickly. This was a consequential advantage to be gained from the appointment of Woodcock to the CIR.

Even if this had been true, however, there was no reason to think that Feather would be more helpful than Woodcock. He was more closely involved in Labour Party politics than Woodcock and his political sympathies had distinctly not been with the left wing of the party. He disliked Castle and in his turn regarded her as having 'no political principles'. He regarded Wilson as a political 'artful dodger' who would find Feather politically 'a more artful dodger'. (His vanity was justified. With the help of the General Council he might be thought to have picked the political pockets of two prime ministers.)

Nor would Feather be inclined to be helpful on proposals which gave Woodcock a leading role as Chairman of the CIR. He had been Assistant General Secretary to Woodcock for too long. In private he had been critical of his General Secretary's advocacy of incomes policy and would be critical of a policy for industrial relations in which Woodcock was a leading figure. He was also unlikely to carry as much influence with the General Council as had Woodcock. As Acting General Secretary until his appointment was confirmed by Congress in September, he would avoid any moves which might jeopardise his confirmation, however remote this possibility. By appointing Woodcock to the CIR, Castle added to her own difficulties, though given the attitude of Jones, Scanlon and other members of the General Council, the addition was marginal. Feather influenced the tone of the early discussions rather than the outcome of the argument.

More important was the encouragement given by the General Council to the opposition within the government and the Parliamentary Labour Party to the White Paper and the proposed legislation. The position of James Callaghan, now the only senior member of the Cabinet since 1964 with practical experience of the trade union movement and who, as Treasurer of the Labour Party and for other reasons, thought it essential to maintain good relations with the unions, was strengthened. There would be strong opposition within the PLP from a wider section than the usual left wing who had opposed the statutory incomes policy.

The White Paper, *In Place of Strife*, was debated in the House of Commons on 3 March 1969. Fifty-three Labour members voted against the government and forty abstained. These figures of disaffection were much higher than the government had expected and higher than in any debates on incomes policy legislation. On 26 March the National Executive Committee of the Party passed by 16 votes to 5 a resolution proposed by Joe Gormley and amended by Callaghan stating that the NEC could not accept legislation based on all the proposals in the White Paper. These divisions within the movement, the government and the PLP made Castle's plan for an extended programme of consultation and conversion of the unions highly unattractive. The divisions would be on public show for months in the run-up to a general election.

A Bill to Reform Industrial Relations
During the months in which *In Place of Strife* was in preparation and under discussion events seemed to justify the view that action beyond Donovan and in line with Castle's proposals was necessary. An interunion demarcation strike at Girlings, a Cheshire motor component firm, directly concerning only twenty or so workpeople, led to thousands being laid-off in the motor industry. There were strikes in the steel and motor industries, the former arising from competition over negotiating rights for non-manual workers between the Iron and Steel Trades Confederation on the one hand and the Association of Scientific, Technical and Managerial Staff and the Administrative Workers' Union on the other and the latter, at Ford, centring on the issue of unofficial strikes. A strike of ten men at the Ellesmere Port plant of Vauxhall virtually stopped operations and caused 15,000 workers to be laid-off.

There was nothing unusual about the strikes. All illustrated – and the Ford strike was an outstandingly good example – the confusion that resulted from existing bargaining procedures and the damage that could follow. They appeared to justify Castle's proposals to deal with the less satisfactory features of collective bargaining – inter-union rivalries, the inability or unwillingness of negotiators to commit their members, disregard of the consequences of strike action and the readiness to break agreements.[4]

Wilson reaffirmed his support for *In Place of Strife* in a constituency speech largely provoked by the Vauxhall strike. He referred to the Girlings and Vauxhall strikes and then to *In Place of Strife*, saying that the strikes had provided powerful support for the government's proposals, which it still intended to introduce in Parliament. The strikes were, in fact, a two-edged weapon. While they supported Castle's argument for more rapid reform than promised by Donovan, they left her open to criticism that her proposals would not be in operation before late 1970 and that, though she talked of urgency, she was showing too little sense of it.

These troubles may have influenced the government in deciding on early legislation, but it was influenced also by considerations of little or no relevance to industrial relations reform. The government had now decided against extension of the statutory powers on wages in the Prices and Incomes Act, 1968 which were due to expire at the end of 1969, though the decision had not yet been announced. Callaghan had favoured dropping any statutory incomes policy as early as 1967, because of the difficulties it caused in the PLP and with the unions. Opposition to the powers was now growing in the Party and there had been difficulties with many unions in 1968. The policy could hardly be enforced during the 1969–70 wage round without worse industrial trouble and a more open breach with the trade unions generally in the months leading up to the general election. The problem was foreign confidence in the pound and the economy and what to put in place of the incomes policy. The answer seemed to lie in industrial relations legislation.

There were other political considerations pointing in the same direction. The authority of the government in the House of Commons

---

[4] During a conciliation exercise in the Ford strike, Barbara Castle had asked the union representatives what agreements were for, if they were to be broken within days of being reached. She was told by Reg Birch of the AEU that agreements were there to be broken. To be fair, if a longer philosophical discussion had been appropriate, Birch would no doubt have explained that he meant some agreements in some circumstances. Such a direct and straightforward reply would, however, have been unlikely ten years earlier; the question would not have been thought worth asking ten years later.

had been damaged by Crossman's failure with the Parliament Bill.[5] Wilson's own standing in the Cabinet and the Parliamentary Labour Party was at a low ebb; Callaghan's opposition to *In Place of Strife* and his alliance with the trade unions might threaten his position.

For these and other reasons some members of the Cabinet, including some who had been opposed to *In Place of Strife*, now favoured early legislation on industrial relations. Jenkins thought the legislation could be presented as some sort of substitute for an extension of the powers in the Prices and Incomes Act, 1968, which might impress foreign opinion; Crossman (who had earlier opposed *In Place of Strife*) and other senior ministers supported it for a variety of reasons. Castle, now aware of the degree of trade union opposition, wished to keep to the original programme but was persuaded to accept early legislation. Wilson supported it and preparations were started to introduce a Bill in the current session of Parliament.

When the possibility of the early introduction of a short Bill became known, the General Council, which had been in consultation with Castle on the assumption of legislation in the next session, but had already been pressing to see Wilson, insisted on meeting the Prime Minister. A meeting took place on 11 April. The General Council reported on the action it was taking on the Donovan Report and argued strongly against the 'penal proposals' of *In Place of Strife*. In reply, Wilson stressed the urgent need to deal with unofficial strikes, saying that the government could be destroyed economically and politically if it had no answer to the problems posed by these. If there was time to solve the problems without legislation there would, he said, be advantages in proceeding in this way. The country as a whole, however, did not think that such time was available.

On 14 April the Cabinet agreed the outline of a short Bill, to be introduced as soon as possible. Feather was informed of the decision, which was announced by Jenkins in his budget speech on the following day. Jenkins explained that the government would not seek a renewal of the powers on wages under the Prices and Incomes Act, 1968. The powers, he explained were viable only in exceptional circumstances and in the short term and to renew them would have prejudicial effects on industrial relations. Not surprisingly, he claimed that the policy had been a success and, by establishing stronger links between increases in pay and productivity, was doing much to improve the

---

[5] The Parliament Bill to reform the House of Lords had to be withdrawn after opposition from backbenchers who regarded its provisions as both inadequate and undesirable.

industrial performance of the country. This success had to be reinforced by more orderly industrial relations and this was why the government had decided to introduce during this session of Parliament some of the more important provisions from *In Place of Strife*.

Details of the provisions to be included in the legislation were given to Feather on 16 April and outlined in a speech by Castle in the House of Commons later that day. The proposed short Industrial Relations Bill would have five provisions: it would establish the statutory right of every worker to belong to a trade union, give the government powers to compel an employer to recognise a trade union, to impose settlements in inter-union disputes and to impose a twenty-eight day conciliation pause in unconstitutional disputes and would also remove disqualification from unemployment benefit from workers laid-off in consequence of a dispute in which they were playing no direct part. Castle had some difficulty when explaining the sanctions against strikers who did not obey an Order imposing a conciliation pause, but gave an assurance that fines would not be permitted to lead to prison and explained that she was ready to discuss ways of recovering payment to secure this. She emphasised that the major proposals could not wait and stressed that they had been conceived 'in the spirit of faith' – faith in the future of the trade union movement in the country and in its power to grow, adapt, accept responsibility and exert its authority in its own interests and the interests of the community.

In introducing the Bill the government regarded itself as presenting two bargains to the unions and the Parliamentary Party. It proposed to drop the powers on wages in the Prices and Incomes Act, 1968 in exchange for powers on industrial relations; with the proposed Industrial Relations Bill it would give benefits to the unions and their members in exchange for powers to deal with inter-union and unconstitutional disputes. The 'bargains' were not readily acceptable to either recipient.

The decision to introduce the short Bill intensified and widened the opposition on the General Council. There was no possibility of acceptance of the proposals for the conciliation pause and government intervention in inter-union disputes. The first and unanimous objective of the General Council was to compel the government to drop these proposals. A majority of its members were, however, still prepared to minimise the conflict by putting forward as an alternative to legislation proposals for action by the TUC in unconstitutional strikes and inter-union disputes. If the proposals had given any real power to the TUC, they would, of course, hardly have been more acceptable to Jones, Scanlon and others than government intervention. Nevertheless, so long as there was no encroachment on the rights and autonomy of individual unions, they, too, would be prepared to go along with a formula by which the government could save face.

Rules 11 and 12 of the constitution of the TUC related to strikes and inter-union disputes respectively. Rule 11 required unions to inform the General Council of strikes likely to affect large numbers of union members and gave the General Council the right to give a considered opinion and advise the unions concerned. Rule 12 gave the General Council the power to adjudicate in inter-union disputes with the ultimate sanctions of suspension and expulsion from Congress if the General Council judgements were not accepted. It was now proposed to change the rules to make it clear that unions were under an obligation in the case of unofficial strikes likely to affect large numbers of the work force 'to take immediate and energetic steps to obtain a resumption of work' and were not entitled to authorise strikes in inter-union disputes until the General Council had been consulted.

The General Council called a Special Congress at Croydon for 5 June (not a Conference of Executives as favoured by Woodcock), the first for 50 years and only the second in 100 years. Preparation was started on a document to put to the Congress as the response of the TUC to the government proposals – later to be published as *Industrial Relations: Programme for Action*. Most of this document repeated the views expressed in *Action on Donovan*, developed to include comments on *In Place of Strife* and the proposals of the General Council on unconstitutional strikes and inter-union disputes which were to be presented as the trade union alternative to the government's proposals.

The Defeat of Wilson and Castle

The first draft of *Industrial Relations: Programme for Action*, containing the General Council's proposals, was sent to Wilson and Castle on 12 May 1969 and formed the basis for the first of a series of meetings with the General Council before the Special Congress at the beginning of June. The discussions centred on the issue of unconstitutional strikes.

The General Council was prepared to make further presentational changes to help: it was ready to amend Rule 11 to underline the fact that a union which refused the assistance or advice of the General

Council could, in the last resort, be expelled; it was prepared to make it clear that a 'recommendation' by the General Council was something which unions were expected to obey and that in doing this, unions would be expected 'to take action within their own rules if necessary'. Scanlon underlined the fact that the changes were presentational: 'let it be clearly understood – we will decide whether action will be taken under our rules or not'.

Neither Wilson nor Castle was satisfied that the proposals were an adequate substitute for the proposed legislation. Wilson wanted a guarantee that sanctions, either in the form of fines or, in the last resort, expulsions, would be imposed on union members who refused to return to work or go through agreed procedures. He emphasised the difficult economic situation and the wider political implications of the situation:

> In our joint consultation what we are talking about is a deep and fundamental split between the two wings of the movement. This is serious – extremely serious in any circumstances. We all recognise and approach it with that degree of gravity. I believe it means something more – whether this Labour Government or any Labour Government can continue.[6]

His appeal to the political commitment of the trade unions was not successful, made as it was on an issue of crucial importance to the internal affairs of the TUC and its affiliated unions. The General Council was not prepared to make concessions which would impair the autonomy of unions. Its proposals would be put unchanged to the Special Congress. Wilson agreed not to introduce the short Bill until after the Congress.

He now faced increasing opposition within the Parliamentary Labour Party to the proposed short Bill. The opponents of the Bill supported the stance of the General Council. Douglas Houghton, the Chairman of the Party and in touch with Feather, came out publicly against the proposed legislation and in favour of an agreement between the government and the TUC. Callaghan supported this line. Some backbenchers made moves to organise an 'action group' against the short Bill – and to replace Wilson as Prime Minister.

At the Special Congress on 5 June the recommendations of the General Council were adopted by 7,909,000 votes to 846,000. Wilson, after private talks with Scanlon and Jones between their last meeting

---

[6] Statement at the end of a meeting with General Council representatives on 21 May 1969. *See* Peter Jenkins, *op. cit.*, pp. 133–4.

and the Special Congress, was convinced that the TUC would not exercise effective authority over affiliated unions and that unions would not take effective action against their members in unconstitutional strikes. In a press statement issued immediately after the Congress he rejected as inadequate the proposals which the Congress had endorsed. The government, he said, recognised the proposals as a major advance and regarded those for dealing with inter-union disputes as broadly satisfactory, but it had 'considerable reservations' about the effectiveness of the General Council's proposals for dealing with unconstitutional strikes, particularly the proposed arrangements for ensuring that any awards and recommendations made after a TUC inquiry into such disputes would be implemented by unions and their members.

The apparently modest and limited government proposal for a conciliation pause in unofficial disputes which many – supporters and opponents alike – doubted would be effective if used had now become a major political issue within the labour movement. It seemed absurd that this and Wilson's reservations, though 'considerable', about the TUC alternative should create a gulf between trade unions and government wider than at any time since 1931. The analogy with the pre-war years was recognised by some of the leading figures involved. Scanlon is said to have assured Wilson, 'Prime Minister, we don't want you to become another Ramsay MacDonald'. Wilson, speaking at a dinner on the night of the Croydon Conference, referred to Stanley Baldwin's comment on certain newspaper proprietors who, Baldwin had claimed, were asserting their claim to power without responsibility; that claim was, said Wilson, being re-asserted not by press lords but by another estate of the realm. 'If that is the claim', he concluded, 'it will get Baldwin's answer'.[7]

Behind the argument over the seemingly modest proposals for a conciliation pause there were, however, more important and farther-reaching political considerations. The issue, while in one sense narrow and concerned with internal TUC and union affairs and rules, was part of the wider problem of industrial relations and trade union power which had become a major political issue which would be important in the next election. There might be serious electoral consequences if it became clear that the General Council could dictate to a Labour government.

Despite these implications, opinion in the PLP gave priority to avoiding a split in the movement and a repeat of 1931. The majority

[7] Peter Jenkins, *op. cit.*, pp. 141–2.

of the PLP was against the proposed legislation and in favour of government acceptance of the TUC proposals. Robert Mellish, the Chief Whip, informed the Cabinet that there was no hope of the short Bill being passed. The only members of the Cabinet in favour of proceeding with it were now Wilson and Castle (even Jenkins, previously a strong supporter, had changed his mind).

The final meeting between Wilson, Castle and the General Council took place on 8 June. Knowing that the Cabinet no longer supported the Prime Minister, the General Council was ready to help (and avoid serious trouble over the leadership), accepting his suggestion that both parties should enter into what he described as 'a solemn and binding undertaking' about unofficial strikes. The undertaking was drafted by Wilson on the basis of a circular the TUC had ready to send to affiliated unions. In unconstitutional strikes where the TUC deemed the strikers to be at fault, it would 'place an obligation on trade unions to take energetic steps to obtain an immediate resumption of work, including action within their rules'. In strikes where it was 'unreasonable to order an unconditional return to work', the TUC would tender its considered opinion and advice. The guarantee of the use of sanctions for which Wilson had pressed was not given. Wilson agreed not to proceed with the short Bill.

The negotiations between Wilson, Castle and the General Council – 'HMS Fruitless' as the exercise was called by a member of the Cabinet Secretariat – came to an end with Castle's demanding (without success) that the undertaking should be signed by every member of the General Council – no doubt in the hope of making it 'binding' – and with the appearance of the Attorney General – perhaps intended to add solemnity to the proceedings. The attempt to reform industrial relations with a degree of urgency greater than that of the Donovan Commission or the TUC had failed.

Re-uniting the Movement – and the Next Election
The government kept to its side of the bargain it had offered the unions and the Parliamentary Party and did not withdraw its commitment to allow the powers in the Prices and Incomes Act, 1968 to expire at the end of the year. The attempt at the 'bargain' ended with the government doing more than simply dropping these powers and its proposals to reform industrial relations: Wilson gave first priority to re-establishing harmony between the Party and the trade unions on trade union terms and, given his position in June 1969 in

the Cabinet and the Party, with an election likely in 1970, he did so without reservations.

Preparatory work was started on an Industrial Relations Bill for the next session which not only excluded the 'penal' proposals put forward by Barbara Castle but which, it was tacitly accepted, would include only such Donovan Commission recommendations as were wanted by the TUC. The proposal to establish a tribunal to supervise trade union rules and protect the rights of members of trade unions was dropped. In unofficial and other strikes Victor Feather took over the role of conciliator – when he so wished – from the Department of Employment and Productivity.

The government went through the motions of continuing an incomes policy aimed at securing some restraint in the rate of wage increase. A White Paper on incomes policy, *Productivity, Prices and Incomes Policy after 1969* (Cmnd. 4237), was published in December 1969, setting out a 'norm' for wage increases within a range of $2\frac{1}{2}$ per cent to $4\frac{1}{2}$ per cent and stating that the government proposed to re-activate Part II of the *Prices and Incomes Act, 1967* to give it power to delay increases for up to four months on reference to the National Board for Prices and Incomes. The continuation of the policy of wage restraint was, however, very largely a formality. The government was anxious to avoid serious industrial troubles, particularly in the public sector, during the 1969–70 wage round. Between June 1969 and the election in June 1970 wage rates increased by 10 per cent. The relaxation on wages, besides avoiding conflict between the government and the unions, had the advantage of reflating the economy at a time when the government was still hesitant about reflating by direct government measures which might have had a more serious effect on the pound and foreign opinion. (The fact that reflation by relaxation on wages would be less easy to reverse was a disadvantage outweighed by the political advantage of avoiding trouble between the government and unions in the months leading to the election.)

The failure of the government to continue an effective degree of wage restraint and to put through its policy for reform of industrial relations, both of which it had insisted were crucial to its economic policy, did not prevent its achieving the major objective of this policy since July 1966. By the end of 1969 there was a continuing surplus in the balance of payments and the pound was no longer under immediate threat. The Heath Government which came into office in June 1970 inherited this success. At the same time it inherited the consequences of the conflict between the trade unions and the Wilson

Government which had been resolved by the assertion of trade union power: a rate of wage increase which was higher than at any time since the war and which, if continued, would threaten a return to the difficulties of 1964–69 and attitudes in the trade union movement which would make it more difficult for it to pursue its own policies to reform industrial relations.

As Wilson is said to have remarked at the end of his discussions with the General Council in June 1969, 'I don't envy Ted having to deal with this crew'.

PART III

Edward Heath, 1970–74 – 'A New Style of Government'

Relations between the Heath Government and the unions were dominated by the government's commitments to legislate to 'reform' industrial relations in a manner which would limit (or at least regulate) the exercise of trade union power and to avoid a statutory incomes policy, and by the need to reverse the trend on wages and inflation which had followed Harold Wilson's retreat on incomes policy after March 1969. Between 1970 and 1974 the consequences of the commitments and the pursuit of the last objective led to a striking change in Edward Heath's views on how government should react to the problem of trade union power and an almost complete reversal of his policies on coming into office.

The period 1970–74 can be divided into three. From June 1970 to February 1972 the government resisted wage claims in the public sector and set out to reduce the power of the unions by the Industrial Relations Act. In the second period, from March to November 1972, Heath searched for a way of avoiding the 'confrontations' between government and unions which had accompanied these policies and finally attempted to reach an agreement (not unlike that of the Wilson Government in 1964–66) on an incomes policy coupled with promises of economic growth. This attempt failed, and in the last period, November 1972 to February 1974, the government introduced a statutory incomes policy – although Heath continued to try to reach an understanding with the unions and to avoid 'confrontation'. Both efforts had failed by the time of the election of February 1974.

8 Industrial Relations Legislation and Confrontation, June 1970– February 1972

A 'New Style' of Government

Edward Heath's relations with the trade unions were determined from the outset by the need to reverse the trend on wages following Harold Wilson's retreat in the face of union power and by his own pre-election commitment to legislate on industrial relations. For Heath, unlike Wilson, wage restraint and 'reform' of industrial relations were not alternatives: he pursued both. The first would have been an extremely difficult operation for a Labour government able, perhaps, to call again on the 'loyalty' of the unions. Heath faced the normal political animosity of the unions to a Conservative government, increased by the hostility to his policy on industrial relations. Personal attitudes expressed in his foreword to the 1970 Conservative manifesto, *A Better Tomorrow*, together with his general approach, seemed unlikely to reduce the intensity of the certain conflict between his government and the unions:

> But good government is not just a matter of the right policies. It also depends on the way the government is run.... This is something which I have thought about deeply. Indeed it has been one of my main interests since I entered the House of Commons....... I am determined therefore that a Conservative government shall introduce a new style of government.... I want to see a fresh approach to the taking of decisions.... And in coming to its decisions it [the government] must always recognise that its responsibility is to the people, and all the people, of this country.... Once a decision is made, once a policy is established, the Prime Minister and his colleagues should have the courage to stick to it. Nothing has done Britain more harm in the world than the endless

backing and filling which we have seen in recent years. Whether it be our defence commitments, or our financial policies, or the reform of industrial relations, the story has been the same.... We must create a new way of running our affairs.

Assertions of resolution and responsibility to all the people are common enough. The foreword was a convenient platform for criticism of Wilson's style of government (and an assurance perhaps that Harold Macmillan's 'flexibility' would not be repeated), but there was more to Heath's 'new style'. He appeared to believe in the 'authority' of government and was critical of institutions such as the National Economic Development Council and the National Board for Prices and Incomes on which powerful interests were represented and which made claims to share that authority. There was no mention of the NEDC, a Conservative creation, in the manifesto and the NBPI had been more or less written off as early as *Fair Deal at Work*. In 1972 Heath would dismiss the suggestion that the government was 'bargaining' with the trade unions – governments did not 'bargain'. His 'new style' was anti-corporatist: the government, though at any one time represented by one party only temporarily in power, should operate above the 'interests' in the country, rather than with them. Whether his 'new style' would now prevail was to be put to the test by trade unions who had asserted their power and shown their own style in dealing with government in 1969.

The Change in Conservative Attitude: Wages and Incomes Policy

The only clear indication in the Conservative manifesto of policy on wages was that 'Labour's compulsory wage control was a failure and we will not repeat it'. On industrial relations, in contrast, the manifesto was positive and included a firm commitment:

> We will introduce a comprehensive Industrial Relations Bill in the first Session of the new Parliament. It will provide a proper framework of law within which improved relationships between management, men and unions can develop. We welcome the TUC's willingness to take action through its own machinery.... Yet it is no substitute for the new set of fair and reasonable rules we will introduce.

It was made clear that the Bill would follow the lines of *Fair Deal at Work*, published in 1968.

On both these issues the manifesto recorded a change of attitude since the party was last in office. On wages there was no longer talk of the need for a permanent incomes policy to combat wage-push inflation. This withdrawal from the position taken by Harold Macmillan and Selwyn Lloyd in 1961 was not surprising. Incomes policy, after all, was thought to have contributed to the electoral defeat in 1964, even after Macmillan had retreated from it. Since then, the incomes policies of the Wilson Government had caused serious industrial and political difficulties and had failed. Incomes policies were thus no longer politically attractive, and by the Conservative Party the Selwyn Lloyd effort might now be judged a short-lived, mistaken and damaging episode.

The manifesto did not make clear what alternative measures a Conservative government would take to deal with the problem of inflationary wage increases, suggesting only that there were to be more palatable policies than 'Labour's compulsory wage control' to check inflation – strengthened competition, reduced taxes, better industrial relations, improved efficiency, all helping to stimulate output: 'This faster growth will mean that we can combine higher wages with steadier prices to bring a real increase in living standards'.

There was, however, a recognition that this might not be enough: 'The Labour Government's policies have unleashed forces which no Government could hope to reverse overnight. The first essential is for the new Government to give a new lead'.

It seemed inevitable that some action would be taken on wages. As a result of the 1967 devaluation and the deflationary measures which followed, there was a substantial favourable balance of payments in 1969 and 1970, but the achievement was threatened. The rate of growth in 1969 had been about 2 per cent, while the rate of wage increase was moving into double figures and for 1970 was to be over 13 per cent. Prices in 1970 were to rise by nearly 8 per cent. Increasing wage costs and the relative rate of inflation were in process of destroying the competitive advantages of the devaluation.

Relations between government and unions on the wages front were certain to be extremely difficult – far more difficult perhaps than Heath and his colleagues might have expected. The more important trade union leaders were very different from those Heath had known when Minister of Labour in 1959–60 or Robert Carr had known when a junior Minister in the same department from 1955–58. More than at any time since the war, the most influential members of the General Council would regard a Conservative government as representing interests in conflict with – and on matters crucial to them, irrecon-

cilable with – the interests of labour. The political views of the two
most important members – Jack Jones and Hugh Scanlon – were
further to the left than those of any of their predecessors in their two
unions since the war. It could be assumed, following their successes
against Wilson in 1969, that the unions would be prepared to oppose
a Conservative government to the limit in defence of their bargaining
power and in pressing their wage claims in the free collective
bargaining system. If on wages 'the first essential was for the new
government to give a lead and stick to it', this would mean direct
conflict in the public sector between government and individual
unions. The possibility of 'moderation' being shown by the unions or
their influence used to limit trouble, as in the early years of the
Wilson Government, would not exist.

The theoretical alternative of securing wage restraint through an
incomes policy agreed with (or accepted by) the TUC – a policy which
had been attempted by Macmillan and had been the hope at times
of all governments since the war – was not a serious practical
possibility. Some advocates of incomes policies within the civil service
(and outside) favoured an attempt by the government to secure this
and, if necessary, the putting aside of the proposals on industrial
relations as a move in such an attempt. The history of incomes
policy gave, however, little hope and there was no reason to think that
the General Council would contemplate an agreement with a Conservative government. The decision to proceed with *Fair Deal at Work*
in the form of the Industrial Relations Bill was of secondary
importance in ruling out the alternative.

The Change in Conservative Attitude: Industrial Relations

The commitment to legislation on industrial relations was more significant for the Party than the decision on incomes policy, representing
as it did the final break with the Churchill and Macmillan policy of
avoiding action which might provoke serious industrial trouble and,
above all, a general conflict with the trade union movement.

Within the Macmillan Government there was, by 1963, frustration
over the limits imposed on government economic policy by the
inflationary consequences of union power in collective bargaining and
resentment that the use of this power was influenced by political
considerations to the disadvantage of a Conservative government. The
industrial power and political hostility of the trade unions had not,
however, prevented the party from winning three elections and

holding office since 1951 and opposition to the policy of 'conciliation' was muted by political success. Events after 1964 strengthened the critics. After two lost elections, the political implications of union power could no longer be disregarded. The unions' agreement on an incomes policy with the Wilson Government revealed more clearly than at any time since the war the importance of their political commitment to the Labour Party and their apparent readiness to modify their industrial activities for political purposes. Industrial relations continued to deteriorate and by the mid-sixties 'reform' was a major political issue. Following *Rookes* v. *Barnard* the Conservative Party had been committed to an inquiry in its 1964 manifesto and the Labour government had appointed the Donovan Commission. By 1966 the leadership of the Party consisted of post-war politicians less influenced by the events of the twenties and the partnership of the war and ready to accept the risk of conflict in an attempt to deal with the problems of trade union power. This was the background to Robert Carr's speech to the Party Conference in 1967, which gave expression to the changing attitudes of the Party towards the unions and which was followed by *Fair Deal at Work*, published in March 1968.

Fair Deal at Work contained what Carr described as proposals for the comprehensive modernisation of the laws governing industrial relations in Great Britain. It recommended: 'measures which, if applied, would transform the British system of industrial relations. Trade union reform is only one aspect and one requirement. It advocates, not a trade union policy, but a new approach to industrial relations as a whole'.

The proposals which concerned trade union 'reform' would, however, regulate by law the activities of trade unions in relation, amongst other things, to their members, recruitment, collective bargaining, the closed shop and (in emergency situations) to the government and would limit both their industrial and political power.

It was not clear how far the Party or a future Conservative government would be committed by *Fair Deal at Work*. There were reservations in Carr's foreword:

We publish it not as a final definitive statement of the detailed actions to which a future Conservative government will be committed but as a considered set of proposals and as a basis for public discussion of what is one of the most important economic and social problems in a modern industrial society. Our studies will continue and we shall want to take account not only of the reactions to this document, but also, of course, of the forthcoming report of the Royal Commission and of the widespread public discussion which we hope will be stimulated.

There was less caution in Heath's preface: 'I consider industrial relations to be absolutely crucial to economic progress and our policy for industrial relations to be a key element in the Conservative framework'.

The framework itself:

> would be able to withstand the pressures which have defeated previous attempts at an economic breakthrough: the critical balance of payments position, the difficulty of reconciling the concepts of full employment and free collective bargaining, the menace of rising prices and the inflationary scramble that ensues.

It seemed likely that the next Conservative government would face up to the facts of trade union power and, in any event, Carr's reservations became irrelevant in the light of developments in 1969. The public discussion he had foreseen following the Donovan Report was submerged within nine months by the political excitement over *In Place of Strife*. The view of the Labour government that the proposals in the Royal Commission were inadequate, the importance given to the reform of industrial relations by Barbara Castle and Harold Wilson (and for a time by some of their colleagues) in terms as emphatic as Edward Heath's preface, the retreat from the central proposals of *In Place of Strife* under trade union and Labour Party pressure and Conservative assessment of the political consequences of this retreat – all combined to establish the Conservative view that legislation to reform industrial relations was not only crucial to economic progress but would be politically advantageous. The events of 1969, moreover, left them little political choice. The Labour government (to the Conservatives' great surprise) had opened a door more or less closed in practical political discussion since 1927 and the Conservative Party could hardly walk away from it. *Fair Deal at Work* was to become the Industrial Relations Bill.

There was no doubt that the legislation would be bitterly opposed. A Conservative government might, however, be in a better position than a Labour government to withstand union opposition. The trade unions had defeated Wilson and Castle through their colleagues and the Party. They could not use their political power directly against a Conservative government and Carr and others assumed that the pressures of industrial action were unlikely to be used for this purpose. In any case, it seemed that union opposition would, with the new

not entirely true

style of government, be met with resolution now that avoidance of
conflict was no longer the first priority.

The Industrial Relations Bill and Union Reaction

The Conservatives accepted that 'reform' of industrial relations was a
long-term process – Carr said that it might be as long as ten years
before the effects of the law were apparent. Given this view and the
fact that the proposed legislation was not immediately relevant to the
problem of wage inflation, the decision to introduce complicated and
highly controversial legislation in the first session of Parliament needs
explaining.

First, there were parliamentary considerations: the government
wanted a reasonably impressive programme for its first session and
an industrial relations Bill would be a major piece of legislation.
Secondly, much preliminary work had been done in opposition: the
new government had already outlined the main principles for the Bill,
which could be prepared quickly. Thirdly, the fact that the benefits
of the legislation would be long-term – the legislation would be
bitterly opposed in Parliament and by the unions and, until it became
law and was accepted in operation, unpopular with an important
section of the electorate – became itself an argument for priority:
legislation early in the Parliament would give time for controversy and
opposition to fade and the benefits to be appreciated before the next
election.

The decision to proceed so quickly, however, had serious consequences. The draft Bill had to be ready before the end of 1970 and
the period for consultation with the unions, employers and other
interests was therefore limited to two months. The unions could
reasonably have expected a much longer period. The radical and
comprehensive nature of the proposals justified the conventional
processes of a White Paper and lengthy discussion. They could not
be expected to accept *Fair Deal at Work*, published two years earlier,
when the Conservatives were in opposition, as a reasonable substitute.
The government was 'rushing' the trade unions just as Wilson had
done with his short Bill in 1969.

A consultative document, for the most reproducing the main
propositions of *Fair Deal at Work*, was published on 5 October and the
TUC and others were asked to comment by 13 November. Carr had
his first – and only – meeting with the General Council on 9 October,
opening the meeting by saying that there were eight 'pillars' in the

proposals which were not open to change. These 'pillars' were the proposals which restricted the bargaining power and regulated the operations of trade unions and which were most violently opposed by them.

Amongst the provisions there was a statutory right to belong or *not* to belong to a trade union. (Equating the right to belong and the right not to belong was contrary to views expressed by the Donovan Commission and a direct blow to the closed shop.) The Act would establish the right of unions to be recognised and would set out the procedures for unions to acquire recognition, through a new National Industrial Relations Court (NIRC) and the Commission on Industrial Relations. The use of these procedures was, however, limited for the most part to registered trade unions. The rules of registered unions would have to meet certain criteria; for example, they would have to prevent arbitrary discrimination in membership, lay down rights to contest and to hold office and to vote and regulate the exercise of union discipline of members.

It would not be compulsory for unions to register, but unregistered unions would be heavily penalised. They could not use the machinery of the Act to obtain recognition (though unregistered unions could be recognised); unlimited damages could be assessed against them if they or their members broke the provisions of the new law concerning industrial action and were involved in 'unfair industrial practices'; they would have no immunity against liability through inducing breaches of contract and they would lose the advantage of tax rebates which, for the trade union movement as a whole, could amount to several million pounds a year. If a union were registered and was faced with proceedings it would be protected by limits on any penalties which might be imposed; it could avoid liability 'if it were able to show that it had used its best endeavours to fulfil its obligations and to prevent any continuation or repetition of the acts complained of'; it could induce members to go on strike in breach of their individual contracts of employment without incurring liability; it benefited from tax concessions.

Collective agreements could be enforceable at law, and would be presumed enforceable unless a written provision to the contrary was included. Various forms of industrial action would be defined as 'unfair industrial practices', including inducing another person to take industrial action in breach of contract or collective agreement unless the action was by a registered trade union or an officer of such a union with authority to call industrial action, industrial action in support of a closed shop or for recognition and certain types of sympathetic industrial action. There were to be emergency provisions, to deal with strikes or other industrial action likely to injure the national economy or imperil national security, which would provide for a 'cooling-off' period and a strike ballot.

The Bill would include other provisions about collective bargaining, protection of employees against unfair dismissal and additional rights under the Contracts of Employment Act and for the new machinery of the National Industrial Relations Court, the Commission on Industrial Relations and a Registrar of Trade Unions.

In reply the General Council made it clear that their terms for entering into consultation were that the government should abandon its proposals and commit itself to the principle of voluntary reform. Heath should accept what Wilson had been offered and had finally accepted. Failing this the General Council was not prepared to have further discussions. The General Council could not conceivably have expected their proposition to be accepted. Victor Feather immediately proceeded to blame the government: 'It is called a consultative document but it is not. Two days earlier Mr. Robert Carr had told the Conservative Party Conference much the same thing. He announced that there was no going back on the central proposals.' The government attitude was, he said: 'wilful denial of the facilities for consultation that have been accorded to the TUC by every government for at least the past thirty years'.

The TUC case against the proposals was published in *Reason: the Case against the Government's Proposals on Industrial Relations*. A public campaign against the Bill was organised. The conflict between the government and unions was thus from the start totally different in form from the conflict over *In Place of Strife*. There was no discussion and a break in effective communication between the government and the TUC.

The situation had some advantages for both the government and the unions. For the government, it was possible to prepare the draft Bill for publication in November. Lengthy consultations would have given the TUC recurrent opportunities to present their case against the government in public, would, anyway, have ended in breakdown – the success of union opposition to *In Place of Strife* made it certain that they would accept no less than total success over what they saw as much more damaging proposals from a Conservative government – and would have delayed the programme.

For the unions, Carr's statement on the eight pillars was used by

Feather to put responsibility for the breakdown on the government. This could help to influence public opinion and made it possible for the General Council to maintain its established posture of always being ready to talk without running into the difficulties which continued consultation would have caused. Extended talks would have laid the General Council open to attacks from militants violently opposed to discussions with government which carried the slightest suggestion of acceptance of any part of the proposed legislation. There would have been demonstrations and industrial action against 'consultation', suggesting division in the trade union movement, which would have been unhelpful with public opinion. As it was, Feather could organise a public campaign on behalf of a 'united' trade union movement. Leaflets based on *Reason* were distributed, training courses and national, regional and local meetings were convened; there was a national petition and open-air demonstrations were organised, including the traditional Trafalgar Square rally and march to Hyde Park and, as a high point, a rally in the Albert Hall. All very different from the meetings in 1969 at Downing Street and Chequers. The government failed to counter this activity with an effective public defence of the Bill. Misrepresentation of its proposals in *Reason* was not rebutted and the extreme position taken by the General Council, which had led to the breakdown of talks, was not effectively exposed.

The union campaign continued until the Bill became law in August 1971. It was the first large-scale 'demagogic' operation nationally organised by the TUC or by any substantial section of the trade union movement since the war. The language was violent: the slogan was 'kill the Bill'. A macabre and over-realistic touch was added by the Angry Brigade, who placed bombs at Carr's house and the Department of Employment.

The campaign added greatly to the atmosphere of 'confrontation' (a word which was now to become fashionable), coinciding as it did with the conflicts which developed between government and individual unions over wages. It was accompanied by a series of unofficial one-day protest strikes. These were not impressive in national terms, but already some employers felt that the government's approach had strengthened the position of militants amongst their workers and damaged their industrial relations. The attitude of an increasing number of employers towards the Act after it came into operation was unenthusiastic and critical.

With the campaign as a background, the government proceeded

with its Bill. It was introduced in the House of Commons on 26 November and the second reading opened on 15 December. The Labour opposition took its cue from the TUC and engaged in total opposition to the Bill, showing no sign of being inhibited by its own attempt to 'reform' industrial relations. As a result, most of the Bill was not debated. The relative futility of the Parliamentary Labour Party in fighting the legislation provided an interesting and significant contrast to the activity of the trade unions.

The Industrial Relations Act

The Industrial Relations Act became law on 5 August 1971. There were no changes of importance from the proposals in the consultative document and the provisions need not be repeated. As it was, however, the first attempt in this country at comprehensive industrial relations legislation which sought to meet criticisms of the system which had been current since the mid-fifties, it is worth some general comment.

Carr had hoped the Act would be short and simple – a document which could be easily understood by shop stewards and workers on the shop floor, explaining their rights and responsibilities. It was, inevitably, very long – more than 170 sections and 20 schedules – and extremely complicated. Within twelve months there were three appeals from the NIRC to the Court of Appeal and one case had gone to the House of Lords. Heath's idea of it as an act 'to curb trade union power' was an over-simplified view. The Act was an all-purpose creation which aimed to deal with the weaknesses deriving from the 'two systems' of industrial relations described by the Donovan Commission, to change the balance of bargaining power to meet the views of those who considered collective bargaining and wage-push inflation a serious threat to the economy, to prevent the kind of maladministration which had been exposed in the ETU on the 1950s, to give legal rights to trade union members and protection to non-unionists and to extend the rights of individuals in their employment by giving legal protection against unfair dismissal and by amending the Contracts of Employment Act. This range of objectives meant that the Act had no clearly apparent, consistent philosophy – but there were four main themes.

First, in an attempt to make industrial relations more 'orderly', it sought to induce or compel trade union officers to exercise greater authority over their members and thus deal with the problems of unofficial strikes or strikes in breach of procedure agreements or in breach of contract. This was the purpose of making collective agreements legally enforceable and making trade unions, as corporate bodies, responsible for the actions of their officers and agents, including shop stewards, and subject to penalities if they failed in their responsibilities. The intention was to bring back to the full-time trade union officers some of the power which had 'gone to the shop floor' and to reverse by law the trend encouraged by full employment and other features of the post-war years. In this sense it was an attempt to deal with the central problem as defined by the Donovan Commission and *In Place of Strife*. The latter had proposed the exercise of government authority in unofficial strikes when trade union authority had failed; the Act tried to change the essential characteristics of existing trade union organisations and impose a managerial pattern – to transform the trade union officer from being a representative of, and spokesman for, his members into being, in certain circumstances at any rate, a trade union 'boss'. These provisions were in direct conflict with the declared philosophy of important trade union leaders, including Jones and Scanlon, and ran counter to many of the realities of trade union organisation and machinery.

Secondly, while seeking to increase the authority of trade union officers over their members for the purpose of securing more orderly collective bargaining, the Act also limited their authority. The rules of a registered trade union had to conform to certain principles to protect the rights of individuals in respect of membership, elections and discipline. The Act gave a right not to belong to a trade union and prohibited the closed shop. These provisions, however justified, were not directly relevant to orderly collective bargaining, and could in some cases be inimical to it. While it could be argued that reasonable control of internal trade union activity need not weaken the authority of officers, legal intervention inevitably challenged it. The provisions were resented by officers responsible for running the existing trade union organisations as reflecting on their honesty and competence. They would also, in the view of these officers, be unworkable, given the manner in which many trade unions were organised.

Thirdly, while some provisions of the Act were directed to increasing the authority of trade union officers in the process of collective bargaining, others were aimed at reducing the power they could exercise in that process. There were provisions limiting the right to strike over recognition, prohibiting sympathetic strikes in certain circumstances, applying special provisions to strikes gravely injurious to the national economy and threatening the health of the population and prohibiting strikes or other industrial action which affected the interests of parties extraneous to the industrial dispute. These provisions were clearly 'anti-trade union' and intended to curb union power.

Fourthly, the Act gave additional rights to employees against their employers by including provisions against unfair dismissal, by improving the provisions of the Contracts of Employment Act and Redundancy Payments Act and by requiring employers to give specified information to unions and their individual employees. It could be argued that these provisions, too, weakened rather than strengthened authority within the trade unions, since they gave protection through the law in circumstances where in the past members would have looked to their union for protection. This argument cannot, however, be pushed too far: when the Act was repealed, the unions insisted on these protective provisions being maintained and increased.

The effect of the Act on trade union activities, particularly the threat to their bargaining power, was in practice likely to be limited – the bark was a good deal worse than the bite. While collective agreements were made legally enforceable, the Act allowed trade unions to negate this in any collective agreement they signed. While an individual could be penalised for inducing a strike in breach of contract, a registered trade union or person acting on its behalf could induce such a strike without penalties. The penalties on registered unions for 'unfair industrial actions' were strictly limited: there was no question of liability for damages as in the pre-1906 days.

It is impossible to assess how far in practice trade union interests would have been damaged, the power of the unions reduced and industrial relations improved by the Act, because it never operated as intended. It went no further in regulating trade union activities than legislation in other Western industrialised countries such as Germany, France, Sweden and the United States. Much of it was modelled on United States legislation. It could not be argued – at any rate in 1971 – that in those countries the unions were not as free and as powerful as in Great Britain, though they might exercise that power differently. Hugh Clegg – an expositor of trade union virtues – thought the implications of the Act for the unions were not very serious and that it in no way destroyed their basic freedom. He described it as 'a Bill compounded of useful but minor reforms and tiresome but hardly fatal irritants to the trade unions'. It is not easy to find a rational, justifiable basis for the intensity and determination of the trade union opposition which continued after the Act was passed.

What about reasons? political/power [handwritten margin note]

The Trade Union Attack on the Act

The TUC knew that its public opposition and the opposition of the Labour Party in Parliament would not prevent the Bill going through and had already decided on its course of action at a Special Congress on 18 March. The Congress adopted the policy of a boycott. Unions were advised not to register (the terms of the Act were such that this meant that unions would have to take the positive step of de-registration), not to co-operate with the NIRC or the CIR, not to sign legally enforceable collective agreements and not to nominate people to serve on the Court, the Commission or industrial tribunals. If the advice were followed, unions would deprive themselves of the protections and advantages provided for registered unions in the Act and make themselves liable to unlimited damages in respect of unfair industrial practices. It would be a voluntary return to Taff Vale.

Though de-registration could thus have the most serious consequences, the proposal for a boycott was not challenged. Any union which favoured acceptance of the law was open to the risk that Jones (and others) would regard it as no longer entitled to the protection of the Bridlington Agreement[1] and there might be other penalties which unions with many votes could inflict. There was discussion about whether unions should be 'advised' or 'instructed' to de-register. The formula of 'advising' (less strong than 'recommending' or 'instructing') helped those trade union leaders who were doubtful about the boycott but were unwilling to stand up publicly against their militants or break the unity in opposition so far shown by the movement. It could be justified as in line with the established reluctance of the General Council to override the policy-making authority of individual unions and it recognised that some unions might be in special difficulties because of their rules. It reflected caution about adopting a resolution which would imply expulsion of unions in breach of it. These doubts were overridden six months later when the more severe resolution of 'instructing' was adopted by the

[1] The Bridlington Agreement, adopted by the Trades Union Congress in 1939, revised the *Main Principles for the Avoidance of Disputes* laid down in 1924. The Agreement lays down recommendations about transfer of members, resolution of inter-union difficulties etc.

Annual Congress in September 1971 to secure universal de-registration, to be followed by the expulsion in September 1972 of thirty-two unions, including the National Union of Seamen and the National Graphical Association.

The decision of the Congress to continue the policy of outright opposition after the Act became law was a setback for the government, which had hoped that, having fought the Bill, the unions would then accept the situation. The government proceeded, however, not surprisingly, to bring the Act into force stage by stage, establish the National Industrial Relations Court and reconstitute the Commission on Industrial Relations, from which all the trade union members appointed by Barbara Castle had resigned. Sir John Donaldson was appointed chairman of the NIRC. The consequences of the Act and the position taken by the unions towards it were now beyond the control of the government and with the Courts.

Wage Claims: 'Giving a Lead'

The campaign to 'kill the Bill' coincided with conflicts between government and unions over wages. The government had ruled out 'compulsory wage control' and with the Industrial Relations Bill eliminated the possibility of talking with the TUC about wage restraint. It had no formal wages policy, but events compelled it to take a line in dealing with two major claims – the docks and the local authorities – within two months of coming into office. It sought to give a lead in 'standing firm' against inflationary wage claims.

As after the election in 1964, there was a wages claim in the docks which had not been settled by negotiation and a dock strike was due on 14 July. Carr and the Department of Employment conciliated. While concerned to settle the dispute, Carr, like his predecessors since the late fifties, did not wish to be associated with a settlement which could be criticised as inflationary. Feather joined the trade union side in the talks. It is not unlikely, though it may seem surprising, that, in spite of the change of government, Feather simply assumed that he would continue in the role of 'public conciliator and intermediary' which he had played since the defeat of Wilson and Castle over *In Place of Strife*. His presence could, however, be interpreted as evidence of general trade union solidarity with any union pressing a 'just' claim and, although the government had not taken any public stand on wages, as a warning that the unions were on the alert to detect any attempt by the Conservatives to repeat the wage restraint policies of Selwyn Lloyd. Carr reacted by inviting Campbell Adamson of the CBI to be present at the conciliation.

Apart from this, the exercise proceeded much as in the past. Jack Jones put an improved offer to a Delegate Conference and this was rejected. Faced by a national dock strike, Carr announced the appointment of a Court of Inquiry under Lord Pearson. The government declared a State of Emergency. The Court recommended further improvements on the offer and its recommendations were accepted 'as an interim measure' by a Delegate Conference. The strike ended on 3 August. The outcome was reasonable. The Court considered that the settlement would add 7 per cent to wage costs – a relatively moderate increase given the state of the current wage round. The course and handling of the dispute had, however, more general implications. The involvement of the CBI and the declaration of the emergency – the first since 1966 and made within weeks of Heath's coming into office – suggested that the government was determined to avoid any accusation of persuading employers to concede unreasonable wage increases and was ready to face the damaging consequences of a dock strike. The involvement of the CBI gave the impression that the government was prepared for the possibility of the dispute being extended into a wider conflict with the trade union movement.

At the same time, the use of the Court of Inquiry could well be regarded as a sign of weakness by some Conservatives who held the view, dating back to the fifties, that conciliation, arbitration, Courts of Inquiry and all the traditional devices for settling disputes were inflationary. Heath had reason to be sensitive to possible accusations of 'buying' industrial peace, since during his short spell as Minister of Labour he had been responsible for conciliation under threat of a railway strike, which led to a settlement which was higher than the figure originally regarded as acceptable by the government and was criticised as inflationary. The fact that settlements in which governments were involved were normally higher than the figure hoped for until faced by an imminent strike was not a universally accepted defence.

These attitudes and past events might partly explain the government's reactions in the second wage dispute, involving local authority workers who threatened strike action in September. Negotiations had started before the general election and the local authorities had committed themselves to an offer of around 13 per cent. The government could do nothing to reduce this, but, in the hope of preventing a higher settlement, made it clear to the local authorities that they should stand firm against 'unreasonable demands'. On 4 September the unions rejected a formal offer of 13½ per cent. Strikes in the public services were threatened and the local authorities asked the Department of Employment for help in settling the dispute. They were informed that 'it would not be right for the conciliation service of the Department to be used to seek a settlement at a higher level'.

There was no conciliation and strikes started in London at the end of September, extending to other towns. A number of local authorities made separate settlements with the unions. The local authority associations and the unions agreed to refer the dispute to a Committee of Inquiry and asked the government to appoint one. The government refused and the parties finally appointed their own committee with Jack Scamp as chairman and Hugh Clegg and Norman Sloan as trade union and employer nominees. The Committee recommended an increase slightly higher than the employers' last formal offer – but the same as a figure which had already been offered informally. For some reason, the Committee, or at any rate Clegg, perhaps still thinking of a contribution to an incomes policy which no longer existed, thought it necessary to justify its sensible recommendations. It argued that the claim had been made at the end of a wage round in which every major wage increase had been high and inflationary and that inflation could not be stopped by giving local authority employees a relatively smaller wage increase: that would be unfair and of no significant benefit to the country. Heath described the argument of the Committee as 'blatantly nonsensical', and later in the year Clegg's appointment as Chairman of the Civil Service Arbitration Tribunal was not renewed.

By the autumn the lead from the government on wages was becoming clearer. There was to be no statutory incomes policy, the Prices and Incomes Board was to be abolished and the traditional devices to assist the process of collective bargaining – conciliation by the Department of Employment, inquiries and arbitration – were out of favour. Two arbitrators well known and active under the Labour government had been publicly rebuked by the Prime Minister. There were proposals for a whole new apparatus in the Industrial Relations Bill. It looked as though the government intended to dismantle the established machinery, old and new, for dealing with industrial disputes and wages. It had reached the point of committing itself to Selwyn Lloyd's position in 1961 without promising a longer-term policy. It would give a lead by refusing 'inflationary' wage increases in the public sector and would expect other employers to follow. Priority would be given to fighting wage inflation, even if this meant industrial trouble. There would be no sheltering behind conciliation and other procedures. The system of collective bargaining and the unions were to be subjected to a form of 'shock treatment'. 'The difficulty of reconciling the concepts of full employment and free collective bargaining' was to be met by standing firm and this, never easy for a government in major industrial trouble, with ministers pressing different interests and holding different views, was to be helped by discarding the devices for retreat.

The government's stand would be extremely difficult to maintain if industrial action was threatened in sectors where it would do serious damage to the economy or cause serious inconvenience to the public. For the time being, however, in spite of the impression of firmness and resolution, there was scope for flexibility: there was no 'guiding light' or 'norm'. The concept of a 'non-inflationary wage increase' was sufficiently vague to provide room for a settlement when it was thought impossible to face industrial trouble.

Wage Claims: De-escalation and Confrontation

The policy saw the government through the wage round in the public sector between October 1970 and June 1971, with some industrial troubles and with qualified success in reducing the level of settlements. The first major claim in the public sector was in coalmining. Robens persuaded the government to allow him to go to a level higher than it originally wished and negotiated a settlement with the NUM Executive at around 12 per cent. There were, however, unofficial strikes in Scotland and Yorkshire while the offer was put to the vote and until it was finally accepted in November.

Meanwhile negotiations had started in the electricity supply industry, on a claim for a 25 per cent increase. The Electricity Council was under instructions to offer just under 10 per cent and was unable to settle the claim in negotiations at this level. A work to rule and overtime ban was imposed on 7 December. There were severe power cuts and a State of Emergency was declared. A power strike had seemed imminent at times in the past but the immediate consequences were recognised by governments and unions as so serious that it had always been avoided. In the light of the realities – the crucial nature of the industry, the bargaining power of the unions, the need for both government and unions to reach a settlement – and past experience, the course of events was predictable: no strike and a Court of Inquiry leading to a settlement higher than the government would have wished.

The appointment of a second Court of Inquiry – and a reversal of the stance taken in the local authority dispute – was not particularly palatable and before the appointment there was talk of alternatives. The possibility of emergency legislation incorporating the 'cooling-off' and ballot provisions from the Industrial Relations Bill was mentioned – Wilson had, after all, taken the 'penal clauses' from *In Place of Strife* for quick legislation. The precedent was not followed. There was, in fact, no alternative to a Court of Inquiry and, following the public criticism of Scamp and his colleagues, no alternative to a Lord of Appeal as chairman – independent and immune (supposedly) from criticism, at least by government. The best the government could do to meet those critical of the procedure was to require the Court to have regard to 'the national interest' as in the seamen's dispute of 1966. On this occasion, however, the Court was to be given an explanation of 'the national interest'. If the consequences of a strike had not been so serious and the leading negotiator not Frank Chapple, the unions might have rejected the proposition as an attempt to prevent their claim being considered on its 'merits'. The responsibility for expounding 'the national interest' before the Court was delegated to officials. Chapple was given the opportunity of making effective debating points against the government.

The dispute was settled, but the wage increase was substantially higher than the level to which the government had limited the Electricity Council and difficult to justify as in line with the government's anti-inflationary policy. The union claimed it was 15 per cent, the government presented it as 10.9 per cent. While the settlement in the docks may have been moderate, those in coalmining and electricity represented little improvement on the level of the wage-round for 1969–70. It proved possible, however, to settle other public sector claims under negotiation at around the level the government claimed for the electricity settlement.

Government action during the electricity dispute heightened the atmosphere of conflict between unions and government. A State of Emergency had been proclaimed for the second time within four months, and at a very early stage in the dispute. This was necessary to enable the Electricity Council to make planned power cuts, but it also served to alert the public to the threat of union power (and might have influenced opinion against the unions). It could be interpreted as showing the determination of the government to resist inflationary wage claims, but government determination was not enough. It was essential to ensure public support and readiness to accept the consequences of 'standing firm'. An injection of melodrama might encourage this. Heath aimed to highlight the national significance of the issue – the dispute should be 'escalated to a new dimension' and public opinion given time to 'peak'. In any case, a State of Emergency which emphasised the serious consequences of a strike would also help to prepare the public in general and government supporters in particular to accept a settlement which might turn out to be a set-back to the government's policy of resistance to inflationary wage claims.

By the spring of 1971 the dock strike, the local authority strikes and the refusal of an inquiry, the attack on Scamp, two 'emergencies' and the opening of the TUC campaign against the Industrial Relations Bill had established the image of 'confrontation'. In public comment from this time on the substance and purpose of the policies on wages and industrial relations were increasingly ignored, the consequences attacked and the responsibility for them attributed to the government rather than the unions. At the same time, criticisms of the size of the wage increase in the electricity supply industry led the government to stiffen its policy. This now became one of de-escalation which, interpreted in its extreme form, meant that each major settlement in the public sector should be lower than the preceding settlement or, at the very least, should not exceed it. With this the element of flexibility disappeared.

Within two months there was a strike of Post Office workers in support of a claim, originally for increases between 15 and 20 per cent but later modified to 13 per cent. The government limited the Post Office to an offer of 8 per cent and when this was rejected was not prepared to arrange any improvement on the figure through conciliation, nor to appoint a Court of Inquiry. The strike, which lasted from 20 January to 8 March, inconvenienced business and the public, but as the Post Office Engineering Union was not involved, tele-communications continued and the government considered the inconvenience supportable. Efforts by Feather to persuade the government to make concessions were not successful and the Union of Post Office Workers (UPW) was given only token support by other unions, in the form of loans when their funds were running low. The government finally appointed a Committee. The union, knowing that there was little prospect of any substantial increase on the offer, called off the strike and the dispute was settled on the basis of increases around 9 per cent.

This was the last major wage claim in the public sector in the 1970–71 wage round which caused trouble. The government's efforts to reduce the rate of wage inflation had not been markedly successful. The increase in wage rates between July 1970 and July 1971 was about 13 per cent, compared with about 10½ per cent between July 1969 and July 1970. The government, encouraged by its success with the Post Office Union decided that its efforts to reduce the rate of increase must be continued. It would hold to its policy of 'standing firm' and fixed a target of 8 per cent for the public sector wage round 1971–72.

The position was, however, becoming more difficult. The consequences of the longer-term policy of limiting the bargaining power of the trade unions through the Industrial Relations Act (for what this was worth) could not be foreseen as a result of trade union refusal to accept the legislation. The government's policy on wages was a challenge to all unions and any union attempting to break it would have the support of the TUC, if only in public argument. It was true that the benefits of the 'solidarity' of other unions with the UPW had not been substantial, but there was the possibility that more effective support might be given in future strikes, particularly through unofficial action by militants who would not be disowned.

Leaving aside this possibility, it was clear that the policy was bound to cause further industrial trouble – and the public preferred industrial peace. They had been seriously inconvenienced by the disputes in electricity and the Post Office. Past experience had shown that even if they supported a firm stand at the opening of a dispute, trouble affecting their convenience or comfort or threatening their jobs meant a shift of opinion in favour of a settlement. Inflation was a less obvious and immediate threat. Unions had the advantage in public argument. Practically all claims taken on their own could be presented as having justifications – low pay, reward for skill, reward for special features of the job, differentials, relativities, cost of living. In the specialised business of bargaining, usually taking place with complicated and debatable 'facts', unions in the public sector were more persuasive advocates than managements or government. They were able to use a range of arguments and to appeal to 'fairness', comparing their treatment by the government with the more reasonable attitude taken by employers in the private sector. Changes in taxation which gave concessions to the higher income groups strengthened the union case in wage claims where it could be argued that those involved were 'low paid'.

The case for the government rested on the threat of inflation – an argument which lost appeal with repetition. The government was at a disadvantage also because of the character of the 'negotiations' between management and unions: Chairmen and Boards of nationalised industries applying a government policy not in the immediate interests of their industry could not be expected to be convincing spokesmen. If the success of government policy depended on keeping public opinion behind it, the odds were not favourable. The government, moreover, had left itself exposed in the argument with the unions: it had abolished the Prices and Incomes Board, condemned arbitrators who challenged its policies, refused conciliation and made clear its doubts about Courts of Inquiry. Business and industrial interests had growing reservations about the policies on both wages and industrial relations, having been affected by the troubles over both wages and the Industrial Relations Bill. Though the CBI had supported the industrial relations legislation, many employers were doubtful about its effects and, in view of continuing union opposition after the Act, were unwilling to take action under the law which might damage relations with unions and their work people.

Finally, as the government had dropped any element of flexibility, a settlement above 8 per cent would now be a clear defeat for its policy. The policy, which had started as a response to immediate problems in 1970, had become formalised. The government had re-adopted a 'guiding light' and pushed it to extremes.

In the autumn of 1971 the situation in the public sector required early decisions on how the government should proceed. Four claims were under negotiation – in coal, electricity, gas and water. In the last two, the unions had in the past been moderate in their bargaining methods and had usually postponed settling until after electricity – though in the new situation past practice was not a certain guide. There had been no national official strike in coal-mining since the war – national negotiations were relatively unimportant until the late sixties – but there had been serious unofficial strikes against the last settlement in 1970. Electricity supply was, as in the past, regarded as the most serious threat. The Boards of all industries had been told to limit their offers to 8 per cent.

Negotiations on the claim in the coal industry came to the point of breakdown first. The NUM imposed an overtime ban on 1 November to strengthen its bargaining position in support of its claim

wage

for increases of £5–£9. The union rejected a Coal Board offer of £1.75–£1.80 and held a strike ballot. Derek Ezra, believing after talks with Joe Gormley that a minor improvement on the offer would be accepted, went marginally beyond the authority given by the government. The improved offer was rejected by the NUM Executive. The strike ballot was favourable and a strike was called for 9 January. The government had to decide whether or not to authorise the Coal Board to try for a settlement before the strike took place. The cost of a settlement would certainly be above the government's target for the wage round; the failure of Ezra's improved offer suggested that it might be well above. It would certainly influence the increase in electricity supply, where a strike could not be faced, and this in turn would influence the settlements in water and gas. The policy would be broken at once.

The government decided to face a coal strike and try to settle the other claims within the limits of the policy, in the hope that these would influence the final settlement in coalmining. The other claims were settled at a reasonable level (8–9 per cent) but the negotiations took longer than hoped. The picketing (particularly the organisation of 'flying pickets') developed by the NUM during the strike was strongly supported by members of other unions and was far more effective and more violent than the government (and probably the union) expected. Coal and other essential supplies to power stations were stopped. The situation was made worse because on this occasion the government delayed proclaiming a State of Emergency. It had been criticised for doing this too quickly in earlier disputes and also feared that it might stiffen union attitudes on the other claims it wished to settle. As a result, the introduction of power cuts to conserve stocks at power stations was delayed. When cuts were necessary, they were introduced with little warning and were extremely severe and damaging to industry.

The government had originally intended to 'conciliate' in the miners' strike immediately the electricity claim had been settled, but now decided that this would mean too open a retreat. A Court of Inquiry, again under Lord Wilberforce, was appointed and, though the Court reported with unusual speed, this necessarily prolonged the period of the strike. By the time of the Report, severe power cuts had been in force for more than a week, industry was on a two-day week and a complete shut-down was threatened unless the picketing was lifted and blacking ended within two or three days. The Court of Inquiry recommended that the miners should be treated as a special case with wage increases of over 20 per cent – far above the government's limits, even though it was recommended that the settlement should run for 16 months. The union was by now in the strongest conceivable bargaining position and did not accept the Wilberforce Report. The government was not able to avoid 'conciliating' – and in the most unfavourable circumstances. There were negotiations on the basis of the Report at the Department of Employment and Downing Street, and further concessions were made.

The de-escalation policy was broken. The public had been seriously inconvenienced yet again and disturbed by the violence of the picketing. Industry had been damaged. The government had not, apparently, foreseen the dangers and the power cuts had been mismanaged. There was public sympathy with the miners, but the appointment of a Court of Inquiry and subsequent conciliation – refused to the local authority and Post Office workers – was an obvious concession to power. No public sector union with industrial power was likely to accept the argument that the miners were a special case without exercising its own power.

The overtime ban and coal strike had coincided with the first clashes between the two biggest unions – the TGWU and the AEU – and the National Industrial Relations Court. As the clashes developed it became clear that the public did not absolve the government from blame even though it could be argued that the clashes were caused by the non-co-operation of the unions. With these troubles following those caused by the government's wages policy, the view spread that 'confrontation' should stop and that it was the government's responsibility to arrange this. By this time, however, Heath was already in search of a new policy.

9 'Backing and Filling', March–August 1972

A Change of Policy

The first public indication that Edward Heath accepted the failure of the wages policy of 'giving a lead' in the public sector was his statement, on the day the miners' strike ended: 'We have to find a more sensible way of settling our differences'.[1] The search by the government for a 'more sensible way' – the beginning of a new policy towards the unions and wages and a change in the 'new style' of government – was part of a wider change of economic policy. For a number of reasons Heath had already embarked on a policy of 'reflation'.

First, unemployment had increased every month since the government had taken office in June 1970. In January 1972 it was over 928,000. Without a change of policy there would have been a threat of over one million unemployed in the winter of 1973 – a symbolic figure which had worried the Macmillan Government in 1960 and evidence that the Conservatives were the party of unemployment. Secondly, a likely date for an election was autumn 1974 and reflation should not be left too late, as some judged it had been in 1962–63. Thirdly, the House of Commons had voted in February in favour of the terms of the agreement to enter Europe and the economy must expand if the country was to benefit fully from entry.

There was change in monetary policy and a reflationary Budget in March 1972. The pound was floated in June 1972 so that maintenance of a fixed rate would not inhibit the pursuit of economic growth. The 'no help for lame ducks' policy proclaimed by John Davies at the Party Conference in 1970 was finally dropped. It had been diluted in 1971 by the decision to nationalise Rolls Royce – though there were special defence, prestige and international considerations in the case – and was openly jettisoned in February 1972 when support was given to Upper Clyde Shipbuilders under pressure from the workers and unions and fear that the loss of jobs could lead

[1] Edward Heath, Television broadcast, 27 February 1972.

to serious unrest and disorder in an area which might be infected by the troubles in Northern Ireland. An Industry Bill, replacing the Industrial Expansion Act, 1968 passed by the Labour Government, was introduced and became law in August, providing a basis for assisting firms in financial difficulty in the private sector. As in July 1962, when Macmillan retreated from incomes policy and embarked on reflation, there were ministerial changes. Peter Walker became Secretary of State for Trade and Industry in place of John Davies and Maurice Macmillan Secretary of State for Employment in place of Robert Carr.

The changes in policy and ministers could not change the reality that Heath faced the dilemma which had faced his predecessors. If the policies of reflation were to succeed in terms of employment and increased exports and too rapid a decline in the value of the pound was to be avoided, the rate of wage increase had to be restrained. At the same time the risk of further industrial damage on the scale caused by the miners must be avoided.

The decision to enter Europe was a major political success which made it easier for Heath to change his policy towards the unions. It could, however, hardly disguise the fact that the change was made following the defeat of the government by the miners and under pressure from employers and other groups whose interests were damaged by confrontation and the weight of public opinion. While the changes of policy and personalities may have been reminiscent of 1962, Heath's position was far more difficult. Unlike Harold Macmillan, he could not, following the miners, present his policy on wages as successful in having taught a permanent lesson and 'slide' away from it: he had either to continue to resist inflationary wage claims in the public sector or find an alternative policy. The Industrial Relations Act could not be wished away and the opposition of the unions to the government, which centred on the Act, was more intense politically and industrially than any previous union opposition to government policies since the war. The stakes were higher – the rate of inflation was more than double the rate of the early sixties, unemployment was higher and industrial trouble much worse.

Until the miners had gone to Downing Street, Edward Heath had not been publicly involved in industrial disputes. He had left them to Robert Carr. He had, indeed, been critical of Harold Wilson's interventions, conciliating at late night meetings with beer and sandwiches. He had given Carr and Geoffrey Howe a surprisingly free hand over the Industrial Relations Bill – he no doubt felt that the principles had, after all, been decided in 1967 – and in 1970 his main preoccupation was with Europe. He was now about to engage in an exercise which in terms of effort and time made Wilson's interventions seem relatively modest – and to claim credit for the degree of his personal involvement and the time he gave to the exercise.

Government and Union Objectives

Following his television broadcast, and partly as a result of the persuasions of the CBI, Heath invited General Council members to meet him and had separate meetings with them and with the CBI in March and April. There was no evidence at this stage that he had decided views about what might be 'a more sensible way of settling our differences'. The meetings served the immediate purpose of making it clear publicly that he wished to avoid 'confrontation' and that, if it continued, the responsibility did not rest solely with the government. His views on future policy would be formed by his assessment of trade union attitudes. The early meetings were exploratory.

In contrast, the General Council members had at least one clear objective – the repeal of the Industrial Relations Act. As a result of their policy of non-co-operation and de-registration they had put themselves in the position of having to expel unions from the Trades Union Congress and the two biggest unions, the TGWU and the AUEW,[2] were already facing heavy fines imposed by the National Industrial Relations Court. The TGWU and the NUR were weakening on the policy of non-co-operation and after a total boycott of the NIRC had decided to be legally represented before it. Jack Cooper of the NUGMW[3] had hinted at a change of policy and officials of other unions who had conformed were not wholly in favour of non-co-operation. A collapse of the 'boycott' could not be ruled out, though it was unlikely to come quickly. Any weakening on it would be bitterly opposed by Hugh Scanlon amongst the national figures and by many militants, and would cause serious dissension within the trade union movement. Repeal of the Act would remove these problems and repeat the success of 1969.

Apart from this wavering on the total boycott of the Industrial Relations Act, the General Council knew that it was in a strong

[2] The Amalgamated Union of Engineering Workers. Formerly the AEU.

[3] National Union of General and Municipal Workers. Also referred to as the General and Municipal Workers Union (GMWU).

bargaining position. The NUM had broken the government policy on wages; other unions with power could also do so. Even if they did not welcome industrial trouble on the scale necessary for this, most of the odium for any trouble attached to the government. The General Council knew the government wanted an alternative and that the CBI was anxious to find a way of avoiding confrontation. The talks with Heath would enable it to assess the chance of obtaining concessions and the price it might be asked to pay. In any case, it was important to prevent Heath transferring responsibility for 'confrontation' from government to unions. This alone was a decisive argument for continuing discussions, in spite of pressure from militants to break them off.

The preliminary phase of discussions between the government and TUC, begun in March, continued until July. Heath, Anthony Barber and other ministers talked of the problems of inflation and the need for wage restraint; the General Council talked of the damage done to industrial relations by the Industrial Relations Act and the difficulty of discussing other problems while the Act continued. The CBI made moves which showed its anxiety for progress towards an understanding which would avoid confrontation and provide some degree of wage restraint. In June it opened talks with the TUC which led to the setting up of a joint independent conciliation service. The project was regarded with disfavour and irritation by Heath, since it appeared to give priority to avoiding industrial trouble and to ignore the need for wage restraint. The battle for the latter had been led by the government in the public sector at considerable political cost. Independent conciliation in the form proposed amounted almost to a repudiation of government policy and authority. There was, of course, no reason why the General Council should reject the CBI proposition – though it could not have thought it important except as public indication of CBI dissatisfaction with the government. The union battle was with the government, not the CBI. The joint independent conciliation service turned out to be misconceived and proved abortive.

A more important CBI initiative was the agreement of its members to a period of voluntary price restraint. This was not expected to secure a direct response from the unions on wages but it was hoped that it would improve the atmosphere of the discussions.[4]

Given the opening objectives of the government and TUC – wage restraint without industrial trouble on the one hand and repeal of

[4] cf. Harold Macmillan's price restraint initiatives in 1955–56.

the Industrial Relations Act on the other – it is not surprising that the talks made no substantial progress between March and July. Heath aimed to persuade the TUC to join in tripartite talks with the CBI, but it was not until July, and then only with difficulty, that he got this far, when the General Council finally agreed to talks 'under the aegis of NEDC'.

The Industrial Relations Act in Operation

Heath's efforts from March to July 1972 were impeded, and his search for a new policy blocked, by the working of the Industrial Relations Act in disputes on the railways and in the docks. The government had some influence on the course of events in the railway dispute but it could not influence events in the docks, which were largely the consequence of decisions by the NIRC and superior courts. The course of both disputes not only delayed Heath's initiative but seriously weakened his bargaining position in discussions with the General Council. (There was justification for Harold Macmillan's comment that the government seemed to have spent its time constructing bunkers and now had to get out of them.)

The railway unions had made a claim for wage increases of 16 per cent. In view of the traditional 'rivalry' in collective bargaining between the long-established great unions, they could hardly be expected to accept the view of the Wilberforce Report that the miners were a special case and settle for an increase in line with government policy before its defeat by the miners. Somewhere between the 8 per cent of the 'de-escalation' period and their claim, and closer to the latter, was the most likely outcome. For the government, however, a settlement in double figures, coming after the miners, would confirm that its wages policy was destroyed and that the 'special case' argument could not preserve it. On the other hand, the possibility of a railway strike so soon after the confusion and damage caused by the miners' strike was unacceptable, and in any case, as always, 'facing up to a strike' would not guarantee a final settlement in line with government policy. The government was undecided whether to try to preserve what it could of the de-escalation policy at the risk of a strike or to avoid a strike by settling the claim at the cost of openly abandoning the policy. Heath wanted the issue out of the way so that the talks with the TUC could proceed, but his authority had been damaged by the miners' strike and settlement and there was, as yet, no alternative policy to de-escalation.

The situation presented difficulties which led to prolonged debate and indecision, repeated discussions of all possibilities and the handling of the negotiations between ministers and British Rail and great government concern about the public presentation of the case. British Rail was authorised to offer increases up to 9 per cent, but this was not accepted and the unions threatened a work-to-rule and ban on overtime. The government could not contemplate another Court of Inquiry after Wilberforce and the miners; the unions were not prepared to accept arbitration; the government was not prepared to authorise British Rail to increase its offer. Maurice Macmillan persuaded the railway unions to meet with British Rail under an independent chairman who would try to secure an agreement and, failing agreement, would make a recommendation. The device gave cover for an advance on the offer. The dispute so far had followed the traditional course. The independent chairman, Alex Jarratt, was unable to secure an agreement and recommended increases of 11 per cent. His recommendation was rejected and the work-to-rule and overtime ban started.

The choice facing the government was now exceedingly dis-agreeable – further inconvenience for the public and industry or a settlement and a further defeat on wages. There was, however, a new factor. As the government was not willing to make any further move to settle the dispute, it played for time by applying to the NIRC, under the provisions governing national emergencies in the Industrial Relations Act, for a 'cooling-off period' of 21 days. The union did not appear before the Court, which imposed a 'cooling-off period' of 14 days and ordered the union to instruct its members to resume normal working. The application was a gamble. There was no reason to assume, in view of the trade union policy of non-co-operation, that the unions would comply with the court order to instruct their members to return to normal working or that their members would obey the instruction. The unions did, however, comply, normal working was resumed and ministers enjoyed a brief spell of euphoria over the success of the Act. The application for a cooling-off period could, however, be criticised as disingenuous. The purpose of 'cooling-off' was to allow moves to be made to secure a settlement, but the government was not yet ready to agree to any advance on the increases recommended by Jarratt. The provision in the Act, conceived to operate in a situation where industrial relations were unaffected by government policies on wages, was being used as a device for supporting what remained of the government wages policy. The time gained did not remove the dilemma.

At the end of fourteen days, the work-to-rule and overtime ban were re-imposed and the government used the second of the emergency provisions, applying to the NIRC for a compulsory ballot. On this occasion the unions were represented before the Court and opposed the application. The NIRC ordered a ballot and the union appealed to the Court of Appeal. The appeal was rejected. The work-to-rule and overtime ban were again suspended and in the ballot over 80 per cent voted in favour of further industrial action. When the unions decided for a third time to impose a work-to-rule and over-time ban the government decided its priorities: the dispute must be settled. British Rail was authorised to go above the Jarratt recommendation and the dispute was settled on its offer of increases of 13 per cent, together with a lump-sum payment. The increases were lower than those for the miners, but were, of course, to run for twelve months only and not sixteen. The use of the emergency provisions of the Industrial Relations Act had failed to support government wages policy and their use for this purpose had discredited the Act. The de-escalation policy had collapsed and was given a final blow by wage increases of around 15 per cent in the building industry in September, following a series of strikes, overtime bans and violent picketing over a period of three months. During 1972 wage rates rose by about 14 per cent.

Heath had removed one obstacle to progress in his talks with the General Council by instructing British Rail to settle with the unions. He could, however, do nothing other than be frustrated about the difficulties in the docks, where the Courts were now deeply engaged. There was unrest amongst dockers because of the loss of work due to the extension of 'containerisation', with packing and unpacking of containers being done at terminals outside the dock area. In Liverpool an unofficial committee of shop stewards picketed terminals, preventing the movement of lorries – 'an unfair industrial practice'. One firm, Heaton's, took the case to the NIRC. The Court instructed the Transport and General Workers Union to stop the picketing of Heaton's terminal, to no avail. The Court then fined the union, unrepresented before the Court in line with the policy of boycott, £5000, which was increased to £50,000 when union attempts to stop the picketing were unsuccessful. Following this, the union was represented before the Court and argued that it had no power to stop the action by shop stewards, which was unofficial and contrary to union policy. The Court reaffirmed the view that the union was responsible and could escape its responsibility only by withdrawing the credentials of the shop stewards or expelling them from the union. The union appealed. The Court of Appeal, under Lord Denning, ruled on 2 June that the union was not liable for the actions of its shop stewards against Heaton's, allowed the appeal against the decision of the NIRC and set aside the fines. Heaton's appealed to the House of Lords.

The decision of the Court of Appeal had immediate consequences for two similar cases of picketing of container depots in East London – at Chobham Farm and the Midland Cold Storage Depot. In the first case, the NIRC, following the ruling of the Court of Appeal, made an order on 12 June to stop picketing by three named individuals. The picketing continued and the NIRC issued an order to desist. The picketing went on and on 21 July, five of the dockers were committed for contempt and put in Pentonville Prison. The Industrial Relations Act had its martyrs. The Conservative government had not avoided the situation which had worried the Labour government at the time of *In Place of Strife*. Picketing continued in London, Liverpool and Hull, accompanied by unofficial dock strikes and limited 'token' strikes in other industries, including the newspaper industry. On 26 July the TUC suspended further participation in the tripartite talks, which had only just started, and called a one-day national strike for 31 July. Also on 26 July, the House of Lords gave its decision in the Heaton's case, upholding the decision of the NIRC against the Court of Appeal. The five dockers were released and the TUC dropped its strike call.

The postscript to these excitements was a national dock strike (threatened since early June) in support of a number of claims over 'containerisation' and terms of redundancy. The government again proclaimed a State of Emergency – but at least Heath could now influence events. The strike was settled by negotiations between Lord Aldington (Chairman of the Port of London Authority and a political colleague) and Jack Jones, with the government paying out money far in excess of its original estimates for a redundancy scheme which in the event proved so attractive that some ports had to recruit dockers within a few months.

By the end of July the position was clear. The government had lost to the unions over wages and the Industrial Relations Act. The policy on wages could not continue. The result of the government 'giving a lead' and standing firm in the public sector had been confrontation and a return to the level of wage increases of 1970. The prospects for the future looked worse. The railway and dock disputes had discredited the Industrial Relations Act. Connoisseurs of the judicial apparatus, procedure and the personalities involved might have appreciated the course of events, particularly the appearances of the Official Solicitor to plead for the dockers, who refused to recognise the Courts but, as martyrs, happily co-operated with the tipstaff who arrested them. To many, however, it seemed that the authors of the Act had produced an ambiguous and unsatisfactory law. Most important, there was now no chance that unions would back down on the policy of non-co-operation. Public opinion, business and many Conservatives decided that confrontation must end. Though much of the trouble had been due to trade union refusal to co-operate with the law and to accept the need for wage restraint and some to the activities of the lawyers and the courts, the responsibility for the confrontation and avoiding it in future was now firmly placed on the government. Many now argued for a return to an 'incomes policy'. The possibility of a prices policy had been foreshadowed by the CBI voluntary price restraint.

Preparing for a Return to Incomes Policy

It was in this atmosphere that the government began the first phase of the tripartite talks with the TUC and CBI, which continued until September 1972. Heath had no choice of objectives. For political reasons he had to seek some basis for co-operation between government and unions; for economic reasons he had to secure some degree of wage restraint. First priority had to be given to securing co-operation or acceptance, for it could be argued that an understanding on wages at almost any level would be less inflationary than the increases necessary to avoid industrial trouble in a situation of 'confrontation'. Heath had regarded a statutory incomes policy, attacked by the Conservatives since 1966, as 'a nonsense' – and in any case there was the risk that a statutory policy would itself lead to confrontation. He now decided, in spite of the discouraging precedents,[5] to negotiate for an agreed prices and incomes policy as 'a more sensible way of settling our differences'.

Following this decision the 'return' to incomes policy was more thorough and intensive than any effort made by previous governments. On the government side, Heath chaired the talks, accompanied by William Armstrong and by ministers concerned, including

[5] Under the Conservatives, 1955–56 and under Labour, 1964–66.

Anthony Barber, Peter Walker and Maurice Macmillan. At official level the operation was controlled by Armstrong who, as Permanent Secretary of the Civil Service Department, was able to draw on the resources of other departments – the Treasury, the Department of Trade and Industry, the Department of Employment, the Ministry of Agriculture and Fisheries, the Department of Health and Social Security. Every issue that arose was analysed, the economic consequences of all propositions evaluated and Heath briefed in the greatest detail. The exercise was to develop into an effort to formulate a policy which could take account of the complexities of the wages 'structure' throughout the country, the varying objectives of different unions and the power pressures behind collective bargaining. It was an extraordinary contrast to the simple policy of resistance to 'inflationary wage claims'. The exercise became increasingly sophisticated, particularly in the second phase from May 1973. The combination of this official activity and Heath's resolution was formidable and politically disastrous. It finally produced a policy of such ingenuity combined with a basic inflexibility that it is difficult to believe that any earlier government would have accepted it. But this is looking ahead.

In this first phase of 'pre-bargaining' sessions Heath analysed the situation, explaining his change of policy, his commitment to economic growth and reduction of unemployment and the need in these circumstances to contain inflation. Supported by Barber, he argued that wage claims should take account of the tax reductions in the April reflationary budget. The trade unions argued the need to meet the problem of the low paid, to restore differentials, maintain relativities and reward productivity. They pressed for statutory price control, criticising the CBI voluntary price restraint as inadequate, and argued for extension of control to the public sector, particularly to rents. They made it clear that the Industrial Relations Act could present an insurmountable obstacle to progress.

The tripartite meetings, chaired by Heath, were supplemented by meetings of William Armstrong, Douglas Allen and Frank Figgures (all, for most of their careers, Treasury officials) with Victor Feather and Campbell Adamson. The representatives of the General Council at the tripartite meetings were the six members on the National Economic Development Council. The leading figures were Jones and Scanlon, as in the 1969 talks with Wilson and Castle. Jones led in widening the scope of the negotiations to cover issues beyond wages and prices, while Scanlon was more concerned with detailed

problems on wages and the Industrial Relations Act and was more
determined – or determined to give the impression of being more
determined – than any of his colleagues to bargain for the last
possible concession. At the meetings in July and August the main
issues were discussed without either government or TUC representatives expressing a view which could be interpreted as a commitment.
The TUC representatives were waiting for the Trades Union Congress
due on 4 September; the Conservative Party Conference was due on
11 October.

10 Conciliation, a Statutory Incomes Policy and Confrontation, September 1972– February 1974

A New Style of Government, Revised Version

At the Trades Union Congress in September, resolutions were adopted declaring that an incomes policy could not be considered unless it was an integral part of an economic policy including control of rents, profits, dividends and prices and designed to secure a re-distribution of income and wealth, and pressing for repeal of the Industrial Relations Act. These issues had already been covered in the discussions with Edward Heath and, to this extent, presented no obstacle to continuing the negotiations. Heath made this clear publicly in his speech to the Conservative Party Conference, which registered an unqualified change of the attitude which had seemed implicit in his 'new style of government' of 1970: 'the trade unions and the employers [must] share fully with the government the benefits and obligations of running the economy'. The essence of the new style, that 'once a decision is made or a policy is decided the Prime Minister and his colleagues should have the courage to stick to it', was, after months of hesitation and indecision, renewed: his policy now was to reach agreement with the unions and he seemed to believe that a sufficient effort of will and resolution would bring success.

In the first phase of the tripartite talks, Heath by August had appeared hopeful that an agreement might be reached with the General Council, and following the Trades Union Congress in September he seemed convinced that agreement was likely. Congress had not rejected the idea of continuing talks with the government, nor had it laid down firm pre-conditions. The resolution on incomes policy could be regarded as a bargaining position. It could be assumed that since the unions were prepared to bargain they were prepared to reach an agreement. This was the optimistic view. Alternatively – and more pessimistically – the resolution could be interpreted as implying no more than a decision not to break off the talks and reject the olive branch offered by Heath, since this might lose public sympathy and transfer responsibility for 'confrontation' to the unions.

So far as the unions were concerned, it was in any case in their interest to see what the government was prepared to offer. Under the conventions of collective bargaining an offer, even if not accepted, could not be withdrawn, and something would be gained. Progress might be made towards repeal of the Industrial Relations Act. Moreover, the new joint liaison committee of the TUC and Labour Party was already in operation and any concessions gained in talks with the government would strengthen the position of the unions on that – if, indeed, given the characteristics of the labour movement and the events of 1969 it could possibly be made any stronger. Jones (and his colleagues) were in a sense in negotiation with both the major political parties. *Problems*

Some features of the negotiations with the government were obvious. First, the concessions the General Council would try to squeeze out of the government would be extraordinarily high. Secondly, whatever concessions it gained, however far the government was prepared to go, it was highly improbable, despite Heath's optimism, that the General Council would face the anger of militants or would embarrass the Labour Party by agreeing with a Conservative government to limits on collective bargaining. It was hardly credible that Scanlon, for one, would accept any agreement so long as the Industrial Relations Act was in operation.

The new 'tripartite' style of government was conducted in circumstances of impressive inconvenience in the Cabinet room. On one side of the Cabinet table there was Heath, with Armstrong, flanked by several ministers and some Permanent Secretaries and backed by other Permanent Secretaries and officials. Facing Heath was Figgures – the 'aegis' of the NEDC – and on each side of him the TUC and CBI members of the NEDC with their advisers behind them. As the talks proceeded the numbers increased.

By late September time for Heath was running short. The public sector wage round was about to start. A settlement in the electricity supply industry was again due in November and the government needed an agreement before then to avoid the possibility of renewed industrial trouble. The second phase of the talks opened when Heath put forward his first proposals on 27 September. The government would aim for a growth rate of 5 per cent; the government and CBI would aim to limit price increases to 5 per cent; the norm for pay increases should be £2 a week, but there would be an additional 20p for every point rise in the Retail Price Index after a rise of six points; help would be given to pensioners. The proposal for a flat-rate increase would improve the relative position of the low-paid and, in addition, the government proposed a new body to help low-paid industries improve their efficiency as a basis for higher wages. It was calculated that the effect of the proposals on pay would be to result in an average increase of around 8 per cent on both rates and earnings. The government was aiming at the figure it had hoped to achieve before its defeat by the miners.

The union representatives made counter-proposals: pay increases should be £3.40 a week and the additions related to the Retail Price Index should start earlier and be higher. They also proposed suspension of rent increases under the Housing Finance Act, statutory price control, measures against property and land speculators, a value-added tax at 7½ per cent instead of the 10 per cent proposed, a wealth tax, a surcharge on capital gains, dividend limitation, higher family allowances and the repeal of the Industrial Relations Act.

If the succeeding meetings in October had, as Heath had expected, been moving towards an agreement, some of the counter-proposals might have been dropped or modified. There was, presumably, scope for bargaining on the pay figure, prices, dividends and capital gains and family allowances. The government was not, however, prepared to repeal the Industrial Relations Act nor to suspend the Housing Finance Act. On the first, Victor Feather produced the formula that it might be 'put on ice'. It was generally understood that both the government and the CBI were desperately anxious that no further actions should be taken against the unions under the Act. It could not, however, be made inoperative without legislation and this would be a politically unacceptable acknowledgement of error and failure on the part of the government. The suspension of the Housing Finance Act also presented political difficulties.

Neither government nor unions changed position in meetings throughout October. At the beginning of November Heath put forward his original proposals with minor changes and said that the Industrial Relations Act and the Housing Finance Act were matters for the government and Parliament and could not be negotiated. The talks ended without agreement. After emergency meetings of ministers, Heath announced on 6 November that the government would be taking powers to freeze prices and incomes for ninety days as the first stage of a statutory prices and incomes policy. A White Paper, *A Programme for Controlling Inflation: the First Stage* (Cmnd. 5125), and a draft Bill, *Counter-Inflation (Temporary Provisions) Bill*, were published on the same day.

The announcement marked the end of the second period of relations between Heath and the unions, which had started with Heath's defeat by the miners in 1972. An assessment of these negotiations with the TUC, Heath's objectives and the outcome might help to explain his decisions, which were politically critical, twelve months later.

Heath had started the talks in March 1972 to make it clear that the government was not 'seeking' confrontation and that if it continued responsibility would not rest solely with the government. He wanted also to discover what other policies, if any, there might be to contain wage inflation and to assess possibilities in the light of union attitudes. Events made this a slower process than he expected. Meanwhile, confrontation continued. By July the government's policy of 'standing firm' appeared to have failed completely and Heath was forced to decide on an alternative. He made the most ambitious choice, aiming at a voluntary prices and incomes policy agreed between the TUC and a Conservative government. Although his negotiating position by then was weaker than it had been in March, he appeared increasingly confident that he would succeed in this aim, despite the failure of earlier Conservative governments which had been in stronger bargaining positions and the move to the left and the more positive political commitment of the members of the General Council. The fact that Harold Macmillan had failed in more favourable circumstances did not rule out the possibility of success for his own attempt.

Heath's apparent confidence was encouraged by civil servants and the CBI. Within the civil service, Frank Figgures, Director-General of the National Economic Development Office, was ready to use his own powers of persuasion and conciliation. The NEDC was the symbol of tripartism. William Armstrong, prevented by the creation of the Department of Economic Affairs from sharing in the development of earlier policies, was now trying his hand. The scale of the exercise itself generated optimism in Whitehall: so much effort and rational argument must secure results. For the CBI, Campbell Adamson and others were optimistic. All those directly concerned in government, together with the CBI, wanted an agreement, some almost desperately. In their view, the need for agreement was so clear that its rejection by the unions was unthinkable. On the union side, Victor Feather, after his spell of organising opposition to the Industrial Relations Act, had resumed his role of 1969 as 'public conciliator' or 'go-between' for unions and government – and with the opportunity of scoring a success equal to that of 1969. He could offer to Heath the prospect of an ultimate agreement in spite of obstacles which only he could help Heath to surmount. Whatever the reasons for Heath's confidence, the fact that his judgement was proved wrong and his new approach ended in failure was to be of major importance in influencing the government's attitude to the unions in the weeks leading up to the election of February 1974.

The talks must not be judged a complete failure because in the end there was no agreement. The decision to try for an agreement and the length of the negotiations meant that Heath established a relationship with the leading national officers of the unions which had not previously existed. Union leaders – or some of them – claimed to have developed a respect for him and for his handling of the talks. The respect did not, however, extend to some of his colleagues nor to his government; nor was it widespread in the trade union movement.[1] It did not influence trade union reaction to his later policies sufficiently to prevent their failure. The negotiations, however, helped to modify, for a time at least, the public impression that Heath was seeking confrontation and was committed to anti-union policies and were useful, perhaps essential, preliminaries to the introduction of the statutory policy and its relative success for the first twelve months.

Incomes Policy: The Standstill

Heath's announcement of a statutory wage freeze on 6 November signalled a return to 1961 and a replay – with variations – of Selwyn Lloyd's pay pause followed by a permanent incomes policy. The promise of a statutory policy was a reversal of the position taken by Heath and the Conservative Party since 1966 and affirmed in 1970 (though the manifesto of 1970 had wisely referred only to 'Labour's

---

[1] Hugh Scanlon described Heath as 'the best of the crew', saying that he did not understand why he was 'thrown overboard' after 1974. (Television discussion with Shirley Williams, text printed in *The Listener*, 27 September 1979.)

compulsory wage control' as a failure which would not be repeated)
and re was no policy prepared in detail for this late, enforced,
conversion. Heath had not encouraged preparation. In any case,
before deciding the details of the policy time was needed for reflection
on union attitudes during the talks and for further consultation.
Without this process the General Council would have been able to
accuse the government of not having been serious in its efforts to
reach agreement and of intending from the start to impose a
statutory policy. The attack on Robert Carr for refusing consultation
on the Industrial Relations Act might have been followed by the
accusation that Heath's consultation was not 'genuine'. The freeze also
gave time to explain the government's conversion to those members
of the Conservative Party who might have failed to keep up with
events.

There were other compelling reasons for the freeze. In the circumstances it was the only immediate action the government could take on
wages. The public sector wage round for 1972–73 had opened on the
day the tripartite talks ended with the settlement in the electricity
industry. Frank Chapple had never expected the General Council to
reach an agreement and, anticipating a wage freeze, had negotiated
to settle before this was imposed. The settlement removed a threat of
disastrous industrial action and at 10½ per cent was not unreasonably
high in the circumstances. Other recent settlements had, however,
been up to 15 per cent and an effort had to be made to avert a wage
round at this or a higher level combined with industrial troubles. The
pound had been doing badly in October when little progress was
being made towards an agreement with the unions; it might do worse
now that the talks had ended without agreement unless quick action
was taken.

A freeze also had encouraging antecedents: during both the Macmillan and Wilson Governments it had been accepted for short periods
without serious trouble – though the possibility of similar acceptance
now was more speculative. There was certainly no possibility of
acceptance without the backing of law and the risk of the law being
defied had again to be taken. Finally, the freeze gave an appearance of
decisiveness. Though substantial negotiations with the TUC had continued for little more than a month, Heath's search for a 'better way'
had started in March. He was open to the charge of indecision and
to criticism for talking to the unions without success and postponing
action to restrain inflation for too long.

In the event the freeze, as in 1961 and 1966, was generally accepted.

The timing was reasonably good. The local authority unions had followed electricity supply and settled their claim by 6 November and the next wage increase for miners was not due until March. There were protest demonstrations and sporadic industrial action, but the main groups of workers in the public sector – water, gas, and the health service – who could have expected an increase following the electricity and local authority workers, decided to await Stage Two of the policy, as did most groups in the private sector. The freeze was extended by Order in Council to the end of March for pay and to the end of April for prices.

Incomes Policy: Stage Two and Success

The shock of the introduction of a statutory prices and incomes policy was softened by Heath's following Wilson's example and presenting it as a less satisfactory and temporary alternative to an agreed policy, which he would continue to work for. The government published a White Paper, *The Programme for Controlling Inflation: the Second Stage* (Cmnd. 5205), and a draft Bill to give effect to the programme in January 1973, a Green Paper, *The Price and Pay Code: A Consultative Document* (Cmnd. 5247), in February, and a final White Paper, *The Counter-Inflation Programme: The Operation of Stage Two* (Cmnd. 5267), in March. In all there were echoes of 1966–69. The first White Paper on Stage Two referred back to the failure to reach agreement on a voluntary policy and emphasised the importance the government still attached to such an agreement. It thus underlined what had been the first purpose of the talks: Heath wanted co-operation, not confrontation. If he was denied co-operation and as a result the statutory policy failed, the responsibility would rest with the unions. They would be refusing to accept a statutory policy after refusing to agree a voluntary policy. The proposals were closely linked with the policies for economic growth which Heath had initiated at the end of 1971: a statutory incomes policy – not the panaceas of the manifesto – was now declared essential for containing inflation, for economic growth and for full employment.

The White Paper and draft Bill proposed the establishment of two new agencies (this at least was an advance on Wilson and the NBPI), a Pay Board and a Price Commission and gave to these agencies and to the government powers to regulate prices, pay, dividends and rents. The agencies were to apply rules set out in a Prices and Pay Code and were to receive information from employers and firms about price and pay increases. The powers were to continue for three years – beyond the next election. In political terms the conversion was as near permanent as a government could make it: there was to be no annual soul-searching as in the Wilson Government. A third (or fourth) change of policy was ruled out unless the unions changed their position so that there could be a voluntary, rather than statutory, policy.

Stage Two was to cover the wage round which had started in November and been interrupted by the standstill and was to run from the end of the standstill on 31 March until the autumn. The main features of the policy were much influenced by the tripartite discussions. On pay, the purpose was to bring increases 'well below the levels reached immediately before the standstill when increases on both wage rates and earnings were running at 15–16 per cent above a year before'. The limit on increases was £1 plus 4 per cent and was applied to groups of workers to give some degree of flexibility within the group, with an individual limit of £250. The policy thus did something to benefit relatively the low-paid (though less than the flat rate increase of £2 offered in the talks) and something to preserve differentials, an issue which had been particularly stressed by Scanlon. There was to be a twelve month interval between pay increases and a special exception to allow movement towards equal pay; normal working hours, if above forty, could be reduced and holidays, if less than three weeks a year, could be increased outside the pay limit. Pensions and redundancy payments could also be improved outside the limit. There were proposals to meet points raised by the General Council representatives on prices and related issues. Subsidies to the nationalised industries would be continued to enable them to limit price increases and an increase due in the price of school meals was postponed. Rent increases under the Housing Finance Act were continued, but allowances to meet need were improved and the rate support grant to local authorities was to be increased.

The two White Papers stressed that the second stage was transitional and would be followed by a more flexible pay policy, prepared after further consultations. As part of this process the Pay Board would be asked to advise on problems of anomalies in the handling of pay agreements which had been interfered with by the standstill and the second stage and – more important – on the problem of relativities (that is, on the possibility of allowing increases beyond the general limits of any pay policy to deal with special cases). With the promise of greater flexibility in the next stage, the government hoped to get through the transitional second stage without undue industrial trouble.

Industrial trouble following the announcement of Stage Two of the policy was, in fact, limited. There were localised strikes and overtime bans in the gas industry immediately after publication of the first White Paper, since the pay increase was less than the increase given in the electricity supply industry, but the Gas Corporation made proposals to postpone redundancies, improve pensions and, at a future date, restructure the pay system, and these proposals, together with the maximum pay offer, were put to a ballot (by the union) and accepted. Three civil service unions called their first ever one-day national strike and followed it with a work-to-rule, but the protest was not pressed. Hospital ancillary staff took part in selective strikes. The General Council suggested that they might be treated as a special case and that other unions would not, in this event, quote the settlement in support of their own claims. The government did not take up the suggestion and the action was suspended in April following an improved pay offer within the limits of the policy. The government was most concerned about the reaction of the miners to Stage Two, but although the NUM balloted members on industrial action, the vote was against it and the union accepted a pay increase within the policy. A special Trades Union Congress was held and the General Council was instructed to call a 'day of national protest and stoppage'. This token action was taken on May Day.

The wage increases gained over the last two years, the level of increases allowed by Stage Two, which had been calculated in the light of the discussions in 1972, Heath's determination to come to terms with the unions even although an agreed policy was denied and the reluctance of many unions to enter another round of strikes contributed to the success of the second stage. In April, after major unions had accepted Stage Two offers, the General Council recorded its 'resentful and reluctant acquiescence'.

Incomes Policy: Stage Three, 'Unacceptable and Probably Unworkable'

In April 1973 the government started preparing for Stage Three. It had decided that this was to run for twelve months from the autumn of 1973. On past form, autumn 1974 was the first likely date for the next election and the outcome of Stage Three might be crucial to the result. It was desirable to show a reduction in the rate of inflation and essential that the policy should not provoke serious industrial trouble and a return to confrontation. Heath was still committed to seeking an agreement with the unions but, having refused to negotiate on the Industrial Relations Act and Housing Finance Act as a matter of principle, he had nothing to offer. In any case, the possibility of the unions agreeing to what would have been a major political success for the Conservatives receded even further as an election came nearer. The best Heath could hope for was that the powerful unions and the General Council would again 'acquiesce' in the terms of the policy and that the general success of the second stage would be repeated. The difficulties in the way of securing this degree of success for the third stage were, however, much greater, for three main reasons.

First, as had been shown in 1961–63 and 1966–69, industrial pressures against any policy of wage restraint increased with time. In recognition of this the government was already committed to making the third stage more 'flexible'. This meant devising formulae to reduce pressures from particular groups by meeting their claims for preferential treatment within the terms of the policy. Variation of treatment could, however, lead to accusations of unfairness. Past experience suggested that the generalised 'unfairness' of a freeze or strictly applied norm was more acceptable for a short period than a policy which, by allowing variations, made it possible for some groups to gain more than others. In 1973 the government judged a policy of greater flexibility to offer the better chance of success. A second difficulty was that the economy was expanding and unemployment was falling rapidly (in January 1972 unemployment had been 3.8 per cent; by mid-1973 it had fallen to 2.5 per cent) – a situation in which, generally, pressure on wages would increase.

The third and most important threat to the policy was that a major break by one important union could destroy it. With a policy agreed by the General Council, theoretically at least on behalf of all unions, industrial action to prove 'a special case' might be prevented by pressure from other unions, or, if not prevented, the 'special case' might be accepted by other unions who would continue to settle within the terms of the agreed policy. This would not apply to an imposed policy, even with the general acquiescence of the General Council. No individual union would be 'bound' to acceptance, the General Council under no obligation to exert pressure and other unions under no obligation to accept a breach as a special case. At best the government's policy was potentially fragile.

The preparations for Stage Three did not repeat the protracted tripartite discussions of 1972. The General Council wanted separate discussions which registered the point that they were bargaining with the government and that the CBI (and employers) were in a secondary position. (The government could have such consultations as it wished with them.)

There were discussions with the representatives of the General Council and private talks with officers of trade unions whose power and militancy might provide the most serious threats as a basis for constructing a policy which could contain the likely demands of special groups without industrial trouble. It was essential for the policy to accommodate the miners and electricity supply workers. Heath explained his proposals at a press conference on 8 October at Lancaster House – the scene of George Brown's *Statement of Intent* – the text of his statement being published as a White Paper, *Counter-Inflation Policy: Stage Three* (Cmnd. 5446). At the same time, a consultative document, *The Price and Pay Code for Stage Three* (Cmnd. 5444), was published.

So far as pay was concerned, the idea of a global sum for groups of workers, within which there could be collective bargaining, was repeated. There was now a choice of £2.25 per head or 7 per cent, with a limit of £350 for any individual and an additional 1 per cent to allow for changes in pay structures (which could, for example, benefit the gas industry) and for productivity bargaining (which could suit the engineering industry, coal mining and others). Where this provision did not suit, the 1 per cent could be used to improve holidays and sick pay schemes. There could be extra payments for schemes which genuinely increased efficiency, subject to the schemes being approved by the Pay Board, and there could be premium payments for those working 'unsocial' hours (which could benefit, for example, the miners, electricity supply workers, steel workers and others). London allowances could be improved (of particular benefit to the civil service). Anomalies created by the standstill and Stage Two could be redressed in stages; there was to be further progress towards equal pay. Provision was made for cost of living increases – or 'threshold payments' as they were described – if inflation, as measured by the Retail Price Index, was greater than the government expected. Finally, there was to be a degree of flexibility 'in reserve' to deal with particularly difficult pressures during the wage round. This would be provided in accordance with a report on relativities by the Pay Board, which was expected by the end of the year. After outlining these proposals Heath concluded:

These proposals give much greater freedom for negotiation and freedom to deal with particular problems in industry both by employers and by trade unions. I expect that what we are doing in these policies for prices and pay, taken together, will keep prices within the limits of what people will be able to afford; but it is right that people should have an additional safeguard against the possibility – and I put it no higher – of world import prices rising exceptionally fast in the year ahead. That is why we propose for the first time a cost-of-living safeguard. This will make it possible for wage negotiators to bargain for a pay increase of up to 40p a week, payable if the retail price index reaches 7 per cent above its level at the beginning of Stage Three, with up to another 40p a week for each percentage point it may rise thereafter until the end of Stage Three. I hope this safeguard may not be needed, but we think it right to provide this additional protection for people's standard of living.

(Unhappily, the hope was proved wrong within weeks and the 'threshold' increases were to contribute to the wages explosion of 1974–75.)

The proposals for Stage Three included continuation of price control as applied in Stage Two, but with some tightening up and extension of the activities of the Price Commission, continued limitation of dividends to 5 per cent and continued subsidies to nationalised industries to enable their price increases to be limited. Special measures in addition to dividend control were proposed to reduce the level of bank profits. As part of Stage Three Heath announced a second Christmas bonus of £10 for old age pensioners (pensions had just been increased by £1 and £1.60), a scheme to enable first time house purchasers to defer part of the interest on mortgages during the first few years – a device to alleviate the hardship of an 11 per cent mortgage rate – and a cut in public expenditure on construction work. The only significant changes of substance between Stage Two and Stage Three were those relating to pay.

In terms of their effect on inflation the immediate aims of the policy were not over-ambitious: given the ingenuity of bargainers it left scope for a wage round in double figures. The policy was, in fact, as much an elaborate and comprehensive conciliation exercise to avoid confrontation in the 1973–74 wage round as it was a counter-inflation operation.

The early omens for avoiding confrontation were not good. The reaction of the General Council came earlier than with Stage Two and was less encouraging: the proposals were described as 'unacceptable and probably unworkable'. The Electrical Power Engineers

Association imposed a ban on overtime working because the standstill and Stage Two had prevented the implementation of an agreement made in November 1972. The ban resulted in power cuts. The miners had on 1 September presented a claim for increases up to 40 per cent (their next increase was not due until 1 March). The Coal Board made an offer of about 13 per cent (with the promise of an efficiency scheme to produce another 3½ per cent) which was within the limits (just) of Stage Three and which they were reasonably confident would be accepted. The Executive of the NUM rejected the offer and imposed an overtime ban, starting on 12 November. Most important, the 'counter-inflation' element of the policy was given a near knock-out blow which the government had not foreseen. The introduction of Stage Three coincided with the beginning of the oil crisis which was to destroy the price expectations on which the 'threshold' payments had been based.

Confrontation and Indecision

Faced with the miners' overtime ban and the oil crisis, the government declared a State of Emergency on 13 November, prohibiting the use of power for advertising and floodlighting and limiting its domestic use. It now had to decide how to react to the threats to Stage Three. Maurice Macmillan was moved from the Department of Employment and replaced by William Whitelaw; the dispute with the power engineers was settled. There remained the problem of the miners.

The situation was not unusual. The militants on the NUM Executive aimed to break Stage Three as they had broken the de-escalation policy in 1972, if necessary – perhaps preferably – by a strike which could be called only after a ballot. Gormley and the moderates were, of course, ready to consider an improved offer which would satisfy a majority of the Executive and could be recommended for acceptance in a ballot. If the government wanted to settle with the miners on an improved offer it had to assess the value of Gormley's judgement and advice, which had been taken in the course of preparing Stage Three, and the balance of power between militants and moderates on the Executive. Given a favourable view by the Executive on an improved offer, the government then had to assess the general effects of such an offer on Stage Three, preferably finding a device for giving more money which would minimise these and would justify treating the miners as a 'special case' for the second time. There was the obvious risk that any improved offer would simply be converted into a basis for further demands, as in 1972 in coalmining and on the railways.

There were different views within the government and civil service. Some ministers and officials thought the militants were in control of the Executive and that no improved offer which could plausibly be presented as not breaking Stage Three would be accepted. Others thought that an attempt should be made to settle on a reasonable increase. In support of the latter view it could be argued that other events, such as the oil crisis and the deflationary measures introduced on 17 December, had in any case destroyed the assumptions of Stage Three and that the oil crisis in particular justified a settlement with the miners and a general revision of the policy. Two things were clear. A settlement with the miners outside Stage Three could be regarded as a retreat by the government which, following the 1972 defeat and the misplaced confidence during the talks in the autumn of 1972, would damage Heath's position. Resistance followed by another extended strike and a capitulation would, however, be even more damaging to Heath and the government. Heath's standing, which had been impaired by the failures of 1972 and temporarily repaired by the success of the standstill and Stage Two, was again in doubt following this early failure of Stage Three to contain the miners. Apart from these obvious reasons for indecision there were positive arguments for delay: time would be given for other unions to settle within the limits of Stage Three (though similar tactics had proved mistaken in 1972).

Heath announced on 13 December that a three-day week would be introduced from the end of the month. Since 1972 preparations had been made for a future confrontation with the miners by building up stocks of coal and other necessary supplies at power stations and holding reserves of emergency generating equipment for hospitals and other institutions. A three-day week would conserve the stocks. The announcement suggested that the government was now resolved to stand by Stage Three and to face a lengthy period of conflict. At the very least, if the consequences of an extended confrontation proved too serious or public reaction adverse, the action would strengthen its bargaining position – or was presumably intended to do this. The announcement anyway removed the possibility of the criticism made in 1972 that the government had made no preparations to deal with the consequences of the miners' strike. It had, however, serious disadvantages.

First, the fact that stocks had been built up left the government open to criticism that the three-day week was unnecessary to conserve supplies and to the accusation that it was seeking confrontation. Secondly, the announcement, made without consultation with the General Council, was a break with the conciliatory approach since April 1972 – and one from which the General Council could make political capital. General Council representatives requested an emergency meeting of the NEDC, at which they asked for postponement of the three-day week to allow for negotiations with the miners and at which they accused the government of confrontation. They argued that the three-day week would reduce production, cut exports, increase prices – in fact, destroy the basis of the government's policies for Stage Three. Heath refused a postponement.

During January, as the three-day week affected employment, a variety of proposals for improving the offer to the miners which would not destroy Stage Three (many unions were accepting offers within the limits) were in circulation. Some, including payments for winding and waiting time, were considered, but without result. The issue became increasingly political, the Labour opposition exploiting all opportunities to show the government as unreasonable and bent on confrontation. (The opposition was concerned that on this occasion, unlike 1972, public opinion might be with the government.) Those government ministers and supporters who thought the actions of the miners and the unions generally as politically motivated and in bad faith were convinced that the government should not attempt to compromise. There was speculation about an early general election to endorse the government's policy and authority.

Against this general background of uncertainty and as the three-day week began to affect employment, the General Council took a further initiative by repeating the move it had made during the strikes of hospital staff against Stage Two. At a meeting of the NEDC on 9 January the trade union representatives reported a resolution of the General Council that 'if the government are prepared to give an assurance that they will make possible a settlement between the miners and the National Coal Board, other unions will not use this as an argument in negotiations in their own settlements'. This was rejected by Barber as inadequate. The rejection may not have been tactically sensible, but it was not totally unreasonable. It was, after all, quite possible that, while other unions might not use the miners' settlement as an argument, they would use their power in the same way as the miners.

The resolution was sent to Heath who, it was thought, had throughout favoured an attempt to reach a settlement, and there were discussions the next day between Heath, Barber, Whitelaw and the representatives of the General Council.[2] Heath wanted some assurance that the initiative would have practical results. He wanted to assess whether, if the miners' settlement was well above Stage Three, the resolution in itself would have any effect in keeping other unions in check (which seemed unlikely) and to discover what action (if any) the General Council might intend to give reality to its formula. The reply of the union representatives was that the government must trust them and the resolution. Their position was much the same as with Wilson in 1969. Their initiative might or might not have practical results, but at the very least they had offered Heath a formula and were not prepared – and, of course, given the lack of authority of the General Council over individual unions were not able – to go further. Heath was not prepared to accept the formula.

An attempt was made also to persuade the General Council representatives to encourage and help the moderates on the NUM Executive to push through a settlement at a reasonable level. (The situation was not unlike that facing Wilson in the seamen's strike.) This suggestion was turned down, though it was clear that a success for the militants on the NUM Executive would encourage militants on the executives of other unions.

The prospect of any rapprochement between the government and unions and the possibility of a moderate settlement with the miners virtually disappeared when a conference of trade union presidents and general secretaries endorsed the General Council resolution on 16 January. Within the government, Len Murray's speech to the conference was regarded as making it clear that the General Council had now decided to present the rejection of its initiative as evidence that the government was choosing to confront the miners and that in this situation the trade union movement would be behind the NUM. After this it was unlikely that the NUM Executive would settle for anything less than virtual capitulation by the government and there was a threat of a general confrontation.

[2] According to Hugh Scanlon, Heath was 'more amenable to some of the things we were trying to say than unfortunately some of his ministers were ... He listened like no other minister. One of the troubles was, having listened, he didn't necessarily act as we wanted him to act [sic], and that ... in my view was because of the pressures within the government.... I thought that the person who did most to prevent an agreement between the trade union movement and the Heath Government was the then Chancellor, Mr. Barber'. (Television discussion with Shirley Williams, text printed in *The Listener*, 27 September 1979.)

The Pay Board produced its report on relativities on 24 January (later than requested) and on the same day the NUM Executive decided to ballot its members on a recommendation for strike action. The Pay Board report suggested a special procedure for dealing with relativities, thus offering a device by which the miners could be offered more money as a 'special case'. It had been hoped originally that other unions might accept 'special case' arguments dealt with by this procedure, but by this date there was little basis for such hope, and little hope, too, that the procedure would satisfy the miners. The government, however, had no alternative but to use the device it had so thoughtfully included in Stage Three. William Whitelaw invited the TUC and CBI to consultations. Heath wrote to Wilson saying that the government, TUC and CBI should agree on the report and co-operate in establishing the necessary machinery and that the miners' claim should be examined as the first 'relativities case'.

The real test of the government's resolution came when the result of the miners' ballot was announced on 4 February. There was an 81 per cent vote in favour of a strike and the NUM Executive announced that this would start on 10 February. Gormley stated that a strike could be prevented only by an immediate increase in the offer: the miners were not prepared to wait for a relativities inquiry. The government, now committed to the relativities procedure for providing more money, refused further talks about money until the Stage Three offer had been accepted and normal working resumed. An offer of talks from Whitelaw on these terms was ignored by the NUM. On 8 February Heath announced – again without consultation with the TUC – that the miners' case would be referred to an enlarged Pay Board under the relativities procedure. His determination to stand by Stage Three of his policy and see through the consequences of a miners' strike was, however, qualified: he also announced that there would be a General Election on 28 February.[3]

'Who Governs the Country?'

The government could have continued in office until June 1975, but there were good reasons for an election before then. The economic prospects for the immediate future had worsened with the certainty of a higher rate of inflation and rising unemployment and the chances of the government's winning an election would get worse as time

---

[3] For a TUC 'calendar of main events' during the miners' dispute, *see The TUC's Initiatives* (TUC, London, 1974).

passed. These were not, however, arguments for an election at this particular time – in the depths of winter, during a period of emergency with power rationing, a three-day week and the oil crisis. The government might have chosen first to settle the miners' strike and end the State of Emergency and three-day working before calling the election. Negotiations to settle with the miners in December would have been a defeat for the Stage Three policy, but could have been justified by the oil crisis. The government could have used the General Council resolution to justify negotiations to settle in January.

There were, however, strong arguments against negotiating for a settlement. An attempt to settle at a reasonable level might not have succeeded at any stage and the chances diminished as time passed. Negotiations to settle outside the terms of Stage Three would have been a further defeat for the government. Heath's policies of 1970 for dealing with union power and inflation – the Industrial Relations Act and de-escalation – had been defeated in 1972 by union opposition, particularly from the miners. His attempt to reach an agreement with the unions following the miners' strike in 1972 had failed. The failure seemed the greater because of his exaggerated confidence during the course of the negotiations. It was not surprising that some government supporters should think that his efforts had not only failed but had been misguided and that he and others immediately involved had misjudged the situation and had been misled by the unions, who had never intended to come to an agreement and because of their political commitment would not come to an agreement with a Conservative government. Because of his failure to reach agreement Heath had been forced to introduce a statutory prices and incomes policy, which many of his supporters disliked. The miners were now seeking to break this and if the government accepted the resolution of the General Council they would be 'conned' again. The extremists in the unions were determined to wreck the government by the use of industrial power and the moderates would in the end go along with them. For those who held these views it was clear that the government should stand by its policy, resist trade union power and certainly make no move to settle with the miners outside Stage Three.

Even if this ruled out negotiations there was an alternative course of action. The government could await the relativities report and meanwhile sit out the miners' strike – a course for which it had made preparations since 1972 and for which it had seemed ready since December. With the three-day week, existing coal stocks should last until the spring. It is true that by now the miners were unlikely to accept the relativities report or to settle for anything less than their claim, but this was a problem which could be faced when it arose. The consequences of non-acceptance by the miners would, however, be extremely unattractive and Heath and his colleagues cannot have been wholly confident in the collective capacity of the government – or the readiness of the public – to face a repetition of some of the events of the 1972 strike nor convinced that their preparations would be adequate. There was the risk that after the relativities report there would be another debacle similar to that following the Wilberforce Report with the destruction of another government policy in a meeting at Downing Street. The political consequences would be serious. The miners might succeed in wrecking the government, at any rate in the form in which it existed.

It is not surprising, therefore, that by January 1974 there were those within the party pressing for an election on the issue of union power – 'who governs the country?' – nor that the proposition should appeal to some of the leading personalities involved, particularly as the opposition, concerned that anti-union feeling would work against them, showed signs of not wanting an election on the issue of union power.

The political 'drama' which had from time to time characterised incomes policy and industrial conflict since George Brown's ceremony at Lancaster House in 1964 and which had built up even more since 1969 had reached a new high point. By this time two of the personalities included earlier in the tripartite talks, Feather and Armstrong, chief designer of the policy and responsible for organising the measures after the declaration of the State of Emergency to preserve and protect the authority of government, had left the scene. Figgures, now Chairman of the Pay Board, had been waiting for his cue on relativities. The leading performers, the government, General Council and NUM Executive had taken up their positions on the stage, but had run out of dialogue. An election would at least provide a new scene, would postpone the need for further decisions by the government about the miners – and would provide a 'cooling-off' period and a ballot. (There was even some hope that the miners might postpone their strike, a hope which, not surprisingly, was disappointed.) When returned after the election Heath could decide what could be rescued from both his earlier and later policies to deal with union power and inflation. His position then was unlikely to be questioned, whatever the course of the strike and the nature of the final settlement with the miners.

The issue of union power had been important in the 1970 election and would obviously have been important in the next, whenever it had taken place. With the miners' strike the government could now make it the predominant issue. Union power could be presented as being used to obtain excessive wage increases, threatening government counter-inflation policies and challenging the authority of the government. The theme was widened and developed in the manifesto, *Firm Action for a Fair Britain.*

The manifesto provided an interesting contrast to that of 1970. Opening with an unusual admission of weakness,[4] it combined statements of determination to contain inflationary wage increases and resist the abuse of trade union power with assertions of an intention to work with the unions and proposals to meet some of their demands. After a relatively brief reference to the inflationary effects of rising world prices, particularly oil ('The Danger from Outside'), it dealt with the 'Danger from Within' at greater length:

> What could destroy, not just our present standard of living, but all our hopes for the future, would be inflation we brought upon ourselves.... We have ... had to deal with the inflation which comes as a result of excessive wage increases here at home.

The miners were now trying to break the prices and incomes policy which had been successful in dealing with wage inflation. The miners' claim should be settled within the incomes policy on the basis of the relativities report:

> We shall, therefore, press ahead with pay and prices policy, if necessary stiffening it in the light of the new developing economic situation....
>
> We shall renew our offer to the TUC and CBI to join us in working out an effective voluntary pay and prices policy, ultimately to replace the existing statutory policy, in the management and evolution of which both sides of industry would jointly participate.... But the Achilles heel of the British economy has long been, and continues to be, industrial relations.
>
> It is largely because of this that our economic progress since the war has consistently lagged behind that of most other industrial nations.... It is in large part because of this that we find ourselves in the present crisis, the gravest since the war....
>
> We shall therefore maintain the essential structure of the Industrial

---

[4] 'It is essential that the affairs of the country are in the hands of a strong government, able to take firm measures in defence of the national interest. This means a Conservative Government with a renewed mandate from the people and with a full five years in which to guide the nation safely through the difficult period that lies ahead.'

Relations Act, but we shall amend it in the light of experience and after consultation with both sides of industry ...

There were other proposals. Industrial relations would be improved by legislation for a wider measure of employee participation. There was, however, a small number of militant extremists who could so manipulate and abuse the monopoly power of their unions as to cause incalculable damage to the country and to the fabric of society itself. The best way of curbing the minority of extremists was for the moderate majority of union members to stand up and be counted. It was manifestly unfair, however, that those who did not go on strike were obliged to subsidise those who did and the unions, not the taxpayer, should accept this responsibility. The social security system would be amended.

The manifesto was thus a collection of policies and views which had prevailed – or had been aired – since June 1970 and earlier, perhaps in part because of haste in preparation and differing views within the Conservative Party, but reflecting also the experiences of government since 1970 and a recognition that 'curbing' trade union power was a more difficult exercise than it had then seemed. In consequence, however, it did not impress as giving a consistent lead on the issue on which the election had been called.

It could certainly not be regarded as showing unqualified hostility to the unions and in the election campaign Edward Heath did not take up an anti-trade union position. His criticism of the unions was less severe than might have been justified by the negotiations in 1972, the talks with union leaders in the preparation of Stage Three and his dealings with them over the General Council resolution offered in the weeks preceding the election. In spite of these experiences, Heath did not, it seemed, accept that the political alignment of the unions ruled out agreement with a future Conservative government – at any rate one under his leadership. Even if agreement were not possible, he recognised that a Conservative government would need to secure some degree of union co-operation and that his earlier policies may have prevented this. While his objectives of 1970 had been right, his policies to achieve them had been wrong in part. After the election he would be in a position to resume negotiations; the chances of obtaining an agreed incomes policy or acceptance of a policy might then be better. They should at least not be prejudiced by the conduct of the election. He recognised that while the electorate might want the government to continue the fight against inflation, it did not want confrontation.

Heath's understandable doubts about the nature of the relations between his next government and the trade unions and the most effective ways of handling the problems of trade union power meant that he was asking for support on the grounds that his objectives had been right and that in his next government his policies to achieve them, improved in the light of experience, would be more effective and less disturbing than in the past.

The election had opened on the apparently simple issue of whether the government should resist the miners' power in the cause of fighting inflation. Heath's approach raised wider questions, which it was more difficult to answer. These were the questions of whether he had governed successfully, whether the responsibility for creating the 'crisis' situation in which he had called the election lay with him or with the unions, whether a counter-inflation policy must necessarily lead to confrontation and industrial conflict and, if so, whether the fight against inflation justified such a state of affairs. The last was a question which post-war governments had never answered consistently and it seemed excessively hopeful to expect a clear answer from the electorate. As many strikes had shown, it was likely that many of the public, while in general against inflation, would in particular situations prefer industrial peace at almost any immediate price, without calculating (or perhaps understanding) the longer term effects.

In spite of his efforts since 1972 and his attitude during the election, Heath was still accused of responsibility for confrontation, and for those who accepted the truth of the accusation, the situation which the opposition declared to be inevitable if the Conservatives were returned appeared as unpleasant, even alarming. Others considered that, having committed himself in 1970 to contain the power of the trade unions and still insisting on the importance of this, it was irresponsible to call an election when faced by the challenge from the miners: in a 'crisis' situation the government should govern and not turn to the country.

There were incidents during the election which did not help the Conservatives. Campbell Adamson, Director General of the CBI, described the Industrial Relations Act (which he had praised in 1971) as having 'sullied every relationship at national level between unions and employers'. Information came out from the Pay Board in the course of its relativities inquiry which gave rise to the suggestion that the figures on which the Stage Three offer to the miners had been based might be wrong. This announcement, exploited by the Labour

Party, was a blow to the credibility of the counter-inflation policy and Stage Three similar in its way to the blow given to the Industrial Relations Act by the judgement of the Court of Appeal in the Heàton's case. Perhaps more important than these events during the election was that in their picketing the miners avoided the violence of 1972 which, had it been repeated, might have turned public opinion against them and the unions.

Edward Heath's election was a failure. He was not given a 'renewed mandate' and the result ensured that the affairs of the country were not 'in the hands of a strong government'. The Labour Party with 301 seats in the House of Commons had 4 more than the Conservatives, so that the balance of voting power rested with the Liberals and other parties. Harold Wilson became Prime Minister of his third Labour Government.

In his broadcast opening the election campaign Heath had asked two questions: 'Do you want Parliament and the elected government to fight strenuously against inflation? Or do you want them to abandon the struggle against rising prices under pressure from one particularly powerful group of workers?'.

Whatever the intentions and wishes of the electorate, the political system and the role of the trade union movement within the system meant that the immediate answer to the first question was to be 'no', and to the second, 'yes'.

PART IV

Jack Jones, 1972–79 – 'A New Social Contract'

The chapters which follow are much less detailed than Parts II and III. The aim is to show how government–trade union relations under the Labour governments of 1974–79 were influenced by the experience of the preceding Labour and Conservative governments and to assess the effects of the 'social contract' period on the relative standing of government and unions. The period March 1974–September 1975 is considered in more detail to show the relationship which developed between government and unions and how their agreed policies both precipitated and were affected by the economic 'crisis' of mid-1975.

From 1974 until 1978 at least the relations between the trade unions and the governments of Harold Wilson and James Callaghan were greatly influenced by the reactions of both union leaders and politicians to the events which took place between 1969 and 1972 and were particularly affected by the view which Jack Jones, General Secretary of the Transport and General Workers Union, took of these events. The years can be divided into three periods. Between 1972 and 1974 agreement was reached by the General Council and politicians of the Labour Party on the policies to which the next Labour government would be committed. These policies were presented as the 'new social contract' in the elections of February and October 1974. After February 1974 there was until June 1975 what should have been a halcyon period for the trade unions: the Wilson Government embarked on the agreed policies in accordance with the priorities favoured by the unions, while the unions pursued their normal business of free collective bargaining. This period ended in the middle of 1975 when the economic and social consequences of inflation accelerating to record levels threatened to destroy the government.

In the second period, or second phase of the 'new social contract', from mid-1975 to mid-1978, free collective bargaining was replaced by incomes policies agreed with or accepted by the unions as necessary to reduce the rate of inflation and save the Labour Government. The final period saw the return of the unions to free collective bargaining and the confrontations between the unions and the Callaghan Government. It ended with the defeat of the government in the general election of May 1979.

11 Collective Bargaining and Inflation

The Origins of the 'New Social Contract', 1972–74

In 1969 the trade unions had compelled Harold Wilson to abandon policies which he had argued were essential to the national interest. The conflict within the movement, exposing the realities of power and the inability of a Labour government to resist trade union pressure, contributed to the defeat of the government in the 1970 election.

The consequences of Labour's election defeat were serious for the unions. Within twelve months of the 1970 election the Industrial Relations Act was passed and they regarded themselves as under serious attack. In response to this Jack Jones took an initiative to prepare for the next election and to prevent a repeat of the 'deep and fundamental split between the two wings of the movement' which had been followed by the defeat of the Wilson Government and the Conservative attack. This split had occurred in spite of the long-established links provided by the Labour Party organisation, including trade union representation on the National Executive Committee and other party committees and overwhelming union voting power at the Party Conference. Contacts between leading members of the General Council and the leading politicians, particularly when the Party was in government, had not been close enough for the former to prevent their political colleagues from going astray.[1]

Jones' initiative led to the establishment of a TUC–Labour Party Liaison Committee with members from the General Council and leading politicians likely to be future ministers. This was to be the instrument for deciding the policies of the next Labour government, and it would give practical effect to the primacy of the unions in the movement and the special position they occupied as a pressure

---

[1] Trade union representation on the National Executive Committee of the Labour Party is almost invariably at a level below general secretary or the equivalent. It is not possible under the rules for an individual to be on the General Council of the TUC and on the NEC and top trade union officers choose to be on the former.

group when there was a Labour government in office. Constituted on an informal basis in 1970, the Liaison Committee took on an official status with regular monthly meetings in early 1972, so that Jones and his colleagues from the General Council were in the enviable position of negotiating with the Heath Government in pursuit of policies to which they could ensure the next Labour government would be committed.

In the discussions with Edward Heath in 1972 and 1973, the unions were bargaining with government over issues which went beyond the traditional collective bargaining area of wages and related subjects and extended to political objectives on which the trade unions had in the past tacitly accepted that the Labour Party should take the lead. It is true that these wider trade union interests had been pressed on governments after 1931 and by different means throughout the post-war period (and had been pursued through the established machinery of the labour movement), but the bargaining with the Heath Government and the establishment of the Liaison Committee can be regarded as significant features in the change of union attitude towards government in general and to both political parties, a change which had been developing since 1961, partly in response to government pressures for wage restraint.

This extension of 'bargaining' was an open affirmation that the real value of what the unions achieved by industrial collective bargaining depended on social and economic conditions which were influenced by government policies. The established demarcation between industrial and political activities was blurred and there began a period in which union leaders more openly pursued political aims and became publicly important political figures, operating outside the party and the parliamentary system. For ten years from 1968 Jack Jones was politically the most effective trade union leader since Ernest Bevin – and arguably the most powerful politician within the Labour Party. Unlike Bevin (and Frank Cousins) he exercised his political power without entering parliamentary politics: the opportunities given by the Wilson Government in 1969 and by the Heath Government in 1972 made this unnecessary.[2]

Not all union leaders viewed this political activity with equal enthusiasm. Many would have preferred governments to leave unions to their traditional business of wage bargaining, and would in turn

[2] In a public opinion poll during the Callaghan Administration 52 per cent of respondents said that Jack Jones was the most powerful man in the country, compared with 34 per cent who named James Callaghan.

have preferred to leave governments to pursue their policies in the light of the effects of this activity. This was not, however, a possibility, and, led by Jones, the TUC now gave practical effect to the role which George Woodcock had seen for it as a bargainer with governments, though Jones was not 'reacting', to use a Woodcock word: he was on the offensive. He was a committed supporter of the left wing of the Labour Party and in bargaining pursued its political objectives. There would be no 'shoddy, shabby compromises' (another Woodcock phrase) in any discussions with the Heath Government. The lead Jones gave in the talks with the Heath Government, his position over the miners' claim in the weeks before the February election and his influence through the Liaison Committee were decisive in settling the policies of the Labour government from March 1974 to June 1975.

The main policies for the next Labour government of direct concern to the trade unions were set out in the first joint statement of the Liaison Committee in July 1972 and in *Economic Policy and the Cost of Living* in February 1973. The documents rejected the incomes policy of the earlier Wilson Governments as a means of containing inflation and, of course, the industrial relations policies by which Wilson had aimed to contain the industrial power which has 'passed to the shop floor'. *Economic Policy and the Cost of Living*, like the Conservative manifesto of 1970, played down the importance of wages as a cause of inflation and emphasised that co-operation between government and unions (still being sought by Heath and still being refused[3]) in a 'coherent economic and social strategy' was essential to solve the problems of inflation.

The 'economic and social strategy' reflected the decisions of the Trade Union Congress of 1972, many of which had been put to Heath in the final stages of the Downing Street–Chequers talks, and included food and transport subsidies, permanent price controls, the repeal of the Housing Finance Act, 1972, the redistribution of incomes and wealth, the abolition of social service charges and the expansion of investment and control of capital. At the same time the role of the government in industrial relations was to be reduced. An independent conciliation and arbitration service would be set up, free from the influence of government views or policies on wages. The Con-

---

[3] Heath's statement at the Conservative Party Conference in October 1972 that trade unions and employers must share with the government the benefits and obligations of running the country and his follow-up to this in the tripartite talks may have influenced the subsequent Liaison Committee stress on co-operation between government and unions which culminated in the idea of a 'social contract'.

servative Industrial Relations Act would be repealed and replaced
by legislation to increase trade union power and workers rights. The
power which had passed to the shop floor would be recognised by
an extension of industrial and economic democracy.

The experience of 1965, when within months the Wilson Government departed from the principles of the voluntary incomes policy
agreed in opposition, was not to be repeated; nor was the experience
of 1969. *Economic Policy and the Cost of Living* ended with the statement:

> ... it will be the first task of the Labour government on taking
> office, and having due regard to the circumstances at that time,
> to conclude with the TUC, on the basis of the understanding being
> reached on the Liaison Committee, a wide-ranging agreement on
> the policies to be pursued in all these aspects of our economic
> life and to discuss with them the order of priorities of their fulfilment.

The Liaison Committee report recorded the acceptance by the
politicians of the need to retain the support of the unions and the
determination of a future Labour government to do this.

The policies of the 'economic and social strategy' agreed on the
Liaison Committee reappeared in the Labour Party manifesto of
February 1974, which also contained promises on public ownership
to meet the demands of particular trade union interests, including
firm commitments to nationalise shipbuilding and ship repairing,
aircraft manufacture and the ports. Against the background of the
union confrontation with the Heath Government, the manifesto laid
great stress on the ability of Labour to work with the unions: a
Labour government would 'control prices and attack speculation and
set a climate fair enough to work together with the unions'.

In facing the problem of inflation, the precise nature of the
response a Labour government might expect from the unions in this
'fair climate' was not elaborated. One thing was clear: the unions
offered nothing on wage restraint. A statutory incomes policy was
ruled out as firmly as in the Conservative manifesto of 1970; nor was
there any commitment to an agreed incomes policy as in 1964. All
the manifesto offered was hope of co-operation in achieving the objectives agreed on the Liaison Committee. There would be policies
dealing with 'high prices, rents and other impositions falling most
heavily on the low paid and on pensioners' and the manifesto
expressed the belief that 'the trade unions *voluntarily* ... will co-operate
to make the whole policy successful'. This was the 'essence of the new
social contract ... which must take its place as a central feature of
the new economic policy of a Labour government'. Even this very

general reference to co-operation was included only after pressure from those politicians who believed that some form of incomes policy was necessary to contain inflation and was accepted only reluctantly by the trade unions.

It is impossible to believe that in 1974 Wilson – or indeed many of his colleagues – had serious hopes of an effective response in terms of voluntary wage restraint in view of the experiences of 1964–70 and the origins of the formula. It was, however, all that could be obtained from the TUC. In spite of its lack of substance 'the new social contract' assumed increasing political importance during the election of February and during the third Wilson administration, itself a prelude to the election of October 1974. The passing reference in the manifesto was described by Wilson as: 'A great new Social Contract ... between Government, industry and trade unions, with all three willing to make sacrifices to reach agreement on a strategy to deal with rising prices'.

Between February and October practically all government measures were presented as part of the social contract. By October it had become the central feature of the general election programme.[4] Within six months the understandings on the Liaison Committee, the commitments from politicians and the ambiguous intentions of the trade unions became a political Holy Grail in which any objective of the labour movement could be found – and indeed many objectives which would be regarded as desirable, if not practicable, by politicians of any party in office or seeking office. For two years or more the social contract was to be proclaimed as the guiding and all embracing principle of the Labour government, the major weapon against inflation – the alternative to confrontation and the 'savage wounds' inflicted by Heath. Until mid-1975 it was a political rallying cry for the labour movement which committed the politicians in government to specific measures while the trade union response exacerbated the inflation which was the central economic and social problem facing the government.

The Flowering of the Social Contract – or Winning the Next Election

The economic and political situation when the Wilson Government

[4] See the Labour Party manifesto, October 1974, particularly p. 5, where the social contract is described as being about justice, equality, protection of the lower paid, fairness – in short, the whole range of government policies.

took office in March 1974 was the most difficult since the early 1950s. The increases in oil prices threatened the economies. of all major industrial countries: they would cause inflation, have adverse effects on their balance of payments and could lead to a general recession with rising unemployment. The British economy was amongst the weakest and likely to suffer most serious economic consequences. The threat from outside was superimposed on the failures of the economic policies of the Health Government, and especially the consequences of its monetary policies. On the crucial issue of inflation Britain's performance had continued to be worse than that of other countries. Prices were rising at an annual rate of about 13 per cent and Heath's 'counter-inflation' policy had been rejected by the electorate. On past form it could be expected that any government was likely to react ineffectively to the additional inflationary problems created by the rises in the price of oil. The prospects of economic growth in the immediate future were nil – and industry was on a three-day week.

The political background, too, was depressing. Governments of both major parties were discredited. Their promises of economic growth since the euphoric years of 1962–66 had proved illusory. The rate of inflation was far higher than rates which governments had declared unacceptable for more than twenty years – and was accelerating. Incomes policy, which with economic growth had been a panacea of politicians, civil servants and commentators for more than ten years, looked a very doubtful political – and practical – proposition.

Trade union militancy had increased during the late 1960s and under the Heath Government it had become clear that governments would not have enough public support to face damaging strikes in the public sector to impose wage restraint. Many companies in the private sector were unable to face strikes. Amongst the public there was anxiety and alarm about 'confrontation'. There was talk of the country being ungovernable and of the collapse of parliamentary democracy, of civil disorder and authoritarianism.

The Wilson Government did not have an overall majority and could be expected to give priority to winning the next election, certain to take place in a very short time. Avoidance of conflict with the unions was the major card for this. In any case the events of 1969 meant that the government, and Wilson in particular, would certainly not risk public argument with the unions. The appointment of Michael Foot, who had long admired the Transport and General

Workers Union and who shared Jones' political views, as Secretary of State for Employment gave assurance of this. Jones himself could not have made a better choice.

The primary purpose of government actions in March and April 1974 was to carry out election commitments to satisfy trade union wishes. The miners' strike was settled with increases, which more or less met their claim, of between 22–25 per cent. The government asked the TUC to state its priorities for legislation and promised swift repeal of the Industrial Relations Act, announced a freeze on council house rents, began preparations for the repeal of the Housing Finance Act and introduced subsidies on bread and a Bill to tighten up control of prices. Denis Healey, Chancellor of the Exchequer, included proposals put to him by the TUC in his budget. This was a considerable down payment on the social contract and both politicians and the public were concerned to see how the unions would respond on wages in helping the government with 'a strategy to deal with rising prices'.

There seemed little promise of an agreed approach on the General Council which might offer some hope of wage restraint and certainly no agreed 'policy' was readily available. Amongst union leaders there were different views on the nature of the social contract and its likely value – the fact that it even existed had been denied (temporarily) by Scanlon during the election campaign. Not surprisingly, these differences extended to the effect the contract would have – or ought to have – on wage claims. An assurance by Len Murray, General Secretary of the TUC, that the TUC would encourage union members to relate collective bargaining to 'the achievement of agreed economic and social objectives' was not regarded by some union leaders as inconsistent with the insistence of Gormley and Scanlon that only their members could decide the size of their next claims. The General Council could hardly, however, remain silent in this situation and despite these differences it was prepared to agree that Stage Three of the Heath Government's statutory incomes policy should continue until the end of July 1974. Unions were urged by the TUC to observe the limits of the policy.

In November 1973 the General Council had described Stage Three as 'unacceptable and probably unworkable'. It would be mistaken, however, to attribute the TUC's change of view entirely to the fact that there had been a change of government – or to a change of heart on wage restraint. Many unions had already settled within Stage Three. Given the rate of inflation, it had the attraction that the threshold payments would provide automatic increases and thus too much 'restraint' would not be imposed. There was no possibility of the General Council agreeing on an alternative policy for some time. Without any general guidance such as Stage Three offered the wage round might become so disorderly as to generate serious tensions within the labour movement.

The immediate response of unions to the TUC–government initiative in retaining Stage Three was mixed. There were some settlements within Stage Three in April, May and June, but there were difficulties on the railways and in other parts of the public sector (and also in the private sector). The government accepted that nurses, teachers and postmen amongst others should be regarded as special cases and announced that money would be available to cover these.[5] The first of the Heath Government's threshold payments was triggered on 24 May following a rise of 3 per cent in the Retail Price Index in April. By May the rate of wage increases was accelerating rapidly, though the Retail Price Index was moving up less quickly, due in part to government subsidies. By this time it was clear that even if there was fairly general observance of Stage Three the rate of inflation would get worse, threatening the economy, full employment and the government's prospects of winning the next election. A policy on wages to follow Stage Three when it ended in July had to be found if the government's claims for its 'contract' with the unions were to carry any conviction.

The General Council accepted the burden of producing guidelines for pay to follow the ending of Stage Three. There was to be a genuine voluntary – trade union – pay policy and this time, unlike that of the late sixties, it would not be running in parallel with a government policy. Woodcock's ambition was to be realised. The proposed guidelines for the policy were accepted unanimously by the General Council on 26 June and published as *Collective Bargaining and the Social Contract*.

The likely value of the guidelines in encouraging any degree of wage restraint in the next wage round could be gauged by the fact that in spite of the open disagreements between unions they were accepted unanimously. The main objective of collective bargaining, according to the guidelines, would be to ensure the maintenance of real incomes, either by claiming compensation for the rise in the cost of living since the last settlement – Stage Three settlements could, in effect, be reopened – or by negotiating arrangements to keep up with the cost

[5] As Edward Heath had indicated earlier.

of living during the period of the new agreement. There should normally be a twelve month interval between increases, though this guidance was qualified. Priority was to be given to a wide range of objectives – beneficial effects on unit costs and efficiency, reform of pay structures, improvement of job security and the attainment of reasonable minimum standards, including the TUC's low pay target of a £30 minimum basic rate. Continuing aims were to be elimination of discrimination against particular groups, notably women, improvement of non-wage benefits such as sick pay and occupational pension schemes and progress towards four weeks annual holiday. Full use should be made of the new conciliation and arbitration service (ACAS[6]) to help towards a quick solution of disputes.

While the General Council was preparing this contribution to the social contract the government, too, was preparing for the next election. Denis Healey presented a pre-election supplementary budget at the end of July 1974, aimed at limiting the rate of price increase – at any rate temporarily – and making some gesture in response to pressures from the General Council for higher public expenditure and other measures to prevent unemployment going above 800,000 in 1975. Other pronouncements by the government were clear indications of preparation for an autumn election. In September Healey claimed that inflation was running at not more than 8–9½ per cent a year. The government announced a range of intentions as part of the social contract, including extension of the Dockworkers Employment Scheme – an objective pursued by Jones for years – a Sex Discrimination Bill, a major government stake in North Sea oil and further legislation on trade union rights, since the Trade Union and Labour Relations Act, 1974 (repealing Heath's Industrial Relations Act) had, against the wishes of the unions, been amended in respect of provisions on the closed shop. The Pay Board was abolished and Stage Three of the incomes policy officially ended. There was a White Paper on a capital transfer tax and a Green Paper on a wealth tax, plans for an extension of state ownership, including the nationalisation of the shipbuilding and engineering industries, and a White Paper, *The Regeneration of British Industry* (Cmnd. 5710).

Trade union leaders rallied to the government in the run-up to the autumn election, though some emphasised that the return of a Labour government was not in itself a recipe for industrial peace and wage restraint. The Trades Union Congress at the beginning of September was a pre-election rally, the main purpose of which was to secure

[6] The Advisory, Conciliation and Arbitration Service.

endorsement of *Collective Bargaining and the Social Contract* as evidence of the unity of the labour movement. It was duly endorsed unanimously, in spite of initial opposition by the AUEW to voluntary wage restraint.[7]

The Congress set the scene. The general election was announced within a few days and the Labour Party made the social contract the central theme – it lay 'at the heart' of its programme to 'save the nation'. The Labour government was returned with an overall majority of 5 and a majority over the Conservatives of 42.

The start of Harold Wilson's fourth administration coincided roughly with what twelve months earlier had been intended as the end of Stage Three of the Heath Government's counter-inflation policy – and possibly the date of a new Stage Four or an election called by the Conservative government. Stage Three had been interrupted by the miners' strike and the February election, but it had been continued until July with the backing of the General Council and the Labour government. There had been, perhaps, more 'special cases' settled at a higher level than if the Heath Government had continued, and between July and September – the interregnum between Stage Three and the formal adoption of the TUC policy – there had been breaches of the twelve-month rule, but the threshold increases included in Stage Three by Heath had contributed to the worsening inflationary situation. Responsibility for developments on wages and prices, the rate of inflation and the general economic consequences in the twelve months from October 1973 to October 1974 can be fairly attributed to both the Heath and Wilson Governments – in so far, of course, as they were not due to the quadrupling of oil prices in December 1973 and the consequent onset of world inflation and recession.

Between October 1973 and October 1974 wages rose by 22 per cent. The Retail Price Index rose by 17 per cent, the rise being limited by subsidies started by the Heath Government and extended and increased by the Wilson Government. If Heath's economic policies could be regarded as ending in failure, Wilson's additions to them might be a preliminary to economic near-disaster.

---

[7] The delegation of the AUEW (where Scanlon was adamant against any interference with free collective bargaining) had decided to vote against voluntary wage restraint and the Technical and Supervisory Section (TASS) had put down a motion which laid down near-revolutionary preconditions for any voluntary wages policy. Political and trade union pressures were brought to bear and the engineers were persuaded to withdraw the TASS motion.

Collective Bargaining and the Social Contract: the TUC Policy, October 1974–June 1975

The Queen's speech on 29 October 1974 emphasised the importance of the social contract in the fight against inflation. Proposals in the speech included the introduction of a capital transfer tax and a wealth tax, the raising of family allowances and other related benefits, the introduction of an earnings related pension scheme, another Trades Union and Labour Relations Bill, an Employment Protection Bill, legislation against the self-employed in the construction industry, extension of the dock labour scheme, legislation to put the Conciliation and Arbitration Service on a statutory basis, nationalisation of the shipbuilding and aircraft industries and North Sea oil, and proposals for planning agreements in the private sector. 'The most urgent task' was 'to seek fulfilment of the social contract as an essential element in [the] strategy for curbing inflation, reducing the balance of payments deficit, encouraging industrial investment, maintaining employment ... and promoting social and economic justice'.

The initiative of the General Council in preparing *Collective Bargaining and the Social Contract* and its endorsement by Congress had been a major contribution to the election campaign. The government was now concerned as to whether it would in practice restrain the rate of wage increase in the wage round of 1974–75 which was now starting. Public anxiety had swung back and had begun to centre on inflation rather than on confrontation. As early as the end of October there was talk of the need for the General Council to adopt more restrictive guidelines or, at least, to press unions to observe the existing guidelines more closely. By December there was every sign that *Collective Bargaining and the Social Contract* would make no effective contribution to wage restraint and the government's 'strategy for curbing inflation'. As the General Council maintained pressure on the government to carry out its commitments, arguing amongst other things for increased pensions and family allowances and for reflation to avoid the further increase in unemployment threatened in 1975, 1974 ended as a year of records. Earnings had risen during the year by about 29 per cent and prices by about 19 per cent. The balance of payments deficit was the largest ever recorded at £3.75 billion. Unemployment was more than 200,000 above the level a year earlier and was still rising. Consumer spending showed a decline for the first time in twenty years, the GDP fell year on year for the first time since 1958.

There was little the government could do. The possibility of penalties against employers giving increases beyond the guidelines of *Collective Bargaining and the Social Contract* was considered, but dropped under pressure from the TUC, who regarded the proposals as a disguised statutory incomes policy, and opposition from the CBI. The government restricted itself to exhortation.

At the beginning of 1975, with wages rising at an annual rate of about 37 per cent, Denis Healey entered the debate on inflation and the operation of the social contract. With the rapid rise in unemployment, the TUC Economic Committee had emphasised the need to protect jobs as part of the social contract and Murray had argued that the maintenance of living standards and the maintenance of full employment were mutually reinforcing. Healey now openly disagreed: 'It is far better that more people should be in work, even if that means accepting lower wages on average, than that those lucky enough to keep their jobs should scoop the pool while millions are living on the dole'.

The level of unemployment would, in effect, be determined by the unions and depended on the practical results of their commitment to the social contract. The unions could choose between wage increases and jobs.

The choice was not acceptable to the General Council. Any suggestion that the wage guidelines should be tightened continued to be ruled out and there was a total refusal by union leaders to accept the possibility that wage rises might have to be less than the rise in the cost of living.

These public disagreements took place during the final stages of negotiations on the miners' wage claim, on which the arguments of Healey, Foot and others had no obvious effect. The settlement of 13 February allowed increases of up to 33 per cent. There was some disarray amongst ministers: Anthony Crosland said that too many groups had settled outside the social contract; Reginald Prentice said that the unions must not 'welsh' on the social contract – and was described as an 'economic illiterate' by Michael Foot and rebuked by Harold Wilson; Healey declared that the main cause of inflation in 1975 had been the increase in wages – it was 'irresponsible lunacy to ignore the fact that wages were the main cause of inflation' (and was not described as an economic illiterate).

The settlement more or less determined the level of other public sector settlements of the wage round. Electricity supply workers settled for around 31 per cent and other public utilities settled in line with them. The railway unions rejected an offer of over 21 per cent and finally accepted an arbitration award of 27.7 per cent. In the private sector the National Union of Seamen rejected an offer of 30 per cent and finally accepted an arbitration award of 37.7 per cent.

By the spring of 1975 it was clear that *Collective Bargaining and the Social Contract* was for the government at least an unqualified failure. More than half of the important agreements had been for increases 10 per cent or more above the rise in the RPI for the preceding twelve months; the highest paid workers had done as well as, if not better than, the lower paid; those in the public sector had benefited most. Between July 1973 and July 1974 wage rates increased by 20 per cent. They were to increase by a further 31 per cent between July 1974 and July 1975. The facts of the situation were that the government had 'delivered' and was delivering on its side of the social contract while the unions for their part had failed and were failing to do so.

The economic situation now compelled the government to adopt policies contrary to those pressed on them by the General Council. In spite of demands for reflation to counter rising unemployment, the budget in April gave priority to improving the balance of payments. The public sector borrowing requirement was reduced for 1975–76 and further 'cuts' were planned for 1976–77; direct and indirect taxes were increased; subsidies were reduced. It was calculated that as a result unemployment would rise to one million by the end of the year, that 3 per cent would be added to prices (without taking account of the reduction of subsidies) and that by the summer the year on year increase in prices could rise to 25 per cent. The failure of *Collective Bargaining and the Social Contract* had made a major contribution not only to destroying full employment (the post-war objective of all governments, the unions and the labour movement) but to the highest rate of inflation for centuries.

The Conversion of Jack Jones

Len Murray disagreed with those who blamed the rate of inflation and the level of unemployment on the guidelines of *Collective Bargaining and the Social Contract*. Most wage settlements had, he said, been within the social contract; they had been high because of the statutory policy effective until July 1974. The government was not reassured. It now feared that a third wage round on the scale of the last two – or perhaps even higher – would lead to uncontrollable inflation, a collapse of the pound, unpredictable social and economic consequences and its own disappearance from office. An assurance that measures were being taken to restrain wages was needed quickly in order to protect the pound. At the beginning of May Healey made it clear that the wage guidelines must be tightened and the level of settlements reduced to enable the rate of inflation to be brought down to at most 15 per cent within twelve months. He suggested that government intervention might be necessary, in spite of the risk of confrontation with the unions. Later in the month Wilson repeated proposals which had been in circulation for some years. The TUC and CBI should, he said, join the government in agreeing the total national income for the year and then apportioning it to personal incomes, social services etc.[8] The TUC staff proposed the re-introduction of wage-vetting machinery (shades of 1965–66) but this, and a suggestion that there should be no increase in the TUC minimum wage target of £30 for a 40 hour week, was rejected by the General Council.

The Budget and Healey's threat on wages meant that there was the possibility of serious open conflict within the labour movement as in 1969 or, given the economic situation, even the possibility of a political disaster comparable to that of 1931. In either event the hopes Jones had had for the Liaison Committee would be proved illusions.

It was obvious to Jones that something had to be done quickly if any credibility was to be restored to the social contract and the government. In May he came forward with a new plan for a flat-rate increase tied to the movement in the cost of living index and based on average earnings, which would have the effect of cutting differentials and benefiting lower paid workers more than higher paid and professional people. Later he went on to argue for wage sacrifices to save jobs. He asked the government to freeze the prices of essential goods and services for up to twelve months in return for union agreement to a flat-rate policy (his own version of previous 'price freeze' initiatives). TUC staff supported his conversion. Although critical of Jones' flat-rate proposal on the grounds that it would disturb differentials and thus lead to opposition, in a confidential document put to the TUC Economic Committee as a first draft of *The Development of the Social Contract* they accepted the government view that the rate of inflation must be brought down to 15 per cent at most to keep the country competitive and admitted that high wage rises were a cause of inflation and that a pay policy of matching pay rises to cost of living rises slowed down the rate of progress to lower prices.

[8] Wilson had himself put forward a similar scheme in 1967.

Jones' conversion was remarkable and crucial to any union–government agreement on an incomes policy. Under the previous Labour and Conservative governments he had been one of the strongest critics of incomes policy. As late as January 1975 he had refused to accept that wage rises might need to be less than the rise in the cost of living. Healey, however, backed by Wilson and Foot, had finally persuaded him that the high rate of inflation and the rapid drop in the pound were unavoidable consequences of the collective bargaining activities of unions since mid-1974 and that the results were contrary to the long-term interests of the unions and their members. Equally persuasive were the political consequences. Unless the rate of inflation could be reduced there was little prospect that the government could implement policies to which Jones and the trade union movement were committed – and, indeed, it might not remain in office. The social contract was very much Jones' creation; he did not want to risk its destruction.

With Jones as an ally, Healey could put pressure on the General Council. The government's anti-inflation plans were to be announced by 1 August. The General Council was given a six-week deadline to tighten up the social contract. Failing this Healey planned alternative action, including additional severe cuts in public spending and possible increases in indirect taxation. Further pressure was added when a fall in the value of the pound on 30 June brought from Healey a statement in the House of Commons that the need for agreement to reduce inflation was 'urgent'. The government would work towards a rate of inflation of 10 per cent, to be reduced to single figures by the end of 1976. A 10 per cent limit on wage increases was suggested, together with cash limits for wage bills in the public sector and action in the private sector through the price code.

Before the 'crisis' at the end of June the General Council had responded to Healey's pressure by producing a set of principles as a basis for negotiations with the government and the CBI which had included the suggestion of a price-target for mid-1976 to which a figure for pay increases – in the form of a universally applied flat-rate – set by the TUC would be related. The pace of any such discussion and agreement was now too slow. A series of meetings was held by Healey at which the details of a policy acceptable to the government and the General Council were worked out by the trade union representatives on the NEDC – Jack Jones, Len Murray, Hugh Scanlon, David Basnett, Lord Allen, Daniel McGarvey (often accompanied by David Lea of the TUC, their economic adviser) – and government ministers who included Denis Healey, Michael Foot, Shirley Williams and Eric Varley. The policy was taken back to the General Council who accepted it by 19 votes to 13. *The Development of the Social Contract*, the formal TUC version, was published on 9 July, followed by the government's White Paper, *The Attack on Inflation* (Cmnd. 6151). There was to be a limit of £6.00 on wage increases (with a cut off point of £8,500[9]) to apply for twelve months from 1 August 1975; the existing statutory powers under the price code would be used to prevent excessive rises being passed on in prices; there would be restrictions on financial help for nationalised industries which exceeded the pay limit and on rate support grants for local authorities doing the same; there would be higher food subsidies in the next financial year and increased grants to keep down council house rents – a response to requests made in *The Development of the Social Contract*. The government also undertook to introduce a temporary employment subsidy which would help to compensate employers for retaining employees who might otherwise have been laid-off. A Reserve Bill for statutory wage control was withdrawn after the TUC accepted the £6 limit. Back-up powers for the agreed policy were provided by the Remuneration, Charges and Grants Act, which was to run for one year and be renewable for one year after that.

It was clear that there would be substantial opposition to the policy at the Trades Union Congress in September, but the commitments and influence of all the larger and more influential unions, except the AUEW, whose National Conference in July had voted against any restriction on collective bargaining, ensured a majority. Murray argued that while the level of unemployment was now intolerable, reflation could not start until inflation was beaten and that the policy was the only way to keep Labour in power. Congress voted by 6.9 to 3.4 million, to support wage restraint.[10]

The relations between the parliamentary party and the trade union movement (or perhaps, more accurately, between the politicians and the TGWU) in 1970–75 had features reminiscent of earlier periods in the life of the labour movement. The trade union reaction following

---

[9] Originally the union representatives had wanted a cut-off point of £7,000 and Healey one of £10,000.

[10] The AUEW, the most serious defector, changed its policy in December 1975 when its National Committee voted to accept the £6 limit. This followed the move of its Executive Council to the right and a change in the views of Scanlon, who told the Trade Union Group of the PLP in 1976, 'I looked over the precipice and I didn't like what I saw'.

the 'deep and fundamental split' of 1969 and the establishment of the TUC-Labour Party Liaison Committee on the initiative of Jones recall the determination after 1931 of the TUC, dominated by Bevin, to ensure that a future Labour government would keep commitments agreed with the unions, and the creation of the National Council of Labour in 1934. As after 1931 the TUC had laid the foundations of much of the programme of the Attlee Government, so the discussions on the Liaison Committee were the origin of many features of the Labour Party manifesto of February 1974.

Harold Wilson had set out in 1964 to re-create the partnership with the unions of the Attlee Government, but it is arguable that his government from 1974–76 presented a closer parallel. In these years, more than in 1964–70, the Wilson Government implemented policies agreed with the unions, as did the Attlee Government after 1945. In each case the actions of the government stored up credit with the unions which to some extent influenced their later acceptance of wage restraint. There were other similar features. The fuel crisis in 1947 put millions of workers on the dole. The crisis was temporary, but enough to be a reminder of the depression of the thirties. The record level of inflation and the rapidly rising unemployment in 1975 presented a similarly bleak prospect. These economic factors, the political fear of the return of a Conservative government combined with the 'down payment' on social and economic policies made by the government (under the social contract) all helped to secure union agreement on wage restraint. The forties and seventies had one other thing in common – the TGWU. In 1948 Bevin and Deakin played major roles in persuading the General Council to recommend wage restraint (on the understanding that the government would introduce a price freeze); in 1975 Jones was converted to wage restraint (and asked the government to freeze the prices of essential goods and services).

For two years or so after March 1974 the trade union movement exercised as much, if not more, influence on government as it had between 1945 and 1950. The reasons were partly domestic to the labour movement – to avoid another split – and partly a recognition by the government of the importance to the economy of union co-operation. The latter increased as the damage done by collective bargaining increased and the need for wage restraint became more pressing: an incomes policy could not simply be 'imposed', it had to be agreed with, or accepted by, the unions. The White Paper, *The Attack on Inflation* (Cmnd. 6151), which set out the details of the policy gave total acknowledgement of this – the section on pay from *The Development of the Social Contract* was attached as an annex. The longer-term economic and political consequences of this relationship between the trade union movement and the government remained, in mid-1975, to be seen.

12 The Death of the Social Contract

Partnership and Pay Policy

From July 1975 to July 1978 pay policies agreed between the government and the TUC were a central feature in the government's attempt to secure wage restraint and reduce the rate of inflation. A close working partnership was established between the government and the most influential members of the General Council. The details of the pay policies and related measures which would help to make them acceptable to the unions were decided at meetings between the ministers concerned with economic and industrial affairs and the six trade union representatives on the NEDC. The decisions were taken back by each side to the Cabinet and General Council and for the most part subsequent meetings between ministers and the Economic Committee or General Council were to endorse the understanding reached and to assist the trade union representatives to obtain the widest possible support amongst their colleagues. The meetings which took place in the summer weeks each year before Parliament rose were an opportunity to consider the statements which would be put to the Trades Union Congress in September and which the government could take into account for the Queen's speech and other preparations for the next parliamentary session.

The operation of the £6 limit succeeded in reducing the rate of increase in earnings to about 14 per cent (compared with the government's target of 10 per cent) and the rate of increase in prices to about 13 per cent between July 1975 and July 1976. This 'Stage One' of the pay policy was followed by a 'Stage Two', also agreed between the government and the General Council despite the impossibility of the government's doing anything about the level of unemployment (one of the main union reasons for accepting wage restraint) other than introduce limited special measures. The basis for agreement on Stage Two of the policy was proposals for higher personal income tax allowances and for possible reductions in the basic rate put forward by Denis Healey in his budget in April 1976.

The reduction in the basic rate was conditional on the General Council's agreeing an increase of around 3 per cent in the next wage round. During the budget debate Healey's conditions changed: he would settle for a higher figure from the General Council if trade union leaders advised him that 3 per cent was too low to be acceptable to their members.

In the event, the General Council agreed to a new pay limit of 5 per cent with a £4 ceiling and a £2.50 lower limit, on the understanding that the tax concessions would be put into effect. (These tactics allowed them to claim a substantial gain from their bargaining with the government.[1]) At a special Conference of Executives, *The Social Contract 1976–77*, which set out the General Council's version of the policy, together with its views on prices, employment, pensions and industrial strategy, was adopted by an overwhelming majority. After this the government was able to publish its White Paper, *The Attack on Inflation: the Second Year* (Cmnd. 6507), which incorporated the TUC version as an annex. Healey's tactics, described by some as 'the unions deciding tax levels', were criticised as a further extension of union power, but his budget presentation was not so much more than an explicit version of Maudling's in 1963.

The unpleasant pill of a second phase of pay policy was sweetened by the publication of a 'new social contract', drawn up by the TUC-Labour Party Liaison Committee as *The Next Three Years and the Problem of Priorities*, which was presented to the government in May and formally approved by the General Council and the Labour Party NEC in July. The document emphasised that a return to full employment was essential and proposed more training (a specific of governments since 1960) and other measures described as a 'manpower strategy' – more, and more effective, investment in manufacturing industry, more selective price controls and an examination of restrictions on imports.

Stage Two of the pay policy was to be remarkably effective in terms of wage restraint. It produced the most severe cut in real wages in twenty years[2] but, like the standstill and the period of severe restraint in 1966–67, it was in a sense a wasted effort. The pound on 28

[1] The bargaining on the pay figure was unfortunately accompanied by a serious fall in the external value of the pound. After an assurance by Murray in April that 'no-one abroad need have any fears. We are going to get an agreement', the pound fell in April to its lowest ever level of 1.80 dollars to the pound.

[2] Between mid-1976 and mid-1977 prices increased by nearly 18 per cent, three times the rate of increase in wages.

September 1976 had its biggest fall since being floated, marking the onset of the worst sterling crisis since the war.[3] Healey immediately announced that the government was approaching the IMF for the largest loan since the war. He explained that the alternative would be 'savage deflationary measures and three million unemployed'. It was obvious that deflationary measures would have to be taken, even if not 'savage', and one of the major justifications for the incomes policy further eroded, but the working partnership which had been established with the unions in June 1975 took the strain. Close contacts between ministers and union leaders were maintained during the discussions with the IMF and the government measures, including cuts in public expenditure and higher indirect taxation, were accepted – though reluctantly – without any real possibility that the pay policy would be jettisoned.

The loan and the measures averted the prospect of the 3 million unemployed, but unemployment would certainly rise during 1977 and the year opened in economic gloom. The leaders of the two wings of the labour movement were in prophetic mood. Jones, in Maoist vein, wrote that 1977 must be the 'year of the beaver'. Callaghan (Prime Minister since April 1976), taking a more fatalistic view, described it as 'the year of the pendulum'. Joel Barnett, Chief Secretary to the Treasury, announced that Healey's objective of single figure inflation by early 1977 had been abandoned. It was in fact running at about 17 per cent.

The Trades Union Congress in September 1976 had adopted a resolution recommending an 'orderly' return to free collective bargaining as a third and supposedly final stage of pay policy for the wage round 1977–78, but at discussions of the 'inner circle' it was fairly quickly clear that there was little chance of a formal agreement. The crisis of September 1976 and its aftermath, particularly the level of unemployment and the rate of price increase, made the trade union leaders feel that it was impossible to agree a policy which they could persuade their members to accept. In the light of their position,

---

[3] Confidence in the pound may again have been affected by a threatened seamen's strike. The strike was threatened in support of a claim which would have broken the twelve months rule and was not supported by the General Council, led by Jones. Faced with the possibility of expulsion from the TUC for the third time and exposure to the expansionist ambitions of the TGWU, the executive of the NUS called off the strike. The terms agreed between the NUS, the General Council and the employers in the General Council of British Shipping preserved the twelve months rule – though it was difficult to reconcile other features of it with the pay policy.

Healey produced a Budget in April which he described as 'a basis for discussions' on pay and which proposed cuts in direct taxation of around £1300m., to be increased by another £1000m. subject to the condition that a satisfactory agreement was reached on a pay policy for the next twelve months. While he knew no formal agreement was possible, he had reason to hope that the General Council was prepared to acquiesce in the government's policy, which he announced in the House of Commons on 15 July, stating that the general level of pay settlements 'should be moderate enough to secure that the national earnings increase is no more than 10 per cent'. The government was prepared to impose sanctions (as it had been since 1975) on companies breaching the 10 per cent limit.[4]

The policy was set out in the White Paper, *The Attack on Inflation after 31st July 1977* (Cmnd. 6882). The White Paper contained as an annex a statement published by the TUC on 22 June advising negotiators not to reopen settlements made under Stage Two and not to defer settlements due before 31 July in the hope of securing an advantage by doing so. (According to Healey, the statement had made 'a major contribution towards preventing a pay explosion'.) The tax cuts proposed as 'conditional' on agreement were, of course, given. As in 1966 and 1967, the government had fixed a norm with an assurance that the General Council would not dissent and in the hope that it would influence the coming wage round.

The pay target of 10 per cent was not achieved. By July 1978 wages had increased by about 16 per cent while prices had risen by about 8 per cent over their levels a year earlier. The rate of wage increase exceeded that of price increase by a larger margin than at any time since the wages explosion of 1974–75. The third stage of the pay policy thus reversed the results of the previous stage. Nevertheless, by July 1978 the government could claim considerable success for its counter-inflation policy and for the results of the understandings with the unions since 1975: the annual rate of inflation had been brought within single figures (about 8 per cent).

Free Collective Bargaining and a Government Pay Policy

By the time the government could claim this degree of success in its fight against inflation, however, the partnership it had established

---

[4] In February 1978 it was announced that all future contracts between the government and private companies would include a clause to ensure that the 10 per cent limit was maintained. (The Remuneration, Charges and Grants Act expired in 1977.)

with the unions in 1975 had broken down and the social contract, which had disappeared as a rallying cry for the labour movement in the economic crisis of September 1976, had ceased to exist. There had been forewarnings of this. Pressure from militants in the unions for a return to free collective bargaining had been increasing since early 1977. There had been serious problems in applying the 10 per cent norm in the public sector over firemen, the police and the armed services and the government had departed from its own policy with various forms of camouflage, including payment by stages. By early 1978 it was clear that the views on pay policy of the major unions were diverging. The NUR, the GMWU, NALGO[5] and others favoured a 'Stage Four'. The NUM and, most importantly, the TGWU, were committed to a return to free collective bargaining.

Changes in the leadership of the TGWU and AUEW, where Moss Evans and Terry Duffy succeeded Jack Jones and Hugh Scanlon, affected the working of the 'inner circle'.[6] There was less knowledge and understanding of the situation and the problems. There was also by this time some resentment in the General Council at the extent to which the 'social contract' negotiations were carried out by the trade union representatives on the NEDC, particularly on the part of some of the public service and smaller unions who felt that they were not properly consulted. On the political side, the government was weaker. It no longer had an overall majority and depended for survival on the 'Lib-Lab pact'. The key facts, however, were the retirement of Jones and the determination of the TGWU to return to free collective bargaining.

In spite of these developments there had to be an election by November 1979. If it were to win, the government had to convince the country that it intended to continue the battle against inflation with the utmost determination. In this situation, as in 1977, it decided on a unilateral statement of policy based on its view of what was necessary and its assessment of what might be acceptable enough to influence the next wage round. Efforts were made before the statement was published in July to procure some indication of support or acceptance from the General Council, and again in the autumn, but without success.

The government's policy was set out in a White Paper, *Winning the*

---

[5] The National Association of Local Government Officers.

[6] There had been changes also on the government side – Albert Booth and Roy Hattersley had replaced Michael Foot and Shirley Williams.

Battle against Inflation (Cmnd. 7293), in July 1978. The White Paper emphasised the government's success in reducing the rate of inflation and stated that there was 'general agreement ... on the economic objectives to be pursued for jobs, prices and output'. On prices, the objective of the government was to reduce inflation below the current level of 8 per cent and this required that wage settlements should not rise above 5 per cent. The sanctions against companies breaching the policy would remain. In the public sector, the government would 'do everything possible' to secure adherence to the guidelines. 5 per cent, the White Paper admitted, might seem 'an ambitious objective', but it was necessary in part because of the outcome of the last wage round:

> ... if we do no better in the coming year than in the past year, inflation will be driven back into double figures, the competitiveness which we are only just holding will be undermined and we could all too easily see prices and incomes spiralling upwards again, dashing our hopes of reducing unemployment.

A challenge to the traditional concept of free collective bargaining was contained in the White Paper. It repeated proposals put forward by Harold Wilson and Edward Heath and, by implication, advocated a permanent incomes policy: it was the government's view that the country should aim at a long-term approach – collective bargaining should be based each year on a broad agreement between government, unions and employers about the maximum level of earnings 'compatible with keeping inflation under control in the following 12 months'.

The Trades Union Congress in September rejected the policy by a large majority and the Labour Party Conference passed a resolution urging the Party 'to organise a campaign ... against control of wages'. The movement was in favour of free collective bargaining or, as Sid Weighell, himself a supporter of pay policy, described it in a speech defending the government, in favour of a policy of 'snouts in the trough'.

The wisdom of the government in fixing a norm as low as 5 per cent was questioned at the time. It certainly put any trade union leader who wished to support government policy in an extremely difficult position. Few would have the authority to control the demands of their members to this degree and their position would be impossible if other leaders had not even the will to support the policy. As one civil servant commented (with hindsight), 'the 5 per cent limit has given the unions over to mob rule'. It was as well that James Callaghan was determined, as he said in October, to win the battle against inflation 'even if it means a long hard winter of strikes'.[7]

The Trades Union Congress had also been staged as a pre-election rally. Union leaders were convinced that there would be an autumn election, of which there were all the signs: the 1977-78 wage round had led to the largest consumer boom since 1975; the ambitious objective of limiting wage increases to 5 per cent (an objective they had rejected) looked like a pre-election show of determination rather than a realistic policy. On the assumption of an election, although Congress had rejected the pay policy trade union leaders had given the government full support with pledges to work 'as never before' to ensure the re-election of the Callaghan Government. In the event there was no election. The 5 per cent limit was put to the test and destroyed by the unions within six months. It almost seemed at times during the course of this exercise that the unions had not only expected an election but had also expected the Labour government to lose, had prepared plans to confront a Conservative government and were not able to put their plans into reverse following Callaghan's decision to carry on.

The Destruction of the Government's Policy

The TGWU, where Moss Evans had succeeded Jack Jones as General Secretary, took the lead in dismembering the government's policy in disputes at Ford's and in the road haulage industry. In the Ford dispute the company settled at around 15 per cent after a nine-week strike. The government applied its sanctions – a penalty difficult to defend as reasonable as Ford had suffered heavy losses as a direct result of government policy and one difficult to reconcile with the fact that the company was receiving millions in grants to expand production. (The government's action contributed to a later defeat for the sanctions policy in Parliament.) The road haulage employers finally settled after a strike for wage increases of around 20 per cent, having been assured that the government's prices policy would not prevent the additional costs being passed on.

The government (shades of Selwyn Lloyd and Edward Heath) decided to set an example in the public sector by standing firm on

---

[7] In 1966, Harold Wilson foresaw enforcement of the government's incomes policy as meaning 'a long hot summer'. The season was different in 1978 and the consequences were worse.

5 per cent in negotiations with the unions in local government, the National Health Service and the civil service (though a dispute in the BBC which threatened Christmas television had already been settled by an increase of 12½ per cent). There were selective strikes and other industrial action and the claims were finally settled for immediate increases above 10 per cent with promises of further increases from August 1979. The government went further and reversed its position: it would no longer adhere to its pay policy in the public sector where it could theoretically exercise control; public sector pay would be determined by comparability. A Standing Commission on Comparability was established. Hugh Clegg, the pay and industrial relations academic doyen of the sixties, reappeared as chairman. It was almost a return to the Macmillan Government and the late-fifties.

The ineffective defence of the 5 per cent policy created serious problems. The strikes in the road haulage industry interfered with the distribution of food and other supplies to the community and industry and threatened serious damaging disruption. The strikes in the public sector affected essential services, including hospitals, schools, water supply and refuse collection. There was extensive and effective picketing reminiscent of 1972 and widespread – in some areas unprecedented – refusal to maintain services if this meant crossing picket lines.

From the start of the road haulage strike the government was pressed to declare a State of Emergency and take steps to ensure the maintenance of essential supplies and services. The government argued that this might make the situation worse by encouraging militants to step up their action and by helping them to obtain sympathetic support in areas not directly involved. If this happened it would expose the very limited services the government could in fact provide. It might widen the split between the government and the official trade union leadership. It would be a disagreeable symbolic admission that Callaghan was no more able to avoid confrontation than Heath. (A State of Emergency had not been declared during the firemen's strike in the previous wage round and care had been taken when using the services to reduce the possibility of encouraging greater militancy.) As an alternative the government had discussions with Evans and other national officers of the Transport and General Workers Union. Foot, devotee of the TGWU (after the block vote went to the left with Cousins in 1955) and appearing at times in 1974 and 1975 almost a delegate of the TUC and TGWU in government, was reduced to exhorting Evans to show leadership.

The union issued advice and guidance to local officers and members, intended to ensure the maintenance of essential supplies. The emergencies organisation of the government provided a link with union officers to ensure that the operation worked as well as possible to sort out particular problems. The effects of the initiative by the union varied according to the militancy of those involved in different areas, but the government could argue that its approach was at least as successful as declaring an emergency. There was a similar approach by the government to the problems caused by the public service strikes which followed.

The *Joint Statement* of February 1979

Recognition of the facts of trade union power – or, for the critics, abdication of government responsibility – was formally recorded in *The Economy, the Government and Trade Union Responsibilities: Joint Statement by the TUC and the Government*, published in February 1979. As in 1969, now that the unions had made their point (and ensured that the government was not yet 'winning the battle against inflation') members of the General Council were ready to close the split in the movement and help the government.

The *Statement* concerned itself with every issue of importance arising from the problems of the economy, inflation, pay and industrial relations which had been in discussion or dispute between governments and the unions for the last twenty years or more. There were pronouncements on collective bargaining and observance of agreements, strikes, picketing, the closed shop, pay comparability, efficiency, productivity and inflation. There were three annexes of TUC advice and guidance to unions on negotiating and disputes procedures, the conduct of disputes and the closed shop. Desks in Whitehall and Congress House had been ransacked for good advice and declarations of intent. Two features of the statement, however, made it clear that there was no immediate assurance of any effective continuing understanding between government and unions about pay and the avoidance of future confrontation or that, if confrontation occurred, the course of events would be different: the General Council, as in 1969, was careful to avoid any statement which might be regarded as infringing the right of any individual union to decide how and when to use its power and, as in 1974, it said nothing to commit itself to a departure from free collective bargaining.

On pay and inflation the disagreement between government and unions was exposed in a statement from which no one could dissent: 'There is no precise arithmetical relationship between, for example, getting prices down to 5 per cent, the economy growing at 3 per cent, and a particular level of pay settlements'.

The TUC and the government did, however, set themselves the task of bringing the rate of inflation down to below 5 per cent 'within three years from now', though this postponed objective was accompanied by a warning of likely failure: the target was 'a bold one, but we must take it as our aim'.

The *Statement* did not at the time seem likely to inspire confidence in the government's ability to deal with either trade union power or inflation and Callaghan himself did not at first go out of his way to exaggerate its value. It was not a successor to the 'new social contract'; he rejected its being described as a 'concordat'. His caution was justified. Industrial troubles were continuing and he could not be confident that union actions would be influenced to any great extent by the *Statement*. Within weeks, in fact, civil service unions called strikes while negotiations were proceeding, in spite of the words of the TUC in its guide to the conduct of industrial disputes annexed to the *Statement*, 'strike action should only be taken in the last resort'. The *Statement* might, however, have been politically helpful in closing the split in the movement in preparation for the election which the government – and by now the General Council – hoped could be put off until October 1979. For the purposes of the election which took place in May 1979 the split had been closed too late.

In the election campaign union power was once again a major issue. Union leaders recalled the horrors of confrontation under the Heath Government and warned that if a Conservative government were returned these would be repeated. Callaghan and the Labour Party made what they could of the *Statement* as evidence that, unlike a Conservative government, they could, in partnership with the trade unions, contain inflation and limit industrial conflict. The troubles over the 5 per cent policy were too recent for this argument to convince. The confrontations between the unions and the Callaghan Government had not been so different from those under the Heath Government. If the economic damage of the industrial disputes had been less, the strikes in the public services had affected or had threatened to affect the interests and well-being of much wider sections of the community. The Callaghan Government had seemed no more effective in dealing with the troubles caused by the unions than had the Heath Government. It had gone through a similar spell of indecision and in the end it had been defeated as obviously as had Heath in 1972 and 1974. For a time in public Callaghan was reduced to deploring the disappearance of the responsible trade unionism of his earlier days as though it was a sudden and recent calamity. Until 1979 the Labour Party had been able to insist that only a Labour government could work with the unions. This had now to be qualified: a Labour government could in some circumstances work with the unions.

Those involved will no doubt enjoy discussion and argument in distributing responsibility for the confrontation between the unions and the Callaghan Government: the government was wrong to adopt the 5 per cent norm pressed by Healey and the Treasury and to defend it for so long[8] – but then any norm reasonable in terms of counter-inflation would have been a target to beat in free collective bargaining; Callaghan, 'the most trade union Prime Minister', failed to understand the pressures within the trade union movement for a return to collective bargaining and the degree of militancy behind them – or perhaps, while understanding them, he believed his appeal to the moderates would defeat the militants. Whatever the reason, he was in any case mistaken – but the alternative – acceptance of the pressures and militancy and a return to free collective bargaining – would, he might have argued, throw away the achievements of the last two years and might lead back to 1974–75. Evans, it could be claimed, did not give the leadership which had been given by Jones – but then, the National Executive of the TGWU had decided on a return to free collective bargaining before Jones retired and even Jones might not have been able to persuade the union or its members to accept a further stage of pay policy.

By 1978 free collective bargaining had been in suspense for three years. The militants were not prepared to accept the situation for any longer; the key trade union leaders accepted this view. The terminal illness of the social contract started with the 'crisis' of 1976; its death coincided with the retirement of Jones. By 1978 the government was no longer in a position to do anything further to meet the objectives of the trade union movement. Trade union leaders had no immediate positive reason to favour its continuing in office for another twelve months. Callaghan was wrong not to accept their view (or advice) that there should be an election in the autumn of 1978.

[8] This was Scanlon's view. (Television discussion with Shirley Williams, text printed in *The Listener*, 27 September 1979). He also said that the government had not delivered on prices – a statement not entirely supported by the facts.

It would be wrong to conclude from the events of the winter of 1978–79, culminating in the defeat of the Callaghan Government, that the social contract was an unqualified failure for the government or the unions. For the government, while it is true that in its first sixteen months the unions by their collective bargaining made a major contribution to pushing inflation to record levels, weakening the economy and threatening its existence, the understanding reached in the middle of 1975 in some degree compensated for the damage which had been done. There were three years of relative wage restraint without serious industrial trouble which assisted the government to regain some control over inflation. The rate came down to 8 per cent, which was a considerable achievement, though the chances of maintaining it were never good and were completely ruled out by the return to free collective bargaining in October 1978.

For the unions the period after March 1974 was a great deal more satisfactory. Before the economic situation and, ultimately, loss of its overall majority in the House of Commons, made it impossible for the government to keep its side of any bargain, the unions secured considerable benefits from 'their' government. Their powers were increased by the Trade Union and Labour Relations Acts and the Employment Protection Act. The shipbuilding and aircraft industries were nationalised. Their involvement in the operation of industry was extended by the new 'industrial strategy', with its proliferation of sector working parties under the NEDC, and by their association with activities flowing from increased government intervention in industry through the National Enterprise Board and in other ways. Although they made little progress towards 'industrial democracy' (largely because other leading members of the General Council did not agree with Jones on the subject) and the legislation to extend the dock labour scheme was defeated (in part at least because it would have benefited the TGWU at the expense of other unions), the ground was prepared for a further advance. Most important, free collective bargaining remained intact. It was suspended when the unions so decided and resumed on their decision.

The final confrontation between the unions and the Callaghan Government was, however, the most significant feature of the period. For the first time the unions openly used their industrial power to wreck the policy of a Labour government. In doing so they exposed more clearly than before the weakness of government in the face of trade union power. Unlike Heath, Callaghan did not *choose* to raise the question, 'Who governs the country?'; the election was forced on him. He had, however, perhaps raised a somewhat different and more useful question – 'How can any government govern the country without provoking a destructive reaction from the trade unions?' His February *Statement* did not offer a convincing answer to the question. In the events leading up to it, however, Evans (unlike Deakin in 1948) had given some sort of answer to the issue raised by Chuter Ede in 1948: 'I sometimes wonder.... who governs this country – the government or the Transport and General Workers Union'.[9]

Prospects

It is easy to be critical of the response of governments to the problems presented by trade union power. In the last ten years governments have clearly failed to reconcile the exercise of trade union power with their own views of the national interest. Between 1974 and 1976 the attempts made to reduce trade union power by law, in 1969 and from 1970–74, were put into reverse and union power increased. Attempts to impose wage restraint by law, between 1972 and 1974, and by a display of government 'authority' in 1978, ended in failure and political defeat. An attempt to secure wage restraint by agreement between 1974 and 1978 was, taking the period as a whole, unsuccessful. During the 1970s trade union power has become a more serious and difficult problem for governments.

Something may, however, be said in defence of governments. They were in a position of weakness for which their policies were only partly responsible. By 1964 the country was in a period of rapid political decline and relative economic decline and the problems created gave them little or no opportunity to claim successes which might have added to their authority. They were operating in a situation which favoured the increase and exercise of trade union power – full employment, the mixed economy, the welfare state and inflation. They were held to blame for the results of their dealings with the trade unions – for strikes, 'confrontation', wage increases causing inflation – because they were in the last resort accountable to the public, while the trade union leaders who shared the responsibility for the failures had no such accountability and could disclaim responsibility for the action of their members if it suited them. Harold Wilson's quotation from Baldwin in 1969 was not unjustified.[10]

[9] Chuter Ede, Home Secretary and Chairman of the Emergencies Committee, to Arthur Deakin, General Secretary of the TGWU. *See* pages xii–xiii with Deakin's reply.

[10] *See* page 125.

It could even be argued that governments have not failed. The refusal of the most powerful interest group in the country to accept government policies has not led to a complete collapse of the economic system or continuing serious social unrest. The moderates of the trade union movement could claim that they have resisted pressures from below which might have caused both; they have been protectors of governments and the established political system. Both they and governments might claim that, in the circumstances of political decline and relative economic failure since the war, this should be judged a success. It is not a claim which Wilson, Heath or Callaghan would be likely to make with the hope that it would be accepted by the country. These final pages try to forecast how governments will react to the problem in the eighties in the light of these past failures.

The forecast on the basis of certain assumptions is pessimistic. The first assumption is that the two party system will not change – governments will be either Conservative or Labour.

Secondly, the relationship between each of the two political parties and the trade union movement will not change. It is worthwhile summarising the essential features of these relationships in view of their importance for government policies.

So far as the Labour Party is concerned, the overwhelming power of the trade unions in the Party – the almost total dependence of the Party on trade union money, the reliance on trade union organisation in elections, the block vote at the Labour Party Conference, the substantial number of parliamentary seats within union gift – does not mean, as some have said, that when in office Labour ministers are puppets of the trade union movement (the events of 1969 and 1979 are evidence of this). The relationship inevitably, however, is at times that of patron and dependant. Ministers are free to form their own view of the public good and act on it on issues where the unions have little or no interest (or there is no 'trade union view'). On matters of concern to the unions, ministers are also subject to pressures from other sources. Their policies must take account of these other pressures – although other groups may be less effective and less pervasive. Union leaders, moreover, still sometimes feel the need to have a regard for the wider political effects of too obvious a show of their power and the proprieties of parliamentary politics. In dealings with ministers, the General Council can be understanding and co-operative as well as demanding and insistent. Ministers may be understanding and grateful, but at times resistant. In some future situation of serious conflict they may again, as in 1969 and 1978, assert their independence – though the consequences in 1970 and 1979 may make them more cautious in future. The relationship between the unions and the Conservative Party is simpler. The unions are political opponents of the Party and the attitude of trade union leaders to Conservative ministers is antagonistic and hostile. They continue to pursue their political objectives, and the use of their industrial power for this purpose has in the past influenced the policies of Conservative governments on some issues and in some circumstances as effectively as their power of patronage has influenced the policies of Labour governments.

The third assumption is that the essential characteristics of the trade union movement, which make dealings between governments and the General Council so difficult, will not change. The TUC will have no real authority over affiliated unions, unions will compete for membership and their leaders for power within the labour movement. Union leaders will be constrained to take account of, and will be influenced by, the 'power on the shop floor' and the views of their activists and militants.

On the basis of these assumptions, the main features of the problem governments will have to face can be outlined. First and most important, the trade unions will continue to insist on free collective bargaining. They may on occasion be ready to accommodate a Labour government with the temporary respite of voluntary restraint, or even to accept a period of restraint imposed by any government. They will not, however, be prepared to accept a 'permanent incomes policy' either voluntary or statutory, involving permanent restraint on the use of their industrial power. Collective bargaining is their business. That is what they are there for – the simple answer to George Woodcock's question. They will continue to use their bargaining power to secure wage increases which seek to protect their members against inflation, but in a way which increases inflation.

Secondly, unions will want changes in the law which will increase their membership, their bargaining power and the freedom to use their power. They will not be satisfied with the Trade Union and Labour Relations Acts and the Employment Protection Act. This legislation has not enabled them to compel recognition (for example, in the Grunwick dispute). It has not prevented the courts from issuing injunctions against their activities, for example in the newspaper industry and in the road haulage strike. The closed shop is not yet universal.

Thirdly, they will pursue their syndicalist objectives and aim to increase their industrial power in the public sector through the extension of public ownership and changes in the management of public enterprise, including trade union representation on Boards, and in the private sector through the use of planning arrangements and trade union representation on company Boards ('industrial democracy').

Fourthly, they will aim to increase their political power, and in particular to have more effective influence on (control of, if possible, on some issues) Labour governments, to avoid a repetition of the events of 1969 and 1979. They may seek this, for example, by more formalised arrangements for joint decision by ministers and representatives of the General Council on issues they consider important, by some form of 'patronage' within the civil service, by the transfer of government activities to bodies on which they are represented, as with the disemberment of the Department of Employment into tripartite commissions, or by other means.

The reactions of governments to these objectives will depend considerably, though not entirely, on which party is in office and the nature of the political relationship with the trade union movement. Conservative governments will aim, as the present government already aims, to reduce trade union bargaining power by legislation, but will hope to avoid repeating the conflicts over the Industrial Relations Act. In response, unions will seek to avoid the law and find alternative ways of exerting their power, and when necessary the law will be broken by militants. The unions will try to ensure that any restrictive laws are changed by a successor Labour government. Labour governments are likely to be prepared to legislate to increase the bargaining power of the unions (though this will add to the problems of governments in dealing with inflation) and generally to extend their industrial power. They may be obliged also to accept arrangements which give the unions increased political power and a more effective influence on government. The pace of advance on these matters will be largely determined by the extent of agreement amongst the more important union leaders and the priority they give to the different objectives.

The first union objective – the continuation of free collective bargaining – will be the central problem for governments and on this their reactions will be less influenced by the political relationships. It can be assumed that governments of both parties will wish to keep the rate of inflation within reasonable limits. They will presumably wish also to avoid repeating the confrontations of 1974 and 1979 and certainly the political penalties which followed. If so, it seems possible that they will accept that wage restraint (or incomes policy) as it has been practised until now is not an effective long-term instrument – whether agreed, accepted or imposed – and can make a limited temporary contribution only to containing inflation. The Heath Government's Stage Three may well have been the apotheosis of the concept of a 'permanent incomes policy' which was promised by Macmillan and born with Brown in 1964. Governments will rely more on taxation, control of public spending and monetary policy as the preferred method of checking inflation, as has been the case, in fact, since 1976. They will not, however, be able to disengage entirely from wages and collective bargaining. The level of wage increases will affect their other policies and, in any case, they can hardly avoid responsibility for wages in the public sector. The use, primarily, of fiscal and monetary policies to control inflation will not ensure that governments avoid trouble with the unions, who may well use their industrial power against some of the consequences of reduced public expenditure (the unions in the public services will certainly try to prevent the policies working as intended) and will certainly use it in wage bargaining to negate the effects of any changes in taxation which they regard with disfavour.

More important than any immediate troubles with the unions, however, will be the results of the reliance on fiscal and monetary policies. The substance of the policies adopted would, of course, differ somewhat between Labour and Conservative governments – the presentation would be different and the reaction of the unions, or at any rate the vocal reaction, might be different. As the Conservative version of these policies is now in operation the prospects for this must now be considered.[11]

If the policies were so successful as to convince the country that the government had established continuing control of inflation, this and the fear of unemployment might reduce the pressure for wage increases, moderate the outcome of collective bargaining and lead to a less destructive relationship between governments and the trade unions. It is very doubtful, however, whether collective bargaining

[11] A Labour government would presumably have sought an understanding with the General Council that the policy should include some elements of voluntary wage restraint, as foreshadowed in the *Statement* of February 1979, but the events leading up to the *Statement* suggest that this would be of little practical significance in controlling inflation and could be as damaging to the economy as the TUC 'incomes policy' of 1974–75.

will respond quickly and the damaging conflict between trade union power and government policy is likely to continue, perhaps taking a somewhat different form, but in similar, perhaps more discouraging, economic circumstances. In face of this it is questionable for how long the present government's policy can be sustained. The social and economic consequences may be judged unacceptable before it is effective in controlling inflation. If so, the government may be unable to evade the problem which has faced its predecessors and may feel compelled to attempt to influence or interfere with collective bargaining. If this point is reached the choices open to the government are limited and the prospects of success will be slight. A limited period of 'wage restraint by understanding' or a freeze may again apply at a time of 'crisis' as an alternative to measures as 'savage' as those threatened by Healey in 1975. As in the past, however, a temporary respite would be inadequate and, as in the past, would commit the government to developing a continuing policy. There is no reason to think that a statutory pay policy following a freeze would be any more successful than the policy of the Heath Government and it seems unlikely that the government would take this course.

An attempt to reach agreement with the General Council on a voluntary pay policy would fail for the same reasons as in 1972 (or 1966). For any voluntary pay policy to be effective the trade union movement would have to accept greater responsibility for regulating the activities of individual unions. It would have to be prepared to do this not only to advance the cause of the Labour movement and in support of a Labour government, as Brown hoped it would in 1964, but to do it whatever government is in office. This would mean radical changes in the organisation and normal business activities of the trade union movement, its ideology and its political role. It is difficult to believe that the movement could make these changes even for the promise of a lower rate of inflation, lower unemployment and greater prosperity. It would also require changes in the attitude of the Conservative Party to the union aim of increased industrial power and influence. It would mean changes within the labour movement and in the relationship between the trade unions and the Labour Party. Given the forces resistant to changes of this degree within both political parties and the trade union movement, the prospects of success for a renewed attempt to establish a voluntary pay policy, even one less ambitious than the 'shared responsibility' contemplated by Heath, are no greater than in 1972.

If, however, such an attempt were made by the government and failed again, there could well be pressure for another move to reduce the bargaining power of the unions by law and to impose responsibilities and restrictions more severe than have been contemplated since 1906. (Even if the government makes no move to interfere with collective bargaining and the process continues as in the past, with inflationary consequences and accompanied by serious industrial troubles, there may well be pressure for such legislation.) The government might be reluctant to risk another confrontation similar to that over the Industrial Relations Act 1971, though the trade union movement would have to be rather more determined and united than in 1971 for its opposition again to be successful. It is doubtful, however, whether legislation would in fact limit the bargaining power of the unions effectively and in any case, given the political system, it could not be a continuing factor in a counter-inflation policy. It seems unlikely that the present government (or a successor Labour government) will be any more successful in dealing with the trade union problem than the governments of Heath, Wilson and Callaghan.

It could be, therefore, that the relationship between governments and the trade union movement in the eighties will continue much as in the past. The economic consequences of attempting to control inflation in face of trade union power and collective bargaining are not, however, attractive, and there are other reasons related to the nature of the trade union movement why at some point governments may find the situation unacceptable.

It is true that the trade union movement is not the only pressure group whose activities cause inflation, or the only pressure group to compel governments to change or abandon policies. It has, however, special characteristics which distinguish it from others. It is a 'mass' group – it claims to speak for millions and to have a continuing mandate which over-rides that of either of the political parties. It exerts its pressure on governments in full view of the public, and often by means which cause serious public inconvenience and hardship. One of the two governing parties is openly dependent on it. The use of industrial power for political purposes, discredited for forty years, is no longer discredited and unions are prepared to employ this power. The traditional view the union movement has taken of itself as being 'outside the law' and of being committed to transforming the system in which it operates has persisted in spite of the effective industrial and political power it now exercises within that system. From this position it can disclaim responsibility for the effect of trade union activities on the way in which the system works. It is a 'movement', not an organisation, and it has no institutions for overall self-regulation of these activities. It has so far successfully resisted attempts by governments to regulate its main activities by law. For these reasons it presents governments with a unique problem. The difficulties this causes for governments and the country may be too serious for the *status quo* to be maintained.

The continuation of the existing relationship between governments and the trade union movement in a situation of continuing economic failure could have unpredictable political consequences. These may compel changes in the trade union movement itself, the party political system in which it plays a key role, the relations it has with governments and the legal framework within which it operates. The assumptions made at the beginning of these final pages seem unlikely to prevail throughout the 1980s.

Appendix I List of Official Papers Cited and Other Publications

Appendix 2 Annual Rate of Change of Wage Rates, Retail Prices and Gross Domestic Product, 1946–78

	Hourly wage rate[1] (October to October each year)	Retail prices, all items (October to October each year)	Gross domestic product at factor cost (year on year increase)
	Per cent		
1946	9.4	—	—
1947	9.0	—	0.8
1948	6.0	7.0	4.4
1949	1.8	3.6	3.6
1950	1.2	2.5	3.7
1951	10.1	11.9	1.8
1952	7.5	6.9	− 0.7
1953	4.4	1.7	4.2
1954	4.8	2.8	4.1
1955	7.0	5.3	3.3
1956	7.9*	3.9	1.1
1957	5.8	4.3	1.7
1958	3.7	2.1	− 0.2
1959	1.1	− 0.2	4.6
1960	5.4	2.0	5.4
1961	6.4	3.9	1.8
1962	4.0	2.9	1.4
1963	2.8	2.3	3.2
1964	5.7	4.1	6.1
1965	7.2	4.8	2.7
1966	5.4	3.8	1.8
1967	5.4	2.0	1.8
1968	5.5	5.6	4.3
1969	5.6	5.4	2.0

	Hourly wage rate[1] (October to October each year)	Retail prices, all items (October to October each year)	Gross domestic product at factor cost (year on year increase)
1970	11.6	7.4	1.6
1971	11.7	9.4	1.5
1972	15.5	7.9	3.2
1973	11.3	9.9	6.1
1974	22.1	17.1	− 1.8
1975	25.4	25.9	− 1.9
1976	15.8	14.7	2.1
1977	5.1*	14.1	2.5
1978	18.0*	7.8	3.0

[1] Male manual workers, all industries and services, except for years marked * when the index for *all* manual workers has been used.

Sources: *British Labour Statistics, Historical Abstract 1886–1968,* successive year books and Department of Employment *Gazette; Economic Trends.*

Index

Index of Acronyms

OEEC   Organisation for European Economic Cooperation
PLP   Parliamentary Labour Party
RPI   General Index of Retail Prices
TASS   Technical and Supervisory Section (of the AUEW)
TGWU   Transport and General Workers Union
TSSA   Transport Salaried Staffs Association
TUC   Trades Union Congress
UPW   Union of Post Office Workers